THE PROPHECIES OF
DANIEL

By LEHMAN STRAUSS

The First Person
The Second Person
The Third Person

Prophetic Mysteries Revealed
The Prophecies of Daniel
Devotional Studies in Galatians
 and Ephesians
James Your Brother
The Epistles of John
The Book of the Revelation

Certainties for Today
The Eleven Commandments
We Live Forever

Demons, Yes--but Thank God
 for Good Angels

THE PROPHECIES OF
DANIEL

BY

LEHMAN STRAUSS

LOIZEAUX BROTHERS

Neptune, New Jersey

FIRST EDITION, JUNE 1969

ISBN 0-87213-812-7
Library of Congress Catalog Card Number: 70-85293
PRINTED IN THE UNITED STATES OF AMERICA
18   17   16   15   14   13   12   11   10

To

Elsie

faithful and loving wife from our youth
loyal and devoted mother of our children
tried and true child of God

this volume is sincerely and affectionately dedicated

PREFATORY NOTE

The chapters in this book were written in longhand over a period of sixteen months, January 1, 1967 through April 30, 1968, while traveling about 40,000 miles and speaking about 400 times. Portions were written in Oregon, California, Texas, Louisiana, Georgia, Florida, Michigan, Indiana, Connecticut, New York, New Jersey, and Pennsylvania. Because of the pressure under which much of the work was done, it is to be hoped that the reader will be patient with some of the imperfections.

The writer is indebted to Mr. and Mrs. Clarence Giencke of Butler, Wisconsin, for their labor of love in typing and indexing the manuscript.

We commit this brief exposition to the continuing ministry of the Holy Spirit with the sincere prayer that through it our Lord Jesus Christ will be glorified.

Philadelphia, Pennsylvania   LEHMAN STRAUSS
1968

FOREWORD

It gives me personal joy to write this introductory word to Dr. Lehman Strauss' helpful exposition of the book of Daniel. Our warm friendship over the years has let me know something of how greatly the Lord has used him—and continues to do so. It has been my privilege to read the manuscript of this commentary—and it has the characteristics of the other writings of this author. Do not look for new interpretations; look for solid and authoritative Bible teaching.

The volume is full of Scripture. My brother is a Bible teacher—and that is good. God has given him the gift of bringing related Scriptures together, so that Scripture interprets Scripture. Others may become engulfed in critical problems or in novel interpretations; Dr. Strauss hews to the line because he attempts to give chapter and verse for the question, "What saith the Scriptures?"

This commentary is for the common Christian. While Dr. Strauss shows awareness of a number of the critical problems in the book, he does not major on them—indeed, they are only mentioned in passing; rarely does he do more than give them passing attention. His burden is the meaning of the text. He presents his study in language we can all understand. Our Lord said concerning one of the prophetic utterances of the book: "Let him that readeth understand" (Matthew 24:15). Our author has attempted to do this for the whole book and for both trained and untrained—and in our judgment has succeeded nobly.

This word would be incomplete without reference to the many practical lessons brought forth chapter by chapter. The applications are developed and applied magnificently.

May the Lord give this exposition wide usefulness.

WILLIAM CULBERTSON

CONTENTS

CHAPTER FOUR 111

CHAPTER FIVE 143

CHAPTER SIX 173

INTRODUCTION

The Bible is the Word of God. All the adjectives and superlatives of all the languages on earth fall short of the necessary adequacies to describe this Book of all books. David wrote by inspiration of the Holy Spirit, "I will worship toward Thy holy temple, and praise Thy name for Thy loving kindness and for Thy truth: for Thou hast magnified Thy word above all Thy name" (Psalm 138:2). If anything can be greater than God's name, it is His precious and plighted Word to man. If His Word is not truth, His name is meaningless.

Outstanding among the books of the Old Testament is the book of Daniel. Some higher critics legendize this book. While some of these men are of profound learning and scholarship, they are, for the most part, opposed to the supernaturalism of Christianity which includes the fact that the Bible is a divinely revealed and supernatural Book. One critic said that the book of Daniel was written after the events occurred and then put into the form of prophecy in order to make it interesting reading. Another critic has told us that the book of Daniel belongs to the Maccabean Era and that it is nothing more than a romance. But they are wrong! Men are to be pitied when they foolishly turn from divine light which makes clear God's future plans.

The Old Testament, or Hebrew canon, comes to us in

three divisions: (1) The Pentateuch, called the Law or Torah, which includes the first five books of the Bible, is so designated because these terms stress the legal element which controlled the religious and civil institutions of Israel's national life. (2) The Prophets, or Nebhiim, consisted of the *former prophets*, comprising Joshua, Judges, Samuel, and Kings; and the *latter prophets*, comprising three major prophets (Isaiah, Jeremiah, and Ezekiel); and twelve minor prophets (Hosea, Joel, Amos, Obadiah, Jonah, Micah, Nahum, Habakkuk, Zephaniah, Haggai, Zechariah, and Malachi). This second division is called *the Prophets* because the penmen of these books were considered as having held the office of a prophet. (3) The Hagiographa, or writings, comprising the *poetical books* (Job, Psalms, Proverbs); *the rolls* (Ruth, Esther, Ecclesiastes, Song of Solomon, Lamentations); and the *historical books* (Chronicles, Ezra, Nehemiah, Daniel).

It could come as a surprise to some when they see the book of Daniel omitted from *the Prophets* and included in *the Writings*. No doubt there are good reasons for this, among them being the fact that Daniel was a statesman rather than an official prophet, and that the book bearing his name is not totally prophetical but more accurately historical-prophetical. If we call Daniel a historian we are correct, and if we call him a prophet we are correct. Daniel was both a historian and a prophet, as the contents of the book of Daniel reveal. Our Lord referred to him as "Daniel the prophet" (Matthew 24:15) thereby putting His seal of approval upon both the man and his message. Though Daniel never claimed to be a prophet, and nowhere in the Old Testament is he spoken of as such, yet part of the book is apocalyptic.

The book of Daniel is a mighty tonic to faith in the absolute sovereignty of God throughout the entire earth.

Two significant phrases in the book reveal this pertinent and precious truth. The first is, "There is a God in heaven" (2:28). I say that here is a pertinent and a precious truth. In this second chapter alone God is referred to as "the God of heaven" not less than five times (verses 18, 19, 28, 37, 44). Also in this chapter He is called "the great God" (2:45) and the "God of gods" (2:47), and later in the book, "the King of heaven" (4:37). The second phrase is that "the most High ruleth in the kingdom of men" (4:24, 32). Both truths are announced in Daniel's statement to Nebuchadnezzar, "Thou, O king, art a king of kings: for the *God of heaven* hath given thee a kingdom, power, and strength, and glory" (2:37). The whole point in these two phrases is that the God of the Bible, who is the Christian's God, is sovereign over the affairs of men and nations. "He removeth kings, and setteth up kings" (2:21) "that the living may know that the most High ruleth in the kingdom of men, and giveth it to whomsoever He will, and setteth up over it the basest of men" (4:17).

Another interesting feature in the book of Daniel is the oft repeated name of God, namely "the most High," appearing not less than thirteen times (3:26; 4:2, 17, 24, 25, 32, 34; 5:18, 21; 7:18, 22, 25, 27). Note this name of God and mark it in your Bible. Its first appearance in the Bible is in connection with an incident in the life of Abraham. Abraham's nephew Lot had been taken captive by some enemy tribes. When Abraham received word of the incident he set out at once in pursuit of the invaders. He overtook them, completely routed them, rescuing Lot and returning with much of the enemy's goods. Whereupon the king of Sodom tried to make a deal with Abraham, offering to Abraham the material goods and suggesting that he be permitted to keep the captives. "Abram said to the king of Sodom, I have lift up mine hand unto the LORD, the *most high God*, the possessor of heaven and earth, That I will not take from a thread even to a shoelatchet, and that I will not take any thing that is thine, lest thou shouldest say, I have made Abram rich" (Genesis 14:22-23). This name for Jehovah, the *most High God*, is the translation of the Hebrew name *El Elyon*, meaning "the possessor of heaven and earth." It is that name God uses when He wants to declare His ownership of His creation. In the book of Daniel He is called the *God of heaven*, but He is declared at the same time to be the *most High God*, the possessor of Heaven and earth. Though His earthly people Israel are in captivity and there is no word to them from God, all men in the earth must know that He rules sovereignly over them.

The book of Daniel was undoubtedly written by Daniel himself. He is the one who received the revelations and who speaks in the first person (7:2, 4, 6, 28; 8:1, 15; 9:2; 10:2; 12:5-8). While the book is in two parts, *history* (chapters 1-6) and *prophecy* (chapters 7-12), the entire book is the work of one writer. There is a literary unity in the book as will be seen in the examination of the text itself. True, the book is written in two languages, Hebrew (1:1-2:4a; 8:1-12:13) and Aramaic (2:4b—7:28). While it is difficult to determine precisely why two languages have been used, the fact that there are two does not reflect in any way upon the claim that one man penned the entire book, and that the writings were given to him by direct inspiration of the Holy Spirit. The book is neither a romance nor a forgery, but it does consist of accurate history and divinely given predictive prophecy. Those arguments, so strongly opposed to accepting Daniel as the author of this book, are specious. If the reference by our Lord Himself to Daniel's book (see Matthew 24:15 and Mark 13:14) were the only statements we had to go by, these would be sufficient, and nothing more need be said in support of Daniel and his book. But we do have, in addition to Christ's testimony, distinct references to Daniel in the book of Ezekiel (Ezekiel 14:14, 20; 28:3) as well as a strong hint that both Ezra and Nehemiah had learned some true and deep prayer lessons from the penitential prayer of Daniel (see Ezra 9 and Nehemiah 9, cf., Daniel 9). Whoever therefore denies the divine authority and authenticity of the book of Daniel casts aspersion on the integrity of the Lord Jesus Christ.

Dr. S. Maxwell Coder, in his "Home Study Series" published serially in *Moody Monthly*, has an interesting comment in the section, "Archaeology Confirms the Old Testament" (January 1967):

"The book of Daniel was for years made the subject of one of the bitterest, most arrogant attacks in the history of the entire anti-Bible movement. Considerable literature was written denouncing the historicity of the book being answered by other works in its defense.

"From 1899 to 1917 the German, R. Koldewey, excavated the ruins of Babylon and proved conclusively that Nebuchadnezzar was responsible for the city's greatness, as claimed in the book of Daniel (4:30). Koldewey found in the remains of the palace of Nebuchadnezzar a great banqueting hall 56 feet wide and 173 feet long, with a niche opposite the main entrance for the royal throne. This was undoubtedly the setting for Belshazzar's feast (Daniel 5).

"To escape the force of Daniel's remarkable fulfilled prophecies, it was said the book of Daniel was written much later than the accepted date. (Daniel foretold the fall of Babylon, the rise of the Medo-Persian empire, the conquests of Alexander the Great, the many outstanding events in the long period which followed Alexander's death to the coming to age of Rome. He predicted the coming of Christ and gave the time of His crucifixion.) It was claimed, for example, that Greek musical instruments were listed in it several centuries too early. Babylonian records answered this by showing that Greek artisans and mercenary soldiers were employed in Babylonia in the time of Nebuchadnezzar.

"One of the most striking examples of the defeat of the opponents of the Word of God is to be seen in the fifth chapter of Daniel, where Belshazzar, king of Babylon, is said to have been slain during a feast on the night of the city's fall. Secular historians named the last king of Babylon as Nabonidus; they said he was not present at the capture of the city, that he was not killed, but taken captive and kindly treated, and lived in retirement as a private citizen. Here, said the critics, was a clear case of error in the Bible.

"No one had any idea how the two accounts could be reconciled until Sir Henry Rawlinson discovered an inscription on a cylinder in the Euphrates valley containing the facts needed to clear up the problem. There were two kings of Babylon during Daniel's later life, a father and son. Nabonidus, who occupied a stronghold outside the city, had made his eldest son, Bil-shar-uzzer (Belshazzar), coregent, and allowed him to use the royal title. Belshazzar was slain while defending the city; Nabonidus was spared. Thus, even the apparently insignificant detail of Daniel 5:7, 29, about the prophet's being made the third ruler in the kingdom, was explained."

Some knowledge of the book of Daniel is necessary if we are to understand future world events as predicted here as well as in other Bible prophecies. Moreover this book is essential to the interpretation of the book of Revelation. The whole course of "the times of the Gentiles" mentioned by our Lord in Luke 21:24 has been dramatically unfolded in this remarkable prophetic preview. The rise and fall of Gentile nations have been within the permissive will of God, and whatever time remains until the coming again of Jesus Christ, and however many nations are yet to rise and fall, the affairs of this world are leading up to that greatest climactic event when "the kingdoms of this world are become the kingdoms of our Lord, and of His Christ; and He shall reign for ever and ever" (Revelation 11:15).

The book is chiefly about the man Daniel and his message. The man himself stands out uniquely among the great characters in the Bible. There are other good men in the Scriptures, but none quite like Daniel. He compares with the highest and wisest of men. He was exposed to the temptations of the flesh and he had every opportunity to be spoiled, yet through it all he remained pure and humble. Possibly some of this could be attributed to the fact that Daniel was born and reared during the great spiritual awakening under the good and godly King Josiah. Those impressions that were made upon him during his early, formative years were carried with him throughout his long and useful life. Like Timothy (2 Timothy 1:5; 3:15), Daniel enjoyed the blessings and benefits of godly training in his youth. The history of the Christian Church reveals that much of the best and enduring work of the Church was accomplished by those persons converted to Jesus Christ in spiritual awakenings.

Recently, while reading through the book of Daniel, I was impressed with the fivefold appearance of the phrase, "He touched me" (8:18; 9:21; 10:10, 16, 18). What a subject for a sermon! *The touch of the Almighty!* Here we may learn the secret of Daniel's greatness. He had the touch of God upon him. Nothing finer could be recommended to the youth of today than a study of the life of Daniel. He is an aristocrat of the Old Testament, a truly great man because God had touched him.

God touched him to make him *see* (8:18-19).

God touched him to give him *skill* (9:21-22).

God touched him to make him *stand* (10:10-11).

God touched him to make him *speak* (10:16).

God touched him to make him *strong* (10:18).

Because God had touched Daniel he was a man of perception, purpose, principle, prayer, purity, and power. He had the touch of God upon him because his trust and confidence were in God. "No manner of hurt was found upon him, because he believed in his God" (Daniel 6:23). Many modern psychologists and psychiatrists would convince us that faith in God, as a rule and principle to live by, is an antiquated concept of an unscientific and unenlightened era that is behind us. Today they tell us, have faith in yourself! But we are learning that faith in ourselves leaves us cold and comfortless when sickness and sorrow come to us. Let a man trust God and the touch of the Almighty will be upon him.

Much more could be written in this Introduction about Daniel. However, it is in my heart and mind to get to the study of the inspired text. But before we proceed with the exposition, I want you to share a paragraph written in 1959 by E. L. Langston of England in *The Prophetic News and Israel's Watchman* (January 1959):

"The book of Daniel should be the textbook of every modern politician. If I had my way I should compel, not only every Christian, but the prime minister, members of the cabinet, ambassadors, the consular service, and all diplomats to study it. It is a panorama of the main political events at the end of 'the times of the Gentiles.' Its predictions concern Europe, Rome, Syria, Egypt, Palestine, and the Jews, the certain grouping of nations and individuals that will be prevalent just prior to the advent of the Messiah. The predictions concern labor and capital, the growth of infidelity and modernistic tendencies. We shall see the idea of a king of Syria or Assyria and a king of Egypt, and the United Nations organization which are not new, but predicted 2,500 years ago, and now being fulfilled before our very eyes. *Do we realize that at least half of the prophecies foreshadowed in this book have literally come to pass,* just as specified 2,500 years ago? Therefore, surely we are to expect the remaining prophecies to be just as literally and minutely fulfilled."

DANIEL—CHAPTER ONE

DANIEL—CHAPTER ONE

THE DEPORTATION OF JUDAH (1:1-2)

In the third year of the reign of Jehoiakim king of Judah came Nebuchadnezzar king of Babylon unto Jerusalem, and besieged it. And the Lord gave Jehoiakim king of Judah into his hand, with part of the vessels of the house of God: which he carried into the land of Shinar to the house of his god; and he brought the vessels into the treasure house of his god (Daniel 1:1-2)[1].

The book of Daniel opens with a statement which is both an accurate historical record and a fulfillment of divine prophecy. The reader should recall that the original kingdom of Israel, as begun under David and Solomon, had divided into two separate monarchies under Rehoboam, the son of Solomon (1 Kings 12). Ten of the original twelve tribes chose Samaria as their capital city and formed the northern kingdom of Israel, and the remaining tribes of Judah and Benjamin remained loyal to Rehoboam, making Jerusalem their capital. This division was followed by a

---

[1] For an excellent discussion on the seeming discrepancy between the "third year" of Daniel 1:1 and the "fourth year" of Jeremiah 46:2, see H. C. Leupold, *Exposition of Daniel,* pages 47-50.

steady decline into apostasy, sin, and idolatry.

Jehovah had been jealous for His people, so much so that when the nation began under God, He warned them through His servant Moses as to the consequences of any willful departure on their part. If ever they would seek false gods and break the covenant that Jehovah made with them, God said, "Then My anger shall be kindled against them in that day, and I will forsake them, and I will hide My face from them, and they shall be devoured, and many evils and troubles shall befall them; so that they will say in that day, Are not these evils come upon us, because our God is not among us?" (Deuteronomy 31:17) God's servants, the prophets, had repeated this warning over and over again, but despite the frequency with which the warning was heard, the people rebelled repeatedly. As a result of their departure from God's law, there were many national disasters. The books of Judges, Kings, and Chronicles record the sad history of Israel's many defeats, which brought eventual destruction.

This first chapter of the book of Daniel comprises that portion of the divine revelation which relates to the nation's downfall at the hands of the Babylonians. The captivity of Judah was the judgment of God, to be sure, but it was not in any sense a display of whim or caprice on God's part. In the plan of God Israel was destined to become a mighty nation through whom the world was to receive blessing. Had the leaders and the people remained faithful to the rules and principles which the Lord had revealed, the judgment upon them would not have been necessary. But their backslidings had incurred the divine wrath and the inevitable punitive action.

The Babylonian captivity was predicted in detail through Isaiah and Jeremiah. We must read with care the following prophecies.

Isaiah wrote: "Then said Isaiah to Hezekiah, Hear the word of the LORD of hosts: Behold, the days come, that all that is in thine house, and that which thy fathers have laid up in store until this day, shall be carried to Babylon: nothing shall be left, saith the LORD. And of thy sons that shall issue from thee, which thou shalt beget, shall they take away; and they shall be eunuchs in the palace of the king of Babylon" (Isaiah 39:5-7).

Jeremiah wrote: "Therefore thus saith the LORD of hosts; Because ye have not heard My words, Behold, I will send and take all the families of the north, saith the LORD, and Nebuchadrezzar the king of Babylon, My servant, and will bring them against this land, and against the inhabitants thereof, and against all these nations round about, and will utterly destroy them, and make them an astonishment, and an hissing, and perpetual desolations. Moreover I will take from them the voice of mirth, and the voice of gladness, the voice of the bridegroom, and the voice of the bride, the sound of the millstones, and the light of the candle. And this whole land shall be a desolation, and an astonishment; and these nations shall serve the king of Babylon seventy years. And it shall come to pass, when seventy years are accomplished, that I will punish the king of Babylon, and that nation, saith the LORD, for their iniquity, and the land of the Chaldeans, and will make it perpetual desolations" (Jeremiah 25:8-12).

"And now have I given all these lands into the hand of Nebuchadnezzar the king of Babylon, My servant; and the beasts of the field have I given him also to serve him. And all nations shall serve him, and his son, and his son's son, until the very time of his land come: and then many nations and great kings shall serve themselves of him. And it shall come to pass, that the nation and kingdom which will not serve the same Nebuchadnezzar the king of Babylon, and that will not put their neck under the yoke of the king of Babylon, that nation will I punish, saith the LORD, with the sword, and with the famine, and with the pestilence, until I have consumed them by his hand" (Jeremiah 27:6-8).

"For thus saith the LORD, That after seventy years be accomplished at Babylon I will visit you, and perform My good word toward you, in causing you to return to this place" (Jeremiah 29:10).

These verses tell us some of the details about the captivity, including the causes. When God's people refuse to hear His prophets, and turn to idolatry in any of its various forms, the people may expect divine intervention. God always settles His accounts with those who refuse to heed His warnings.

While there were repeated acts of insubordination toward God's laws, we cite here one illustration of the willful sin in the nation, a sin that continued over many years. It was the sin of stealing God's sabbatic years. Very early in the nation's history God had set forth a proposition for His people. That proposition concerned the use of the soil for agriculture, and it was known as the law of the land. Simply stated, the law read that the land was to be tilled and planted for six years, and that every seventh year the soil should remain idle. God's command was accompanied by the assurance that enough food would be produced in six years to provide for the people during the sabbatic year. The people were not left in ignorance regarding this law because God had spoken clearly: "And the LORD spake unto Moses in mount Sinai, saying, Speak unto the children of Israel, and say unto them, When ye come into the land which I give you, then shall the land keep a sabbath unto the LORD. Six years thou shalt sow thy field, and six years thou shalt prune thy vineyard, and gather in the fruit thereof; But in the seventh year shall be a sabbath of rest unto the land, a sabbath for the LORD: thou shalt neither sow thy field, nor prune thy vineyard. That which groweth of its own accord of thy harvest thou shalt not reap, neither gather the grapes of thy vine undressed: for it is a year of rest unto the land. And the sabbath of the land shall be meat for you; for thee, and for thy servant, and for thy maid, and for thy hired servant, and for thy stranger that sojourneth with thee, And for thy cattle, and for the beast that are in thy land, shall all the increase thereof be meat" (Leviticus 25:1-7).

Nothing is said in these verses about the judgment of God in the event of disobedience on the part of the people. However, in the very next chapter the solemn warning is sounded with unmistakable clarity. "Ye shall keep My sabbaths. . . . If ye walk in My statutes, and keep My commandments, and do them; Then I will give you rain in due season, and the land shall yield her increase. . . . But if ye will not hearken unto Me. . . . And if ye walk contrary unto Me. . . . I will bring the land into desolation. . . . And I will scatter you among the heathen, and will draw out a sword after you: and your land shall be desolate, and your cities waste. Then shall the land enjoy her sabbaths, as long as it lieth desolate, and ye be in your enemies' land; even then shall the land rest, and enjoy her sabbaths" (Leviticus 26:2-4, 14, 21, 32-35).

Now the leaders in the nation knew precisely what was expected of them in relation to God's law of the land. But instead of tilling the land God's way, the people disregarded the law of the Lord and went about their own agricultural program totally ignoring what the Lord had told them. Maybe they thought that God had forgotten, or that He did not mean what He had said, or that He might overlook their transgression. The human heart is capable of varied and numerous excuses and explanations when confronted with its wrongdoing. But sin pays wages. Pay day will surely come someday. Judah's sin against the law of the land continued for some 490 years in all. They worked the soil for everything they could derive from it year after year, ignoring the law which said they must allow the land to remain idle every seventh year. In their mercenary and materialistic spirit they thought they had outmaneuvered God. But whatever a nation or an individual soweth, that is what will be reaped. "Be not deceived; God is not mocked: for whatsoever a man soweth, that shall he also reap" (Galatians 6:7).

The inspired chronicler relates the law of sowing and reaping as that law applied to the Babylonian captivity: "Moreover all the chief of the priests, and the people, transgressed very much after all the abominations of the heathen; and polluted the house of the LORD which He had hallowed in Jerusalem. And the LORD God of their fathers sent to them by His messengers, rising up betimes, and sending; because He had compassion on His people, and on His dwelling place: But they mocked the messengers of God, and despised His words, and misused His prophets, until the wrath of the LORD arose against His people, till there was no remedy. Therefore He brought upon them the king of the Chaldees, who slew their young men with the sword in the house of their sanctuary, and had no compassion upon young man or maiden, old man, or him that stooped for age: He gave them all into his hand. And all the vessels of the house of God, great and small, and the treasures of the house of the LORD, and the treasures of the king, and of his princes; all these he brought to Babylon. And they burnt the house of God, and brake down the wall of Jerusalem, and burnt all the palaces thereof with fire, and destroyed all the goodly vessels thereof. And them that had escaped from the sword carried he away to Babylon; where they were servants to him and his sons until the reign of the kingdom of Persia: To fulfil the word of the LORD by the mouth of Jeremiah, until the land had enjoyed her sabbaths: for as long as she lay desolate she kept sabbath, to fulfil threescore and ten years" (2 Chronicles 36:14-21).

I do not know how my reader will respond to this gripping account of the tragic decline of a nation. I can speak only for myself. This has been a stern and solemn lesson to my own heart. I cannot persist in disobedience to God's laws and escape the inevitable judgment. The first important lesson in Daniel for us, then, is that God hates and judges sin.

"And the Lord gave Jehoiakim king of Judah into his hand" (1:2). In Jeremiah 25:9 God calls Nebuchadnezzar "My servant." Here we are struck immediately with the fact of God's sovereign control over kings and nations. It is good for us to recognize that the hand of God is in the rise and fall of nations. "He removeth kings, and setteth up kings" (2:21). Daniel said to Nebuchadnezzar, "The God of heaven hath given thee a kingdom" (2:37). Sometimes it is difficult for us to understand the strange providential ways of the Lord, and yet we dare never forget that "the most High ruleth in the kingdom of men, and giveth it to whomsoever He will, and setteth up over it the basest of men" (4:17). We may learn from the book of Daniel a philosophy of history, namely that God is sovereign over the destinies of men, even ruthless despots such as Nebuchadnezzar. Such tyrants have certain liberty, but they are definitely bound by divine limitations. Under the sovereign rule of God the most powerful and proudest of rulers must come to nought. "The powers that be are ordained of God" (Roman 13:1). God might raise up a despot like Nebuchadnezzar to cause him to become an instrument of judgment upon a man like Jehoiakim. Why? Because "Jehoiakim . . .

did that which was evil in the sight of the LORD his God"
(2 Chronicles 36:5). The Psalmist said in his prayer to God,
"Surely the wrath of man shall praise Thee: the remainder
of wrath shalt Thou restrain" (Psalm 76:10). The Babylonian
captivity clearly illustrates this principle. God has had
more to do with the affairs of nations than most world
historians know. The purpose of the book of Daniel is to
show how God, by His providence and power, controls and
directs the history of nations.

Much discussion and debate have arisen over the fact
that Daniel records that only "part of the vessels of the
house of God" (1:2) were taken by Nebuchadnezzar, but
that Isaiah prophesied to Hezekiah, "Behold, the days
come, that *all* that is in thine house, and that which thy
fathers have laid up in store unto this day, shall be carried
into Babylon: nothing shall be left, saith the LORD" (2
Kings 20:16-17). There is no contradiction between these
two verses when we remember that Jerusalem was invaded
by Nebuchadnezzar on three distinct occasions, resulting
in three deportations. Let us say that the destruction of
Jerusalem and the deportation of the goods and the captives
were in three stages. The *first* attack took place in the year
606 B.C., during the reign of Jehoiakim, at which time the
city was not destroyed, but the first group of captives was
taken to Babylon, among whom were Daniel and his
friends. The *second* invasion was in the year 598 B.C.,
during the reign of Jehoiachin, the son of the deceased King
Jehoiakim. Again the city was not destroyed, but the king
and his mother and the vessels of the house of the LORD
were taken to Babylon along with a second group of captives (2 Kings 24:6-16). The *third* and final invasion was in
587 B.C. This time the Temple was destroyed, the city
burned, and the remainder of the vessels were taken along
with the final deportation of captives. From Daniel 1:2 it

appears quite clear that Daniel was writing about the first invasion by Nebuchadnezzar in 606 B.C. at which time he himself and his three companions were deported.

When Nebuchadnezzar brought "the vessels of the house of God . . . to the house of his god," he no doubt was acknowledging by this act the help of his god, whom he felt had given these trophies into his hands. The god of Nebuchadnezzar is not named here, however Young believes it is probably Marduk. We shall leave these "vessels" for the present time since they reappear in chapter 5 and will therefore come up for discussion later in our study.

THE DESIGN OF NEBUCHADNEZZAR
(1:3-7)

And the king spake unto Ashpenaz the master of his eunuchs, that he should bring certain of the children of Israel, and of the king's seed, and of the princes; Children in whom was no blemish, but well favoured, and skilful in all wisdom, and cunning in knowledge, and understanding science, and such as had ability in them to stand in the king's palace, and whom they might teach the learning and the tongue of the Chaldeans. And the king appointed them a daily provision of the king's meat, and of the wine which he drank: so nourishing them three years, that at the end thereof they might stand before the king. Now among these were of the children of Judah, Daniel, Hananiah, Mishael, and Azariah: Unto whom the prince of the eunuchs gave names: for he gave unto

Daniel the name of Belteshazzar; and to Hananiah, of Shadrach; and to Mishael, of Meshach; and to Azariah, of Abed-nego (Daniel 1:3-7).

From these verses it is clear that Nebuchadnezzar had designed a plan whereby the most promising of his captives should serve him. He commanded the chief marshal of his court to examine carefully all of the young men of Israel and select those who were of royal lineage, intellectually sound, and physically fit, and commence a training program for them in the school of the Chaldeans. The king wanted the finest young men for the service of his government and to grace the royal court. From this we may conclude that Daniel and his friends had a wide range of knowledge, were handsome in appearance, and of royal stock. These men possibly were descendants of the good king Hezekiah.

At this point in our study we turn again to Isaiah's prophecy to note a detail simply that we might see the accuracy with which the Holy Scriptures were given. "Then said Isaiah to Hezekiah, Hear the word of the LORD of hosts: Behold, the days come, that all that is in thine house, and that which thy fathers have laid up in store until this day, shall be carried to Babylon: nothing shall be left, saith the LORD. And of thy sons that shall issue from thee, which thou shalt beget, shall they take away; and they shall be eunuchs in the palace of the king of Babylon" (Isaiah 39: 5-7).

Now take special note of that seventh verse, "Of thy sons . . . shall they take away; and they shall be *eunuchs* in the palace of the king of Babylon." Daniel tells us that they were given into the custody of the master of the king's eunuchs. The eunuchs were leading men holding positions of authority, such as the Ethiopian eunuch "of great authority" (Acts 8:27). We are not to limit this word to our modern use of it, because in ancient times "the word translated 'eunuch' was used in a broader sense, as of Potiphar, who was married (Genesis 37:36)."[2] Whatever the exact meaning of the term, we see in Isaiah's prophecy one more detail in support of the divine inspiration and infallibility of the Holy Scriptures.

In verses 5 through 6 inclusive there is every evidence that the king's design had in it a clever device through which he had hoped to <u>convert completely the Hebrews to the Chaldean way of life</u>—intellectually, socially, and religiously. After enrolling them in the <u>royal college for a three-year</u> course, the king prepared their diet of food and drink. This meant that these four young men would be assured of an ample supply of rare delicacies from the royal pantry, for theirs was to be a regular daily portion. I take it that they were really being permitted an unlimited indulgence, which was a part of Nebuchadnezzar's brain-washing device. It was the king's subtle method of orientation, a clever scheme to denationalize them completely. This same form of denationalization and brain-washing is being carried on by communists in our day.

The four young men who play an important role in this dramatic unfolding in the book of Daniel are mentioned by name. They are Daniel, Hananiah, Mishael, and Azariah. The <u>speculation as to the age of these four vary from four</u>teen to <u>nineteen years of</u> age. A conservative estimate would be seventeen for Daniel, so that we are safe in concluding that they all were teenagers. There is no way of our knowing how many were selected for this special training, but these four are specifically named since they play an important role in the narrative which follows.

There is some difference of opinion as to the meaning of these names, so we consider it wise not to be dogmatic in asserting the meaning of these and other proper names. The important fact here is that in changing the names of

[2] Edward J. Young, *The Prophecy of Daniel*, page 39.

the four (verse 7), it was the intention of Nebuchadnezzar
to erase every vestige of identification between them and
their own people and land. The new names imposed upon
them was a device to aid in obliterating the name of Israel's
true God. Leupold says that "the change of name involved
the idea that the god of those who bestowed the new name
was to be honored rather than the god of the vanquished."
Each of the four original names contain some form of the
name of Jehovah, so that Israel's God was honored when
the parents named their children at birth. But Nebuchadnezzar intended to change all of that.

So that the reader might have some idea as to the possible meaning of the names and their significance, I have
gathered the following from several other writers on the
subject:

Gaebelein:

Daniel (God is my judge) to Belteshazzar (Bel's prince).

Hananiah (Beloved of the LORD) to Shadrach (Illumined
by the sungod).

Mishael (Who is as God) to Meshach (Who is like Venus).

Azariah (no meaning given) to Abed-nego (The servant of
Nego).

Epp:

Daniel (God will judge) to Belteshazzar (The god Bel
favors).

Hananiah (Beloved of the LORD) to Shadrach (Illuminated
by the sun god).

Mishael (Who is as God) to Meshach (Who is like unto
Venus).

Azariah (The LORD is my help) to Abed-nego (The servant
of Nego).

Leupold:

Daniel (My judge is God) to Belteshazzar (Leupold simply
refers to Daniel 4:8).

Hananiah (Gracious is Jehovah) to Shadrach (Command of Aku).

Mishael (Who is He that is God?) to Meshach (Who is what the moon-god is).

Azariah (Yahweh hath helped) to Abed-nego (Servant of Nego).

These three meanings are recorded here merely to show that, though some difference does exist among the students of Scripture as to the meaning of these proper names, there is a close resemblance in them. At any rate, in each instance the change, insofar as Nebuchadnezzar was concerned, was intended to obliterate any reference to the true God of Israel and keep before the four youths a continuous reminder of the gods of the Chaldeans. All of the commentators I have read agree on this point. Therefore the changing of the names was a device used by the king to accomplish his own design.

THE DEPORTMENT OF DANIEL (1:8-16)

But Daniel purposed in his heart that he would not defile himself with the portion of the king's meat, nor with the wine which he drank: therefore he requested of the prince of the eunuchs that he might not defile himself. Now God had brought Daniel into favour and tender love with the prince of the eunuchs. And the prince of the eunuchs said unto Daniel, I fear my lord the king, who hath appointed your meat and your drink: for why should he see your faces worse liking than the children which are of your sort? then shall ye make me endanger my head to the king. Then said Daniel to Melzar, whom the prince of the eunuchs had set over Daniel, Hananiah, Mishael, and Azariah, Prove thy servants, I beseech thee, ten days; and let them give us pulse to eat, and water to drink. Then let our countenances be looked upon before thee, and the countenance of the children that eat of the portion of the king's meat: and as thou seest, deal with thy servants. So he consented to them in this matter, and proved them ten days. And at the end of ten days their countenances appeared fairer and fatter in flesh than all the children which did eat the portion of the king's meat. Thus Melzar took away the portion of their meat, and the wine that they should drink; and gave them pulse (Daniel 1:8-16).

The prince of the eunuchs could change Daniel's name but not his nature. Putting a man in a different culture will not necessarily change his character. This new and different environment brought Daniel to a crisis in his life. He knew that he had been powerless to prevent his deportation, but he knew also that he could be defiled only by his own behavior. This was the crucial test for Daniel and his friends, and the test was not an easy one. After all, he had been taken captive, not because of his own sins, but as the result of the sins of his fathers. Now as a slave in a foreign country he might have become bitter or discouraged and falsely concluded, "What's the use? I might as well live it up and enjoy Babylonian life to the full, for tomorrow I might be put to death." Or he might have followed the vain reasoning, When you are in Babylon, do as the Babylonians do. But this teenager, far from home and loved ones, solemnly resolved in his heart that he would not defile himself with the king's delicacies.

It has been pointed out by T. Kliefoth that there were three things of a distinctly heathen character which Daniel and his companions had to decide upon daily: the acquisi-

tion of heathen learning, the bearing of heathen names, and
the eating of heathen food. The first two of these did not
necessarily involve conscientious scruples. Though they had
to learn heathen wisdom and sciences, they would not have
to accept as truth everything that was taught them. But in
the matter of eating heathen food more serious issues were
involved. The portion of meat on the king's table would
first be dedicated to some heathen god in sacrifice, so to
share in such a feast would mean sharing in honoring the
god in whose name the animal was sacrificed. For that
reason Daniel refused to contaminate himself. His great
decision was both a moral and spiritual one and it marked
him as a young man of purpose and high principle. It was
here that Daniel took his first stand. He was not exempt
from temptation, but he refused to yield to that temptation.
No man is of any use, nor will be ever of any use, if he is
not a man of high purpose when faced with temptation to
do wrong. When Barnabas came to Antioch, he exhorted
the believers there "that with *purpose* of heart they would
cleave unto the Lord" (Acts 11:23). Paul wrote to Timothy,
"Thou hast fully known my . . . *purpose*" (2 Timothy 3:10).
Our times call for young people who, like Daniel and his
friends, will exhibit a steadfast devotion to high and noble
principle. The source of Daniel's momentary victory and
the secret of the blessing that attended him thereafter can
be summed up in the statement, "But Daniel purposed in
his heart that he would not defile himself."

What did Daniel have to guide him at this crucial time?
What determined his proper deportment when he stood at
the crossroads? Personally I can see but one answer to this.
Daniel's decision resulted from the knowledge he possessed
of the Holy Scriptures, those inspired writings penned by
Moses, David, and the prophets. Such knowledge controlled the spirit and manner in which he refused the king's

food. Along with the strength of character to discern and
decide, he displayed sound common sense, at the same time
being courteous. There was neither rudeness nor fanaticism
in his stand for what he believed to be right, but merely a
polite request to be excused from eating and drinking forbidden fare. Daniel would not surrender his faith nor renounce the Word of his God, and in his deportment he has
left an example for all believers. Let every young believer be
well assured that it matters tremendously how you make
decisions in your teens. Guard your deportment at all times,
and watch your manners.

"Now God had brought Daniel into favour and tender
love with the prince of the eunuchs" (1:9). Leupold renders
the words, "*tender love*," to read, "sympathy." The idea to
be emphasized here is that the chief eunuch was convinced
that Daniel's request was made in sincerity and upon the
basis of principle, therefore he was sympathetic and had
respect for the request. Do not overlook the fact that it was
God who caused the chief eunuch to react sympathetically
toward Daniel. Daniel was true to his God and honored
Him, and God honored the true witness of His faithful
servant.

There is much in this first chapter that we can learn from
Daniel. If we will live a separated life in obedience to God's
Word (see 2 Corinthians 6:14-18), God can and often does
control the hearts of men for our good. Surely God was
dealing with the heart of the chief eunuch. Dare to be a
Daniel and determine that you will be true to your Lord
whatever the cost or consequences. Don't trifle with your
conscience. Stand for God's principle of separation, never
fearing that you might be dubbed narrow-minded or
bigoted. "When a man's ways please the LORD, He maketh
even his enemies to be at peace with him" (Proverbs 16:7).

The first response from the prince of the eunuchs grew

out of fear for his own safety. Even though he was sympathetic toward Daniel, he replied to Daniel's request in the following words, "I fear my lord the king, who hath appointed your meat and your drink: for why should he see your faces worse liking than the children which are of your sort? then shall ye make me endanger my head to the king" (1:10). In substance the prince of the eunuchs was saying to Daniel, "I respect your convictions and your high principles, and I would like to grant you your request but I dare not. If you lose weight because of a change of diet and appear pale and undernourished, then I could be beheaded." The difficulty of this man's position we must recognize. He was answerable to his superior who was in this case the ruling monarch of the empire.

From the contents of verse 11 it seems as though the prince of the eunuchs then delegated to one, Melzar, the oversight of Daniel and his companions, for we read, "Then said Daniel to Melzar, whom the prince of the eunuchs had set over Daniel, Hananiah, Mishael, and Azariah, Prove thy servants, I beseech thee, ten days; and let them give us pulse to eat, and water to drink. Then let our countenances be looked upon before thee, and the countenance of the children that eat of the portion of the king's meat: and as thou seest, deal with thy servants" (1:11-13). In the same courteous manner with which Daniel answered the chief of the eunuchs, he now approached the chief's subordinate, who was appointed the specific responsibility for his training. This second appeal is simply another sincere effort by Daniel to keep from sinning against his better knowledge and therefore against his conscience, for "to him that knoweth to do good, and doeth it not, to him it is sin" (James 4:17). Daniel's request was a display of faith, courage, and fairness. Neither the "pulse" (a vegetable or grain food), nor the water, would be included in the forbidden foods. Daniel was so certain that God would honor his stand for the right, he proposed that a comparison be made at the expiration of "ten days." Here is a display of faith, courage, and wisdom which characterize Daniel's behavior throughout the entire book. Let not one of my readers come to the hasty faulty conclusion that an undue amount of emphasis is being given here to a matter of little importance. The great care that Daniel and his friends exercised in doing the will of God at this point shows how clearly they discerned the issues at hand and how correct they were in getting their bearings at the very start.

The stand which these youths took paid off in rich dividends. The one who had custody over them gave them their request: "So he consented to them in this matter, and proved them ten days" (1:14). And the results were exactly what one might expect them to be. When the four young men were brought before the king after the ten days of testing they were healthier physically and keener intellectually than all those who had been eating the food which the king had appointed. "And at the end of the ten days their countenances appeared fairer and fatter in flesh than all the children which did eat the portion of the king's meat" (1:15). There is a beautiful lesson for us all in this. I see here a demonstration of both the grace and power of God. Daniel and his friends were enjoying the provision of divine grace while the Babylonians were commencing to see a demonstration of divine power. It was nothing short of miraculous that Daniel and his friends flourished physically on such a meager diet. We Christians should take note of this to our own blessing and advantage. The believer who adheres to the will of God shall not be found wanting. "Thus Melzar took away the portion of their meat, and the wine that they should drink; and gave them pulse" (1:16). The test was so successful that Daniel's requested diet was continued. What a testimony to those Babylonian leaders of the power of Israel's God! "Wherefore let them that suffer according to the will of God commit the keeping of their souls to Him in well doing, as unto a faithful Creator" (1 Peter 4:19).

THE DEVELOPMENT OF DANIEL (1:17-21)

As for these four children, God gave them knowledge and skill in all learning and wisdom: and Daniel had understanding in all visions and dreams. Now at the end of the days that the king had said he should bring them in, then the prince of the eunuchs brought them in before Nebuchadnezzar. And the king communed with them; and among them all was found none like Daniel, Hananiah, Mishael, and Azariah: therefore stood they before the king. And in all matters of wisdom and understanding, that the king enquired of them, he found them ten times better than all the magicians and astrologers that were in all his realm. And Daniel continued even unto the first year of king Cyrus (Daniel 1:17-21).

The emphasis in the remaining verses of this chapter lies in the progress and growth, especially in Daniel, in knowledge and understanding in the literature and sciences of the Babylonians, and a special insight into every sort of vision and dream. Remember, Daniel was soon to demonstrate the calling and gifts of a prophet. The first qualification to become a prophet Daniel met in his resolute purpose to be holy, undefiled, and separate from sin. The second qualification he met by giving himself diligently to his studies. But an important fact not to be overlooked is that "God gave them knowledge." Daniel's <u>attainments were gifts from God</u>. <u>Daniel learned this for himself, and we must learn the same truth for ourselves</u>. As we grow and progress in Christian experience let us never lose sight of the fact that <u>all we have obtained has come from God</u>. If ever we do become proud of our learning, then we have fallen into the snare with those of whom it is written, "Knowledge puffeth up" (1 Corinthians 8:1).

The wisdom and understanding which God gave to Daniel was not merely the wisdom of this world, but knowledge of a discerning kind. There can be no doubt that he gathered much in the way of the superstitious practices of the Chaldeans, for in order to serve effectively the Babylonian government, it wa<u>s necessary that he should be instructed in the ways and wisdom of the Babylonians.</u> But God gave <u>to him the greater gift of discernme</u>nt, that divinely <u>directed insight to distinguish things which diff</u>er, that <u>enlightenment that comes from on high and which no man can achieve by his own strength or endeav</u>or.

The progress and development was so noticeable that the king found Daniel and his companions "ten times better than all the magicians and astrologers that were in all his realm" (1:20). "*Ten* days" testing time and "*ten* times better"! Nebuchadnezzar had never witnessed such powers of perception and insight. It was superior to anything that his court professors had ever displayed. Daniel's was a high type of learning never before known by the most learned among the Babylonians, "Because the foolishness of God is wiser than men; and the weakness of God is stronger than men" (1 Corinthians 1:25).

"And Daniel continued" (1:21). Of course he continued. It is exactly what one might expect. This entire first chapter serves as an excellent introduction to the book of Daniel, showing how, in the providence of God, Daniel was protected, preserved, and came into a position of prominence and influence. It should give us courage to continue boldly in the way of life that God demands of His own. Whatever the Word of God teaches us to be His unalterable will, by that we must stand fast. Every believer must be one with Daniel in this, at least. We as God's people are in the midst of a world which is just as strongly opposed to God and His people as were the Babylonians in Daniel's day. The modern Babylon of our time, prophesied in Revelation 17 and 18, would crush the Christian completely, if this were possible. Many are becoming drunk with her wine and engaging in her spiritual adultery. The Babylon of the last days has taken captive many who are unprincipled and untaught.

The Word of God is plain. We must take a positive stand, dare to stand with the few, and trust the grace and power of our faithful Lord. "Wherefore come out from among them, and be ye separate, saith the Lord, and touch not the unclean thing; and I will receive you, And will be a Father unto you, and ye shall be My sons and daughters, saith the Lord Almighty" (2 Corinthians 6:17-18). "Daniel purposed in his heart. . . . and Daniel continued." Certainly he continued, because, "When a man's ways please the LORD, He maketh even his enemies to be at peace with him" (Proverbs 16:7). If Daniel had failed or compromised in his first test, how great would have been his loss! But he did not fail; thus he lived to see the downfall of the very same empire into whose power he was taken captive.

Now no one will deny that times have changed since Daniel lived on the earth, but Daniel's God, who is our God, has not changed nor has the Word of God changed. The peculiar tendencies of our day are to render obsolete the principles upon which the men of yesteryear stood firm. But the principles of modern psychology are poor pillows upon which to lay our weary heads. Psychology would have us conform to the present world system, so that when we are in Babylon we do as the Babylonians do. But the Bible admonishes the Christian to be not conformed to this world. It is possible to succeed in high school, college, or business and remain a truly separated Christian according to the standard taught in God's Word. When Daniel faced a crisis in his moral life he did not parley or postpone the decision. He answered the temptation to do wrong with an immediate, "No." Better to stand for the right principle, as did Daniel, than to betray a Christian profession upon the slightest pressure from the world. Dare to be a Daniel!

CHAPTER TWO

CHAPTER TWO

The second chapter of Daniel is possibly one of the most famous chapters in the Bible because it contains one of the most amazing prophecies in the Bible. Indeed we have here a mountain peak of Biblical prophecy. Someone has called it "the ABC of prophecy." Dr. Ironside said, "I suppose it contains the most complete, and yet the most simple prophetic picture that we have in all the Word of God."[1] Among the forty commentators whose books on Daniel I have read, almost all of them have emphasized the importance and significance of chapter 2. The reievance of the prophecy is seen in the fact that here is depicted the development and decline of world power in the rise and fall of kingdoms and empires.

There was need for such a revelation at that particular time because the conquest of Judah by Babylon introduced the first major Gentile world power. What did the future hold for the people of God? Did the destruction of Jerusalem and the deportation of the people of Judah seal with finality the fate of the nation? It was the proper time for God to declare Himself as to the future of His people on earth.

Inasmuch as this chapter, and later chapters in Daniel, are associated with dreams, I am constrained to say a few

[1] H. A. Ironside, *Lectures on Daniel,* page 25.

51

words on the subject of dreams. A dream is a vision in sleep, to be distinguished from a vision when one is awake (cf., Acts 2:17). Evil men who give their minds over to vile imaginations in sinful practices are spoken of by Jude as "filthy dreamers" (Jude 8), godless men who exercise their minds in waking visions of a sensuous and defiling character. These are "idle dreamers."

Then there are dreams which occur in sleep, the stimuli of which are either physical or mental. Each of us has had his night's sleep disturbed at some time by a dream.

But the dreams spoken of in Daniel's prophecy are different from the dreams we experience today. In ancient times God said, "If there be a prophet among you, I the LORD will make Myself known unto him in a vision, and will speak unto him in a dream" (Numbers 12:6). Three verses in the book of Job will aid us here: "For God speaketh once, yea twice, yet man perceiveth it not. In a dream, in a vision of the night, when deep sleep falleth upon men, in slumberings upon the bed; Then He openeth the ears of men, and sealeth their instruction" (Job 33:14-16). Here it is clearly stated that God spoke to men in dreams to write His ways in their hearts and minds. It was His silent revelation to men through a method chosen for reasons known only to Himself. Thus He appeared to Abimelech (Genesis 20:3), to Joseph (Genesis 37:5), to Pharaoh (Genesis 41:1, 25), to Solomon (1 Kings 3:5).

This information will serve to show us that the method of dreams has been used of the Lord to communicate His plans and purposes to men. God no longer speaks to men in dreams because His full and final revelation to man has been given in the Scriptures and through His Son Jesus Christ. Dreams in our day are not the result of inspiration, but of physical, emotional, or psychological causes.

THE DREAM OF NEBUCHADNEZZAR (2:1)

And in the second year of the reign of Nebuchadnezzar Nebuchadnezzar dreamed dreams, wherewith his spirit was troubled, and his sleep brake from him (Daniel 2:1).

With the overthrow of Jerusalem and the Jews, Nebuchadnezzar had been elevated to the lofty position of the world's greatest ruler. His conquests did not bring to him peace of mind, but instead he was troubled about the future of his empire, wondering just how long he could maintain his grip on the then known world. We know from verse 29 that it was the king's anxiety over "what should come to pass hereafter," that is, how things might shape up for him in the future, that caused him to dream. The dream did not merely arouse curiosity but rather frightened him, which is the meaning of the word "troubled."

Here we are reminded that power and wealth do not in themselves produce peace of mind. Laxity and luxury are not conducive to tranquility. He who reaches for power and possessions in this life is never satisfied. The man of the world who has his portion in this life only (Psalm 17:14) is living for a world that is passing away (1 John 2:17), so that his "assets" actually become his burden. Conscience, which makes cowards of us all, was troubling the pagan king. Even Job said, "Thou scarest me with dreams, and terrifiest me through visions" (Job 7:14). What really troubled Nebuchadnezzar was the fact of the "hereafter" (Daniel 2:29). His dream was God's answer to his problem.

Before we proceed with an explanation of the chapter, examining the verses in order, I would point out at this time the important phrase, "the latter days," in verse 28:

> *But there is a God in heaven that revealeth secrets, and maketh known to the king Nebuchadnezzar what shall be in* the latter days *(Daniel 2:28).*

Now I am not insisting that every usage of the expression, "the latter days," in Scripture is a predictive prophecy referring to God's people and is to be consummated in the times of the Messiah. However, to stop short of the Messianic import and apply the expression to mean the end of the days of Nebuchadnezzar's reign is misleading. Robert Culver says, "Whenever the scope of an Old Testament prophecy is measured by these words, either in the Hebrew or Aramaic sections, the times of Messiah are always within the scope of that prophecy. The expression appears in the following passages, each one a predictive prophecy: Genesis 49:1; Deuteronomy 4:30; 31:29; Numbers 24:14; Isaiah 2:2; Jeremiah 23:20; 30:24; 48:47; 49:39; Ezekiel 38:16; Daniel 2:28; 10:14; Hosea 3:5; Micah 4:1."[2] The point for emphasis here is that Nebuchadnezzar's dream and its interpretation contain a prophecy of the course of the nation from his own time down to the second coming of Messiah to the earth to set up His final kingdom.

To further elucidate the term, "the latter days," we turn to another term which our Lord used, "the times of the Gentiles" (Luke 21:24). This expression is not found in the book of Daniel. It was used only by our Lord, therefore it is a New Testament term exclusively. Jesus said, "And they shall fall by the edge of the sword, and shall be led away captive into all nations: and Jerusalem shall be trodden down of the Gentiles, until *the times of the Gentiles* be fulfilled" (Luke 21:24). Now we should not confuse "the times of the Gentiles" with "the fulness of the Gentiles" (Romans 11:25). These two terms do not mean the same

[2] Robert Culver, *Daniel and the Latter Days,* page 107.

thing. *The fullness of the Gentiles* ends with the removal of the Church from the earth to Heaven by our Lord before the tribulation. While it is true that the believing Jews of this present dispensation who trusted in Christ are in the Church, such are surely in the overwhelming minority in the company which make up the Church. The true Church of Christ consists mainly of saved Gentiles, so that *the fullness of the Gentiles* means that total number of people, taken chiefly from among Gentiles, who will make up the completed Church finally. When the Church is removed from the earth Jewish history will be resumed. So then, *the times of the Gentiles* commenced with the Babylonian captivity under Nebuchadnezzar and will conclude when Christ returns to the earth, after the tribulation, to set up His kingdom. It includes the Church Age in which we now live, so that we are living in the latter days. That the time of Gentile rule should not continue indefinitely, and that Messiah would come in due time to set up the kingdom for the Jews, is clearly taught in the interpretation of Nebuchadnezzar's dream.

THE DEMANDS OF NEBUCHADNEZZAR
(2:2-11)

Then the king commanded to call the magicians, and the astrologers, and the sorcerers, and the Chaldeans, for to shew the king his dreams. So they came and stood before the king. And the king said unto them, I have dreamed a dream, and my spirit was troubled to know the dream. Then spake the Chaldeans to the king in Syriack, O king, live for ever: tell thy servants the dream, and we will shew the interpretation. The king answered and said to the Chaldeans, The thing is gone from me: if ye will not make known unto me the dream, with the interpretation thereof, ye shall be cut in pieces, and your houses shall be made a dunghill. But if ye shew the dream, and the interpretation thereof, ye shall receive of me gifts and rewards and great honour: therefore shew me the dream, and the interpretation thereof. They answered again and said, Let the king tell his servants the dream, and we will shew the interpretation of it. The king answered and said, I know of certainty that ye would gain the time, because ye see the thing is gone from me. But if ye will not make known unto me the dream, there is but one decree for you: for ye have prepared lying and corrupt words to speak before me, till the time be changed: therefore tell me the dream, and I shall know that ye can shew me the interpretation thereof. The Chaldeans answered before the king, and said, There is not a man upon the earth that can shew the king's matter: therefore there is no king, lord, nor ruler, that asked such things at any magician, or astrologer, or Chaldean. And it is a rare thing that the king requireth, and there is none other that can shew it before the king, except the gods, whose dwelling is not with flesh (Daniel 2:2-11).

Because of the nature of the dream Nebuchadnezzar awoke from sleep in a spirit of agitation and nervousness, a condition that grew until he became "angry and very furious" (2:12). He summoned his magicians, enchanters, and sorcerers, which made up his entire university of scholarly experts, and proceeded to tell them why he sent for them. He experienced a dream that greatly disturbed him, leaving him in a state of fear. Instead of telling his court of scholars what the dream was about, he insisted that they tell him what he had dreamed and then interpret the dream.

A matter of interest right here is whether or not the king remembered the dream. The commentators are divided, some saying he did and others insisting he did not. Personally I do not believe that the king had forgotten the dream. My viewpoint is based upon verse 9 where Nebuchadnezzar says, "Tell me the dream, and I shall know that ye can shew me the interpretation thereof." How could the king know if their statement of the dream was correct unless he had remembered the dream? This tyrannical and unreasonable demand seems almost deliberate, as though he wanted to expose and ultimately dispose of these men who made pretense of having access to deep and hidden things. In further support of my viewpoint on this matter I refer my readers to the more literal rendering of the statement, "The thing is gone from me" (verses 5 and 8). The Authorized Version has led some to the conclusion that the king was saying, "I have forgotten the thing (i.e., the dream)." But both Leupold and Young give their translation of the Hebrew. Leupold translates it, "The thing is certain with me" (page 60). There is little difference between the two. Being in an ugly mood, the king is stating plainly that his demand is irrevocable. He had made up his mind and didn't intend to change it.

The Chaldeans appealed for leniency from the king on the ground that he was demanding the impossible. They said, "There is not a man upon the earth that can shew the king's matter: therefore there is no king, lord, nor ruler, that asked such things at any magician, or astrologer, or Chaldean" (2:10). Theirs was a desperate effort not to say anything further to irritate their king, but they finally took courage and told him that it just could not be done. They were at once confessing their own limitations and their acknowledgment in a sovereign and supreme God who is greater than any human (2:11). Indeed "the natural man receiveth not the things of the Spirit of God: for they are foolishness unto him: neither can he know them, because they are spiritually discerned" (1 Corinthians 2:14). God also challenges the underworld of evil spirits and false gods to foretell the future (see Isaiah 41:21-23).

THE DECREE OF NEBUCHADNEZZAR
(2:12-13)

For this cause the king was angry and very furious, and commanded to destroy all the wise men of Babylon. And the decree went forth that the wise men should be slain; and they sought Daniel and his fellows to be slain (Daniel 2:12-13).

Little wonder the king issued his strong decree. I don't blame him at all. I admit the penalty to be severe, however. These men who were trained in the king's university to interpret mysteries were frauds. They had a knowledge of the religions, arts, philosophies, and sciences of their time, yet they were powerless to interpret God's inspired message to man. They were like some modern ministers of our own day who spend their time studying philosophy, psychiatry, psychology, social science, political science, and then continue under the pretense of being God's messengers to men. I am not surprised at the resentment of the man on the street against our modern churches, nor do I blame him. I don't look for men in our government to stand up and declare with authority, "Thus saith the Lord," but I do expect it from men who occupy the pulpits of our churches. If you call yourself a minister of God, but have failed to declare with authority the whole counsel of God as revealed in His

Word, the Bible, then do not be surprised if you are held in contempt. The true servant of Christ might not have the world at his feet, but at least he is respected by many for being true to his high calling. Babylon the great of the last days, that mother of harlots, the growing world church, meets her doom at the hands of the world's political powers, because she too is a fraud (read Revelation 17).

But I wonder if the decree of the godless Nebuchadnezzar was not Satan's plot to destroy Daniel, for we read, "And the decree went forth that the wise men should be slain; and they sought Daniel and his fellows to be slain" (2:13). It is a matter of no consequence to Satan that many should be killed in order to accomplish his ends. Paul wrote to the Thessalonians, "Wherefore we would have come unto you, even I Paul, once and again; but Satan hindered us. . . . Finally, brethren, pray for us . . . that we may be delivered from unreasonable and wicked men" (1 Thessalonians 2:18; 2 Thessalonians 3:1, 2). Every detail of Nebuchadnezzar's decree might have been a diabolical plot of Satan to dispose of Daniel and his godly companions. There was to be a mass execution, to be certain, but the goal of it seems to be the extermination of Daniel and his friends. It seems strange that Daniel was included in the king's fatal order, and yet he was not summoned before the king to tell and interpret the dream (verse 2). Daniel was not given an opportunity to tell the king his dream, nevertheless he was sentenced to die. What would you or I do in such a predicament?

THE DECISION OF DANIEL (2:14-23)

Upon hearing the king's decree, Daniel was faced with an important decision. He had to act and act speedily, for there was not a minute to be lost. His decision showed the marks of a man of God.

The Exercise of Prudence.

> *Then Daniel answered with counsel and wisdom to Arioch the captain of the king's guard, which was gone forth to slay the wise men of Babylon: He answered and said to Arioch the king's captain, Why is the decree so hasty from the king? Then Arioch made the thing known to Daniel. Then Daniel went in, and desired of the king that he would give him time, and that he would shew the king the interpretation (Daniel 2:14-16).*

Mark the words, "Then Daniel answered with counsel and wisdom." In a display of unusual tact, Daniel gave a discreet and prudent answer. He began by approaching the chief executioner who was already on his way to round up the victims. Daniel must have won the friendship and confidence of Arioch, for Arioch arranged a meeting between Nebuchadnezzar and Daniel so that Daniel could plead his case before the king. Apparently the king was still desirous of learning the meaning of his dream, for in spite of his anger and harsh decree, a stay of execution was granted to Daniel and his friends as well as to the Chaldeans. All of this called for rare courage and faith on Daniel's part.

The Exercise of Prayer.

> *Then Daniel went to his house, and made the thing known to Hananiah, Mishael, and Azariah, his companions: That they would desire mercies of the God of heaven concerning this secret; that Daniel and his fellows should not perish with the rest of the wise men of Babylon. Then was the secret revealed unto Daniel in a night vision. Then Daniel blessed the God of heaven (Daniel 2:17-19).*

Having received a grant of time on the promise that he would show the king the interpretation of the dream, Daniel proceeded at once to call his companions to prayer. Taking to their knees, they brought the whole matter before the Lord. The men of Babylon were marked by spiritual poverty and panic, while the men of God were marked by prudence and prayer. Daniel did the thing that was right and reasonable. The modern leaders in some present-day churches, finding themselves in a similar predicament, would call a committee together or consult the textbooks on dreams. The prayer of Daniel made known to God that they came to "desire mercies." These men saw no worth in themselves, so they cast themselves upon the God of mercy. In prayer meetings such as this history has been made. From these verses we should be reminded that prayer is essential to understanding spiritual truth. The secrets of God are not revealed to those who do not know Him and pray to Him. He Himself said, "Call unto Me, and I will answer thee, and shew thee great and mighty things, which thou knowest not" (Jeremiah 33:3). Nebuchadnezzar took his worries to bed with him; Daniel took his to God in prayer. If you are a Christian, cultivate the good habit of taking everything to God in prayer. (Read Psalm 37:5; Philippians 4:6-7; Hebrews 13:5; James 1:5; 1 Peter 5:7).

The Exercise of Praise.

> *Then was the secret revealed unto Daniel in a night vision. Then Daniel blessed the God of heaven. Daniel answered and said, Blessed be the name of God for ever and ever: for wisdom and might are His: And He changeth the times and the seasons: He removeth kings, and setteth up kings: He giveth wisdom unto the wise, and knowledge to them that know understanding: He revealeth the deep and secret things: He knoweth what is*

in the darkness, and the light dwelleth with Him. I thank Thee, and praise Thee, O Thou God of my fathers, who hast given me wisdom and might, and hast made known unto me now what we desired of Thee: for Thou hast now made known unto us the king's matter (Daniel 2:19-23).

The actual prayer, that is, the words which made up the prayer, are not recorded. But verse 19 does tell us that Daniel requested of God the unknown secret of the king's dream and its interpretation, and that God answered the prayer. Daniel had prayed in faith. When God had granted him his request, he immediately gave praise and glory to God. His praise commenced with the ascription that God's name should be eternally blessed. While we could not prove that Daniel was quoting passages from the Scriptures, certainly there was much material from which he could draw and with which he was no doubt acquainted. (See Job 12:13-22; Psalms 31:15; 41:13; 75:6; 103:1-2; 113:1-2). Daniel praised God for His revelation, His power, His providence in controlling the time element and the duration of the seasons, and His absolute authority over earthly monarchs. If a man has true wisdom, his only source of that wisdom is God. If a man is a ruler or leader of others, his tenure of office is owed to God whether or not divine control is in evidence to the ruler or his subjects. In verse 22 Daniel acknowledged divine omniscience. All of the deep and dark things unknown to man are surely known by God, and He only is able to reveal them to man (see 1 Corinthians 2:9-11). There is no doubt that Daniel praised God specifically for the revelation of prophecy through Nebuchadnezzar's dream. Finally, in verse 23, Daniel expressed thanks because his petition was heard and answered. I am much impressed at this point with the deep spirituality of this young man, because I detect no mention of the fact that his life had been spared, and this tells me that his prayer was selfless. It is not infrequent that our prayers are selfish requests, the answers to which we hope will contribute to our comfort, good health, and prosperity.

One of the needed lessons we all might learn from our chapter up to this point is the fact that, though He stands ready to reveal the deep things to His children, God refuses to reveal Himself to just any casual passer-by. We must have a spiritual attitude toward God and His Word, because "the natural man receiveth not the things of the Spirit of God: for they are foolishness unto him: neither can he know them, because they are spiritually discerned" (1 Corinthians 2:14). Our Lord had this in mind when He said, "Give not that which is holy unto the dogs, neither cast ye your pearls before swine, lest they trample them under their feet, and turn again and rend you" (Matthew 7:6). It appears that He was thinking in this same vein when He prayed, "I thank Thee, O Father, Lord of heaven and earth, because Thou hast hid these things from the wise and prudent, and hast revealed them unto babes" (Matthew 11:25). One must have a spiritual attitude that flows out of a spiritual life in order to understand the deep things of God. Daniel was that kind of person.

THE DISAVOWAL OF DANIEL (2:24-30)

Therefore Daniel went in unto Arioch, whom the king had ordained to destroy the wise men of Babylon: he went and said thus unto him; Destroy not the wise men of Babylon: bring me in before the king, and I will shew unto the king the interpretation. Then Arioch brought in Daniel before the king in haste, and said thus unto him, I have found a man of the captives of Judah, that will make known unto the king the interpretation. The king answered and said to Daniel, whose name was Belteshazzar, Art thou able to make known unto me the dream which I have seen, and the interpretation thereof? Daniel answered in the presence of the king, and said, The secret which the king hath demanded cannot the wise men, the astrologers, the magicians, the soothsayers, shew unto the king; But there is a God in heaven that revealeth secrets, and maketh known to the king Nebuchadnezzar what shall be in the latter days. Thy dream, and the visions of thy head upon thy bed, are these; As for thee, O king, thy thoughts came into thy mind upon thy bed, what should come to pass hereafter: and He that revealeth secrets maketh known to thee what shall come to pass. But as for me, this secret is not revealed to me for any wisdom that I have more than any living, but for their sakes that shall make known the interpretation to the king, and that thou mightest know the thoughts of thy heart (Daniel 2:24-30).

When he had possession of the much coveted answer to the mystery of the king's dream, Daniel was prepared to appear before the monarch. His first words were to the royal executioner, requesting him to spare the wise men of Babylon and to escort him to the king's chamber. Losing no time, Arioch led Daniel before the king and made known to him the claim of Daniel. I see here a vastly different attitude on the part of Daniel and Arioch. Arioch desired credit for himself as is obvious in his words, "I have found," as though he through his own effort discovered the man who could interpret the king's dream. Daniel, on the other hand, displayed dignity and humility, disavowed any ability of his own, and pointed Nebuchadnezzar to God. Arioch was excited about being a figure in so important an event, while Daniel meekly gave God the glory. Actually Arioch did not find Daniel at all, rather Daniel found him. The courage, wisdom, grace, poise, and humility displayed by Daniel are rarely found among us these days.

Daniel was like Joseph on a similar occasion (Genesis 41:16). Both admit to human weakness and point to God as the revealer of prophetic secrets. Too frequently some of us miss opportunities like this to glorify God. We discover some truth in the Bible that no one had previously brought to our attention, and then we go about preaching it as though we wrote it. When will we living mortals disclaim any wisdom of our own and give to God the glory and honor which are due Him? Let us remember at all times that "there is a God in heaven that revealeth secrets."

It is not easy for any of us to escape the sin of intellectual pride. Not infrequently pride accompanies, or else follows, the acquisition of knowledge. The unspiritual man is proud that he knows so much; the spiritual mind is humbled because of lack of knowledge. Do not forget that the sin of intellectual pride began with Satan. One of the requirements for spiritual leadership is "Not a novice, lest being lifted up with pride he fall into the condemnation of the devil" (1 Timothy 3:6). Had Daniel fallen into this sin the entire record might have been different. *Daniel continued*, but he could not have continued if he had had a high opinion of his own ability, because "Pride goeth before destruction, and an haughty spirit before a fall" (Proverbs 16:18; 18:12). "Seest thou a man wise in his own conceit? there is more hope of a fool than of him" (Proverbs 26:12). Later in our study we shall see how Nebuchadnezzar's failure to learn this lesson from Daniel resulted in the king's shameful downfall (Daniel 4:37; 5:20-21). O, that Nebuchadnezzar had learned from Daniel when he said, "But as for me, this secret is not revealed to me for any wisdom that I have"!

THE DISCLOSURE OF THE DREAM
(2:31-35)

Thou, O king, sawest, and behold a great image. This great image, whose brightness was excellent, stood before thee; and the form thereof was terrible. This image's head was of fine gold, his breast and his arms of silver, his belly and his thighs of brass, His legs of iron, his feet part of iron and part of clay. Thou sawest till that a stone was cut out without hands, which smote the image upon his feet that were of iron and clay, and brake them to pieces. Then was the iron, the clay, the brass, the silver, and the gold, broken to pieces together, and became like the chaff of the summer threshingfloors; and the wind carried them away, that no place was found for them: and the stone that smote the image became a great mountain, and filled the whole earth (Daniel 2:31-35).

These five verses bring to light exactly what Nebuchadnezzar had dreamed. One can imagine the excitement that prevailed throughout the king's court when the word spread that Daniel was to disclose the dream. With skill Daniel reviewed the essentials of the dream. He recalled to the king how he lay gazing upon a huge statue. I take the word "great" to refer to the size of the image; it was an immense statue. The second thing was its "brightness," the extraordinary splendor of its shining metal. While no doubt beautiful and attractive, its size and appearance were terrifying. The disclosure to this point is accurate. The king had admitted the morning after he had the dream that he was "troubled" (2:1, 3).

The statue was that of a man, the particulars of which are made to pass quickly before the king. The head of the statue was of pure gold, the chest and arms of silver, the belly and thighs of brass (or bronze), the legs were of iron, and the feet were a mixture of two materials, iron and clay. (There is no specific mention of toes at this point.) There is no action coming from the statue; it merely stood. Nevertheless this polymetallic colossus was very impressive. The student might note the descending value of the metals.

Then, quite dramatically, a stone appeared, "cut out without hands," meaning that the stone was formed by God without human power or assistance (verses 34-45). With the appearance of the stone action commenced and the picture became a moving picture. As the stone moved swiftly toward the earth, it was noted that the statue lay directly in its path. The stone struck directly upon the feet of iron and clay with such vehemence that the entire statue was crushed to pieces. So thorough was the destruction of the image, we are told the metals were reduced to powder, "like the chaff of the summer threshingfloors," so that no trace of them could be found. "The sweeping away was so complete that the dust found no visible resting place" (Leupold). The climax of the dream shows the stone, which had smitten the image, growing to such gigantic proportions that it became a huge mountain which filled the whole earth.

There is neither incongruity nor superfluity in Daniel's entire word description of Nebuchadnezzar's dream. It is a masterpiece because it is divinely revealed. It is genuine and authentic. Criticism and change are offered without warrant. These are the details in the dream exactly as Nebuchadnezzar saw them in his night vision. The king made no attempt to correct or contradict Daniel in one little point because Daniel's description was accurate. One can imagine with what emotion and trepidation the king listened to Daniel, for while he was listening to the voice of a young Hebrew man, he was actually hearing a Voice from another world. The *God of Heaven* was speaking to a king on earth. Nebuchadnezzar must have recognized immediately that the words of Daniel were inspired and authoritative. "This is the dream," declared Daniel. And the king knew it!

THE DETAILS OF THE DREAM (2:37-45)

Thou, O king, art a king of kings: for the God of heaven hath given thee a kingdom, power, and strength, and glory. And wheresoever the children of men dwell, the beasts of the field and the fowls of the heaven hath He given into thine hand, and hath made thee ruler over them all. Thou art this head of gold. And after thee shall arise another kingdom inferior to thee, and another third kingdom of brass, which shall bear rule over all the earth. And the fourth kingdom shall be strong as iron: forasmuch as iron breaketh in pieces and subdueth all things: and as iron that breaketh all these, shall it break in pieces and bruise. And whereas thou sawest the feet and toes, part of potters' clay, and part of iron, the kingdom shall be divided; but there shall be in it of the strength of the iron, forasmuch as thou sawest the iron mixed with miry clay. And as the toes of the feet were part of iron, and part of clay, so the kingdom shall be partly strong, and partly broken. And whereas thou sawest iron mixed with miry clay, they shall mingle themselves with the seed of men: but they shall not cleave one to another, even as iron is not mixed with clay. And in the days of these kings shall the God of heaven set up

a kingdom, which shall never be destroyed: and the king-
dom shall not be left to other people, but it shall break in
pieces and consume all these kingdoms, and it shall stand
for ever. Forasmuch as thou sawest that the stone was
cut out of the mountain without hands, and that it brake
in pieces the iron, the brass, the clay, the silver, and the
gold; the great God hath made known to the king what
shall come to pass hereafter: and the dream is certain, and
the interpretation thereof sure (Daniel 2:37-45).

Daniel commenced his definition of the details of the
dream by paying deference to the king, acknowledging that
until that present hour he was the greatest among earthly
monarchs, "a king of kings." Then, without blurring the
issue so as to gain favor with the king, Daniel stated fearlessly and forthrightly that the monarch's rise to success
was a gift from Israel's God, the only true God, "the God
of heaven." The capacity to rule his kingdom and solve its
problems, along with the glory resulting from such a rule,
were not in himself nor did they come from the Babylonian
gods.

The first major item in the interpretation was the fact
that the statue represented a succession of *kingdoms.* "The
God of heaven hath given thee a *kingdom.* . . . And after
thee shall arise another *kingdom* inferior to thee, and
another third *kingdom* of brass. . . . And the fourth *kingdom*
shall be strong as iron. . . . And in the days of these kings
shall the God of heaven set up a *kingdom,* which shall never
be destroyed" (2:37, 39, 40, 44). Nebuchadnezzar's was the
first in this series of kingdoms represented by the statue,
for Daniel said to him, "Thou art this head of gold" (2:38).
The head of gold included the kingdom of Babylon as well
as Nebuchadnezzar the king. This is evidenced by Isaiah's
prophecy, "Take up this proverb against the king of Babylon, and say, How hath the oppressor ceased! the golden

city ceased!" (Isaiah 14:4) The second major item in the interpretation of the dream was the absolute sovereignty of God in all of these kingdoms. They commenced with God giving the kingdoms to men (2:37) and they will conclude with God taking them from men and finally setting up His own kingdom in the earth.

Little was said here about the second and third kingdoms. Both were confined to one verse (2:39) with the mere mention that there would be two. The only thing said, for the present, about the second kingdom was that it was to be "inferior" to Nebuchadnezzar's. This is important, however, and it calls for further comment. This inferiority is a striking feature and it follows through at each transition, from gold to silver to bronze to iron and finally to iron mixed with clay. From the head to the feet there is a decrease in worth and weight. (By weight I refer to the specific gravity of these metals.) The statue cannot stand forever because it is on a weak and insecure foundation. The inferiority means deterioration, not in mere size, but in the moral and ethical quality of rule. No Gentile power would ever be strong enough to control the world's growing and rebellious population. The head was the strongest, but there was a definite division of sovereignty in the two arms, two legs, and eventually ten toes.

The *second kingdom* I understand to be the Medes and Persians, the two representing one realm rather than two separate realms. There is no evidence, to my knowledge, for supposing that the Medes were the second kingdom which suppressed Babylon, and the Persians a third kingdom which supplanted the Medes. On this point Culver writes, "Darius the Mede took the kingdom from the last Babylonian king (Daniel 5:31), but the Median king is said to represent the 'Medes and the Persians' (Daniel 5:28), and he ruled his kingdom by 'the law of the Medes and Persians'

(Daniel 6:8, 12, 15). He is mentioned with Cyrus the Persian' as if head of the same realm as that which Cyrus ruled (Daniel 6:28). Furthermore, Daniel 8:20 speaks of Media and Persia as parts of one realm rather than two separate realms. Not only so, 2 Chronicles 36:20 shows that the Bible writers thought Persia followed the Babylonian kingdom without any intermediate Median kingdom."[3]

The *third kingdom* to succeed the Medo-Persian Empire was identified by name as Greece (Daniel 8:21; 11:2). Its inferiority is seen in the division of power, for in the belly and thighs there is represented a combination of two countries, Greece and Macedonia. This is the Greco-Macedonian Empire, ruled over by Alexander plus his four successors after his death. I find very little disagreement in the commentaries I have read as to the identifying of this third kingdom.

The *fourth kingdom* was not identified by Daniel, nor does it bear a name elsewhere in Scripture. The name of the first is Babylon; the name of the second is Persia; the name of the third is Greece; the fourth is unnamed. Yet it is the fourth which received more extensive treatment than do those three that precede it.

The distinctive feature of the fourth empire is strength, "strong as iron," commented Daniel. The strength is not a moral or religious strength, not the strength of inner unity, but destructive strength that ruthlessly "breaketh in pieces and subdueth all things" (2:40). This fourth kingdom I take to be Rome. A consistent interpretation of the image, in view of Daniel's explanation of its first three parts, suggests at least that the entire image is intended to set forth in prophecy a historical succession of kingdoms. I conclude therefore that the fourth kingdom is the Roman Empire.

[3] Culver, *Daniel and the Latter Days,* page 112.

One critic of this view objected to it on the ground that Rome was merely a little village on the banks of the Tiber when Nebuchadnezzar dreamed his dream. Such argumentation is weak when one considers that the Hellenic states were a group of small warring tribes when Babylon's monarch experienced his dream. I call the fourth kingdom the Roman Empire because it succeeded the Grecian and it originated in Rome, which did become the center of world rule. Furthermore Daniel's description fits the Roman Empire, for Rome had the reputation of crushing all opposition and resistance with an iron heel. When our Lord was born in Bethlehem the tramp of Rome's legions was heard and felt throughout the then known world. In the New Testament we read, "And it came to pass in those days, that there went out a decree from Caesar Augustus, that all the world should be taxed" (Luke 2:1). It is a matter of historical record that the Roman Empire succeeded the Grecian in 63 B.C., and that for almost five hundred years after the death of our Lord Rome's power was known by all. It is only of divine providence and foretelling that this fourth kingdom is described in such detail.

One detail in this fourth kingdom, not mentioned heretofore, is the matter concerning the "toes." The implied ten toes, like the breast and arms, the belly and thighs, and the two legs, suggest a kingdom in parts. While one kingdom is suggested, there is a sense in which there is division in the union. The fourth part of the image exactly corresponds to the "fourth beast" in Daniel 7:7, and this in turn corresponds to the "ten horns" in Revelation 17:12. Assuming that there were ten toes upon the feet of Nebuchadnezzar's dream image, we can come to one conclusion, namely "the ten horns which thou sawest are ten kings" (Revelation 17:12).

Of significance is the fact that the iron of this kingdom

is in its later stages mixed with clay. "And whereas thou sawest iron mixed with miry clay, they shall mingle themselves with the seed of men: but they shall not cleave one to another, even as iron is not mixed with clay" (2:43). What is the clay? It is "the seed of men" in the fourth kingdom, that is, mankind in general in contrast to one particular race or nation or empire. One has only to read Roman history to know how large a variety of peoples were assimilated into the Roman Empire. Pember wrote: "In the days of Augustus, the Roman Empire extended from the Atlantic in the West to the Euphrates in the East; from the Rhine, the Danube, and the Black Sea in the North, to the deserts of Africa and Arabia, in the South. In the reign of Domitian, Britain was added; while the emperor Trajan acquired the vast tract of Dacia, and organized as provinces Armenia, Mesopotamia, and Assyria. In the reign of Diocletian, Persia was forced to a formal surrender of Mesopotamia, together with five provinces beyond the Tigris. Such was the greatest extent of Rome in her first, or iron development. In the brief time of her second, or clay-iron power, the prophecy seems to require that her boundaries should be pushed still farther in more than one direction."[4]

Here we must guard against the wrong conclusion that the ten-toed condition of the fourth empire has finally been reached at some point in past history. While it is true that the Roman Empire was divided into several different kingdoms, few writers agree as to the actual number of those kingdoms. Furthermore there was neither unity nor union between them because they fought among themselves to destroy one another. Then, too, we should not overlook the point made by Dr. Ironside, namely the divisions in the old Roman Empire were spread over a period of several centuries, whereas the ten kingdoms represented by the

[4] G. H. Pember, *The Great Prophecies of the Centuries,* page 212.

toes on the image exist at one time and form one confedera-
tion. From the concluding verses in this section of our
study (2:44-45) it is clear that this last form of Gentile world
power exists when the stone crushes the image. The following verses must be studied closely:

> *And in the days of these kings shall the God of heaven*
> *set up a kingdom, which shall never be destroyed: and*
> *the kingdom shall not be left to other people, but it shall*
> *break in pieces and consume all these kingdoms, and it*
> *shall stand for ever. Forasmuch as thou sawest that the*
> *stone was cut out of the mountain without hands, and*
> *that it brake in pieces the iron, the brass, the clay, the*
> *silver, and the gold; the great God hath made known to*
> *the king what shall come to pass hereafter: and the dream*
> *is certain, and the interpretation thereof sure (2:44-45).*

Verse 44 is clearly the eschatological portion of Daniel's
interpretation of the dream, and every student recognizes in
this prophecy the beginning of the Messianic kingdom on
earth. What we are here to study is not now historical but
prophetic. The time of this prophecy is fixed then at the
second coming of Christ to the earth. It states that God
is going to set up a kingdom on earth which will destroy all
other kingdoms, and that His kingdom shall never be
destroyed. This is the very heart and soul of all prophecy
because it anticipates that day when "The kingdoms of
this world are become the kingdoms of our Lord, and of
His Christ; and He shall reign for ever and ever" (Revelation 11:15). It shall never be destroyed. This is the "stone"
kingdom.

The stone in the dream is the Lord Jesus Christ. It is one
of the many figures of speech used in Scripture to describe
Christ and His dual office of both redeeming Saviour and
reigning Sovereign. The stone is of supernatural origin

(2:34-35) as seen in Christ's miraculous conception and virgin birth. Isaiah wrote of Him, "Therefore thus saith the Lord GOD, Behold, I lay in Zion for a foundation a stone, a tried stone, a precious corner stone, a sure foundation: he that believeth shall not make haste" (Isaiah 28:16). Again, "Behold, a king shall reign in righteousness, and princes shall rule in judgment. And a man shall be as an hiding place from the wind, and a covert from the tempest; as rivers of water in a dry place, as the shadow of a great rock in a weary land" (Isaiah 32:1-2). That eternal rock of ages provided *satisfaction* (Exodus 17:3-6) and *security* (Exodus 33:22) for the children of Israel while in the wilderness, for Paul added an inspired word when he wrote that they "did all drink the same spiritual drink: for they drank of that spiritual Rock that followed them: and that Rock was Christ" (1 Corinthians 10:4). Our Lord Himself said, "Whosoever shall fall on this stone shall be broken: but on whomsoever it shall fall, it will grind him to powder" (Matthew 21:44). When this stone falls upon the Gentile nations who have rejected Him, they will be ground to powder.

The stone has not yet fallen upon the image, nor will it until world power is vested in the masses of humanity as represented in the whole image. Do not lose sight of the fact that the judgment is not limited to the legs, feet, and toes of the image; rather the striking of the image at the feet brings down the whole image so that "it brake in pieces the iron, the brass, the clay, the silver, and the gold" (Daniel 2:45). The Babylonian rule was *autocratic,* the Medo-Persian rule was *oligarchic,* the Roman rule was *imperialistic,* but the rule at the end of the age will be *democratic,* a government by the people. The latter might appear to be the soundest form of government, but it will prove to be a total failure. Today all races, religions, and rationalizations are clamoring for a hearing, insisting upon their rights. Uneducated students insist upon controlling the policies in our colleges and universities. Lawlessness abounds everywhere, even among the lawmakers themselves. America might serve as a classic example of one nation which has become a melting pot for the peoples of all nations. There is no mistaking the present trend and the bitter end. Our democratic form of government is doomed to crumble, along with all other forms of rule. It will give way to a *theocracy*, which is the rulership of God. The stone will appear! "The dream is certain, and the interpretation thereof sure" (Daniel 2:45).[5]

In summarizing we simply state that the dream presents a panorama in prophecy of the "times of the Gentiles" which includes their dawn, duration, and doom. It is doubtless one of the most important time periods in the prophetic Scriptures. These times relate to God's dealings with the Gentiles through a succession of four great world powers, commencing with the Babylonian captivity when Jerusalem was overthrown by the first great Gentile power. Daniel 2 presented the commencement, course, and consummation of this period. The consummation of the times of the Gentiles will be manifest at the end of the great tribulation when Jesus Christ comes back to earth.

Before we approach an examination of the concluding verses in chapter 2, let us have a look at the final form of Gentile power at the time of Christ's return. We must not fail to see that there is not a fifth kingdom before our Lord returns to establish His theocracy. From this I draw only one conclusion, namely the final form of Gentile power is an outgrowth from and final redevelopment of the fourth empire, the Roman. It is a hard saying to some, but it is one

[5] Other texts to be examined on the subject of "Christ the Stone" are Psalm 118:22; Isaiah 8:14; Zechariah 3:9; Acts 4:11; 1 Peter 2:4-8.

which the facts fully substantiate, that there is no escaping the continued existence of the influence of the Roman Empire. From out of the smolderings of that fourth empire there has been a gradual rising of a Roman system that has influenced the whole world religiously, intellectually, and politically. It is no new system, but the oldest in human history, easily identified by name. While related to the head of gold, it goes back far beyond the time of Nebuchadnezzar to Nimrod, "And the beginning of his kingdom was *Babel*" (Genesis 10:10). The times of the Gentiles commenced with Nebuchadnezzar, but the kingdom of Babylon predates him. The system of Babylon is seen in the end time revived from the fourth empire and called BABYLON THE GREAT (Revelation 17:5). Her headquarters never removed from Rome and remains there till this day (Revelation 17:9). She has taken the lead in recent years in forming a one-world church, her ecumenical church. Her power will increase politically until she is recognized and given political and military authority by the Beast (Revelation 17:3). The political empire and the false religious empire are so closely united at the end of the age that both are called by the same name, Babylon. Political Babylon destroys ecclesiastical Babylon (Revelation 17:15-18), but finally the political Babylon is destroyed by the return of the Lord Jesus Christ (Revelation 18).

There are possibly many drastic changes forthcoming within the Roman Catholic Church. It will not surprise this writer if the word Roman is eventually dropped entirely. It will be no surprise if she removes her headquarters from Italy altogether. It will be no surprise if word is announced that a new city called Babylon is to be built and that ecclesiastical Rome will make it her new headquarters. I am predicting nothing at all. But when my Lord returns to this earth (and I expect to be with Him) He will smite the image at its feet. In the ten toes there will be a realignment of nations that will make up the final form of the fourth world empire. While old Babylon as an empire will have disappeared, the gold from the head of the image will still be prominent (Revelation 17:4). The head of the new Babylon will be a blasphemer and a persecutor of the saints of God (Daniel 7:8, 25). But the doom of the system and the city is certain. Babylon is to experience a destruction as sudden and complete as that of Sodom and Gomorrah, from which there is no escape (Isaiah 47:11; Jeremiah 50:40; 51:61-64).

THE DECLARATION OF NEBUCHAD-NEZZAR (2:46-49)

Then the king Nebuchadnezzar fell upon his face, and worshipped Daniel, and commanded that they should offer an oblation and sweet odours unto him. The king answered unto Daniel, and said, Of a truth it is, that your God is a God of gods, and a Lord of kings, and a revealer of secrets, seeing thou couldest reveal this secret. Then the king made Daniel a great man, and gave him many gifts, and made him ruler over the whole province of Babylon, and chief of the governors over all the wise men of Babylon. Then Daniel requested of the king, and he set Shadrach, Meshach, and Abed-nego, over the affairs of the province of Babylon: but Daniel sat in the gate of the king (Daniel 2:46-49).

The details of the dream produced a profound effect upon Nebuchadnezzar. He was deeply impressed both with

Daniel and with Daniel's God. And this might have been one of God's purposes in disclosing to Nebuchadnezzar this prophetic panorama of the last days. It was not merely that the king should know these facts that his dream was interpreted, but that he might know and acknowledge the sovereignty and authority of the true God over earthly rulers.

We should not hastily judge the king for his attempt to worship Daniel (2:46). He was doing honor to Daniel's God the best he knew how, and Daniel must have recognized that fact. In the king's eyes Daniel had accomplished a mighty task, and in his aroused state of mind he was paying honor to whom he felt honor was due. After all, Nebuchadnezzar could not see God with his physical eyes, but he did see God's representative and spokesman. At any rate, whatever was in the king's mind, we can be certain that Daniel's heart was pure in the matter and that his only desire was for the glory of his God. Daniel had proved himself perfectly from the day of his arrival in Babylon.

Nebuchadnezzar did acknowledge the supremacy of Daniel's God over all other gods (2:47). While the king's profession was that of a polytheist, so that he had not come to see that Daniel's God was the only one true and living God, he could not miss seeing the superiority of the Jehovah of Israel. Such a demonstration of divine omniscience as witnessed by Nebuchadnezzar caused him to admit that Daniel's God was in a special way the God of revelation and rulership. But there was much the king was yet to learn about Him.

Daniel received gifts, honor, and power (2:48), which he humbly shared with his three friends (2:49). The Holy Spirit did not permit Daniel to elaborate on the honor bestowed upon him, but we may assume that it involved wealth, a luxurious dwelling (possibly a palace), a retinue of servants, all commensurate with his new position of "ruler over the whole province of Babylon, and chief of the governors over all the wise men of Babylon" (2:48). Such a promotion was not unreasonable. The particular duties of Daniel's office are not explained. Whatever they were, we know that Daniel remained true to God by not engaging in sorcery, astrology, heathen rites, or the eating and drinking of forbidden food and drink. Daniel never sought nor asked anything for himself, but because he exalted God and humbled himself, he was in due time exalted and honored.

THE DETERIORATION OF CIVILIZATION

Let me emphasize an important lesson the image teaches us. Each of the metals which made up the image is inferior to the one preceding it. The image commences with a head of gold and concludes with feet of iron mixed with clay. Gold, the most precious metal, is used as a symbol of Babylonian rule, and then follow the less precious metals in order. This is a striking feature since it suggests a deterioration in both quality and cohesion. When we come to the feet and toes, which symbolize the ten-kingdom empire of the "latter days," we see that the iron and clay will not mix (or hold together). "They shall mingle themselves with the seed of men: but they shall not cleave one to another, even as iron is not mixed with clay" (2:43). The United Nations cannot solve the problems of this world. While it appears at times that the United Nations is succeeding in its efforts to establish international peaceful relations, whatever peace comes to the world now is but temporary. We are deeply grateful to God that, in the divine plan, the UN has met with a measure of military success in stopping the aggression of the warmongering, communistic countries, but all Christians who are acquainted with the prophetic Scriptures are aware of the fact that the nations will not grow stronger in their united efforts for peace, but rather will they collapse, as has every previous peace pact. The end of the age is to be marked by an increase of wars and rumors of wars. The world situation is anything but settled in spite of the united efforts of many nations. God has taken the Gentile nations into His laboratory and has weighed them, and they have been found wanting more and more with each succeeding generation.

Richard H. Seume has pointed out that we have here "a test case for evolution." I heartily agree to this. Here we are able to see whether we are to expect world betterment or a world breakdown. Those who accept the philosophy of evolution insist that there are sufficient remarkable improvements in the world to support their theory. Now the Christian does not deny that, in certain ways, the world is better than it was centuries ago. Great progress has been made in the field of medicine. Half a century ago lepers, dying by the thousands, were hopeless victims of a then incurable disease. Discoveries of the past fifty years have prolonged the lives of thousands, and in many instances brought a complete cure of that dread malady. More could be added concerning the recent developments and discoveries to aid victims of cancer and arthritis. It is almost impossible for my mind to measure the progress in the field of medicine.

The world has been spanned by the invention and use of modern methods of travel. In 1920 I, as a small lad, scarcely gave thought to the "fuzzy-wuzzy" in the islands of the Pacific; now he is my neighbor. In three days I can pay him a visit and return home. Add to this the fact that I can speak and be heard in any part of the civilized world by telephone. This is truly progress.

The writer knows nothing about nuclear science and all of the intricacies connected with the atom and hydrogen bombs, but he is certain that this dread discovery is a terribly historic fact and not mere theory. While a curtain of secrecy still surrounds the A-bomb, the H-bomb and the HT-bomb, I know, in some small measure, what happened at Hiroshima. The late G. B. Shaw said, "At last man has the power to destroy himself and the world." I must go along with those who call this progress.

Let me add one word further concerning the almost unbelievable progress in the matter of missionary enterprise. At this point I am reminded of the words of our Lord: "And this gospel of the kingdom shall be preached in all the world for a witness unto all nations; and then shall the end come" (Matthew 24:14). Since World War II our missionaries have penetrated islands and jungles to take the gospel where white men have never been before. Obviously in these ways, and doubtless in many others, the world is growing better.

But the issue does not rest there. The image was not intended to teach that everything everywhere will deteriorate and collapse as such. However, there are certain aspects in which deterioration has shown itself. In other words, we can see how the world is growing worse. Note first, a keyword in verse 39: "And after thee shall arise another kingdom *inferior* to thee." Mark that word "inferior." Now let us see how the image testifies of deterioration.

(1) There has been deterioration in man's *worship*. In Daniel, chapter 3, Nebuchadnezzar made an image and issued an order that all men everywhere must fall down and worship his image. Turning completely from the God of

Israel, Nebuchadnezzar exalted himself. Then history shows how Darius and Alexander the Great demanded the worship of their subjects. Political Rome followed with her worship of pagan gods, and later the worship of the state. This was later replaced with the suppression of the Bible, the rise of the Roman priesthood, the dogma of transubstantiation, the cult of Mary, the imagery and idolatry in worshiping "saints," all of which have resulted in the papal bondage of millions.

(2) There has been deterioration in man's *word*. The truth becomes more scarce as we approach the end of the age. One of the signs of the times and outstanding characteristics of the last days will be the telling and believing of lies, opposition to the truth. Men will "believe a lie" (2 Thessalonians 2:11-12), and "resist the truth" (2 Timothy 3:7-8), "And they shall turn away their ears from the truth" (2 Timothy 4:4). Deliberate deception is running wild in our day. Some of our own scientists who have pledged allegiance to the United States have turned traitor. In the last days men shall be "trucebreakers" and "traitors" (2 Timothy 3:1-4). Men are becoming more treacherous and undependable. In order to gain his end a man will cast away completely his bond, which is his word. There was a time when treaties were regarded with respect. Now pacts are broken and agreements are treated as scraps of paper.

(3) More could be said about man's moral *worth*: men degenerating into moral reprobates, waxing worse and worse, the breakdown of the home and family life, more divorces than marriages, the consumption of an almost unbelievable amount of liquor and drugs, an increase in crime, and the rise of a host of amateur prostitutes. Indeed the world is growing worse.

Modernists and evolutionists have been spreading a lie about the world getting better, but deterioration and decay

mark the course of Gentile dominion. The feet of the image
is part of iron and part of clay. Permit me to call it "mud,"
for the feet contain in them the elements of decay. The
course of Gentile dominion is a coming crisis because man's
glory cannot be supported for long on a weak foundation.
The modernist who thinks he is saving the world has the
image upside down: he has it standing on its head. The
modernist seldom sees things in their proper perspective.
But according to the image and the interpretation, the whole
superstructure of civilization in these last days is doomed,
for it is seen here to be resting on a marshy foundation.

I know of no more fitting way to close our study in this
chapter than to quote an excellent paragraph from the mind
and pen of Dr. H. C. Leupold: "One impression remains
with the attentive reader rather clearly, and that is the
thought that it always has been and always will be the lot
of the kingdoms that the might of man establishes to go the
way of all flesh and to collapse. Each new combination of
forces or nations that has tried to achieve the result of a
lasting kingdom invariably meets with the same overthrow.
So history is a succession of defeats. But for the one who
knows the Almighty God there is hope. History cannot be a
mere futility to Him, for the Omnipotent One will in due
season make it apparent, as His own already now know it
to be, that He has a kingdom that will never be overthrown,
and that will finally stand out as eternal and entirely successful. This kingdom is the hope of mankind and God's vindication in the course of history that He has not labored in
vain. The labors of His Christ shall be crowned with ultimate and perfect success."[6]

[6] Leupold, *Daniel*, page 130.

CHAPTER THREE

CHAPTER THREE

Most vital at the outset of our study of chapter 3 is the insistence that here is an event that is historical in character and accurate in detail. Not one line in the narrative savors of myth, fiction, or unreality. It is pure truth because it is divinely inspired. The critics attack this chapter because it contains the record of a miracle. And so they approach it in much the same way they approach every miracle, namely because it is a miracle, it could not actually have taken place. But I claim accuracy and inerrancy for the entire book of Daniel, and that claim includes every miracle recorded in it. Totally unsatisfactory are those stock-in-trade objections of unbelieving men. Perish the satanically inspired notion that the writer invented the story, or that he gathered its materials from well-known legends of that time. This is the Word of God.

THE DESCRIPTION OF THE IMAGE (3:1)

Nebuchadnezzar the king made an image of gold, whose height was threescore cubits, and the breadth thereof six cubits: he set it up in the plain of Dura, in the province of Babylon (Daniel 3:1).

There is a close resemblance between this chapter and chapter 2, which precedes it. The resemblance lies in the fact that both chapters have in them an image, or a statue, and I am inclined toward the view that there is a relationship between the two images. This raises the question, what did this image in chapter 3 represent? Conjectures and suppositions vary quite widely on this from one of Babylon's gods, to the symbol of Babylonian power, to Nebuchadnezzar himself. Though much might be said for the first of these three, the second and third seem to be the most logical. The image possibly represented the king himself and the world power of which he was the head. The fact that he made this image of gold could have resulted from Daniel's interpretation of the dream image in chapter 2, when Daniel told the king, "Thou art this head of gold" (2:38).

Some striking contrasts between the two images are obvious. The image which Nebuchadnezzar saw in the dream in chapter 2 was of divine origin; the image in chapter 3 was the king's own idea. The former was purely imperialistic and nationalistic; the latter is religious and is made an object of worship. The first had in it a variety of metals showing deterioration from the head to the feet; the second was all of gold.[1] It is possible that, with the exception of the materials used, the second was a replica of the first. The pride of Nebuchadnezzar's heart caused him to erect this image to represent himself and his empire, and it showed the true condition of his heart in the deification and worship of man. The dream image in chapter 2 predicted the eventual overthrow of Babylon when she would come to nought and give way to the Medo-Persian Empire. And

[1] This does not necessarily mean that the image was of solid gold. There is Biblical reason to believe that the statue itself was made of wood and overlaid on its surface with gold. The "golden altar" for the Tabernacle was actually made of "shittim wood" and Moses "overlaid it with pure gold" (Exodus 37:25-26; 39:38; 40:5).

so, after giving thought to God's plan, Babylon's king comes up with a plan of his own. If Babylon could start the procession of Gentile world powers, she might just as well continue. If she could commence world rule by being the head of gold, why should she not continue? Why shouldn't the whole image be of gold? Thus did Nebuchadnezzar reason.

Now *why* did Nebuchadnezzar do this? Actually we are not given the reason. But when we give consideration as to *when* he did it, we might venture a guess as to the reason. There is much agreement among the students of Scripture that between eighteen and twenty-three years elapsed between those events recorded in chapter 2 and the erection of the image in chapter 3. We establish an arbitrary figure of twenty years. Now twenty years in one man's lifetime is a long period, long enough for him to change his mind about many things. The king had not forgotten the rest of the revelation in chapter 2, namely the foretelling of the downfall of his kingdom. Did he fear this and therefore try to strengthen his position? Did he begin to doubt Daniel's prophetic interpretation of the dream image? Did he think he would not die but live on to hold the reins of power? Whatever prompted him to construct the image of gold, he behaved exactly the way some professing Christians behave today. None of us are immune from the temptation to cling tenaciously to our little earthly possessions, and that almost blindly, having lost sight of the brevity of life and the transitoriness of the things of this world. We hold to our earthly possessions with a tight fist, falsely imagining that we shall have them forever. I would not expect that Nebuchadnezzar would have erected such an image near the beginning of his reign (606 B.C.) while Daniel's prophecy was fresh in his mind, nor in 598 B.C. when he returned to Jerusalem to plunder and kill again, but sometime after 587 B.C. when he completed the overthrow of Jerusalem and burned the city. After he completed his major conquest and was feeling the magnitude and might of his empire, it was easy to forget the Word of the Lord through Daniel. It is in the time of our health and strength and prosperity that most of us forget God.

A significant item for consideration is the fact that Daniel is not mentioned in chapter 3. We are not told of his whereabouts and activities during those intervening years. Because of his high position of responsibility he could have been sent by the king to one of the conquered cities. Frankly, it is not conceivable that the king would have proceeded with the erection of the image if Daniel had been present. From chapter 2 we may conclude that Daniel exercised an influence and a restraint upon Nebuchadnezzar. The king had rewarded Daniel richly and had put much confidence in him, but he was not fully committed to Daniel's God. Whatever impressions were made upon him, after Daniel interpreted the dream, had now become dimmed by the passing of time and the lust for power.

The measurements of the image are worthy of note. The height was 60 cubits and the breadth 6 cubits. The ratio of 60 to 6 (or 10 to 1) does not disturb me. For all we know, the measurements might include the pillar or pedestal on which the figure of the man stood. But I am impressed with the three sixes (666) as well as the fact that there are six musical instruments mentioned. In Scripture the number 6 expresses humanity; it is the number of man. God created man on the sixth day (Genesis 1:26-31). Seven is the number of completion or perfection, a state toward which man strives in his own strength and wisdom but one which he never achieves. The number of the world's greatest genius to come is 666 (Revelation 13:18), but it is still short of seven. The measurements of the proud and boastful Goliath were in sixes (1 Samuel 17:4-7). Six days were appointed for man's labor (Exodus 20:11). Six steps led to Solomon's throne, a throne of human judgment (1 Kings 10:19). But more about this when we come to the prophetic aspect of our chapter.

THE DEDICATION OF THE IMAGE (3:2-5)

Then Nebuchadnezzar the king sent to gather together the princes, the governors, and the captains, the judges, the treasurers, the counsellors, the sheriffs, and all the rulers of the provinces, to come to the dedication of the image which Nebuchadnezzar the king had set up. Then the princes, the governors, and captains, the judges, the treasurers, the counsellors, the sheriffs, and all the rulers of the provinces, were gathered together unto the dedication of the image that Nebuchadnezzar the king had set up; and they stood before the image that Nebuchadnezzar had set up. Then an herald cried aloud, To you it is commanded, O people, nations, and languages, That at what time ye hear the sound of the cornet, flute, harp, sackbut, psaltery, dulcimer, and all kinds of musick, ye fall down and worship the golden image that Nebuchadnezzar the king hath set up (Daniel 3:2-5).

The dedication of the image was an elaborate affair. All of the nations and tribes that were made subject to Babylon were ordered to send a delegation to the ceremony. The capital city was alive and crowded with people from all over the empire. It was doubtless one of the greatest days in the history of Babylon. The orchestra was in place, waiting for the signal to begin playing the musical instruments. When the world sells its wares and presents its programs it must have music. While driving many thousands of miles across our country I use my car radio frequently and I have heard almost every known product advertised with singing commercials, including the weather report and call letters of the radio station. There is something about music that stirs and grips our emotions. There are professing Christians who will attend church to listen to a musical program but who find an excuse to stay away when the Word of God is to be preached. Music is wielding tremendous influence in the religious world. Mind you, some of it is good and a part of worship, but much of it is highly entertaining, and even Christians enjoy being entertained in God's house of worship. Music that is spiritual is an aid to worship (Ephesians 5:19; Colossians 3:16), but much of what I am subjected to is an appeal to the flesh, having in it nothing that exalts our Lord Jesus Christ. On more than one occasion I have suffered through long periods of the poorest kind of music for a worship or gospel service, and then I was expected to take a mere few minutes to expound God's Word to people who came to be entertained. Nebuchadnezzar knew the power of music, and from the context we may conclude that his use of it pretty much followed the pattern set by the originator of the world's music, Jubal of the godless line of Cain (Genesis 4:21).

As I read Daniel 3:3-4 there is a serious question in my mind as to whether or not the official call to the dedication of the image included the announcement that the dedication service was to be religious and not political or patriotic. There is no mention of it in these two verses. As a matter of fact, it was not until after the people were assembled that the king's carefully laid plan was made known to the mass of people. With his knowledge of human nature, Nebuchadnezzar was too astute to ignore the religious part of man's being. Man is intuitively religious, and something inside of him longs to be stirred. This desire responds more readily when the object of worship is a person. And so the golden image, though representing the Babylonian Empire, was designed to draw attention to its leader, the "head of gold" (2:38). To honor the state was to honor its head. In 1936, Herr Baldur von Schirach, who was in charge of the entire youth program in Germany, said in an address to the German youth, "One cannot be a good German and at the same time deny God, but an avowal of faith in the eternal Germany is at the same time an avowal of faith in the eternal God. If we act as true Germans we act according to the laws of God. Whoever serves Adolf Hitler, the führer, serves Germany, and whoever serves Germany serves God."[2] This is the devil's form of worship, and so religion becomes a tool of the state as a means of holding the people in subjection. The Roman Catholic Church has always used this satanic principle, holding up the pope as the one man on earth who can speak infallibly as God's representative to man. And so millions bow to him, calling him "Holy Father." Babylonianism is with us still.

THE DEMANDS AT
THE DEDICATION SERVICE (3:4-7)

Then an herald cried aloud, To you it is commanded, O people, nations, and languages, That at what time ye hear the sound of the cornet, flute, harp, sackbut, psaltery, dulcimer, and all kinds of musick, ye fall down and worship the golden image that Nebuchadnezzar the king hath set up: And whoso falleth not down and worshippeth shall

[2] G. H. Lang, *The Histories and Prophecies of Daniel*, page 39.

the same hour be cast into the midst of a burning fiery furnace. Therefore at that time, when all the people heard the sound of the cornet, flute, harp, sackbut, psaltery, and all kinds of musick, all the people, the nations, and the languages, fell down and worshipped the golden image that Nebuchadnezzar the king had set up (Daniel 3:4-7).

After the people were gathered together, the real motive behind the dedication of the image was announced. An announcer made known the royal edict. It was a stern demand that, when the symphonic sound was heard, all persons present were to prostrate themselves before the image and do homage to it. The word used in the inspired text is "worship," appearing not less than eleven times (verses 5, 6, 7, 10, 11, 12, 14, 15, 18, 28). At once it is clearly seen that the religious significance of this act is not merely incidental but primary (see 2:12, 14). We would not underestimate its political and patriotic significance; however, it was a gathering at which worship was demanded from all subjects of the Babylonian Empire. The golden image, representing the state and its monarch, was to be worshiped. There was one religion for all the "people, nations, and languages" (3:4). All must conform to state worship.

The demands were strict, and the punishment for all who rebelled so severe that none dare refuse to participate. By means of the music the emotions of the people would be aroused, and that in itself should produce the desired results. In the event of a few holdouts, the threat of being cast alive into a fiery furnace should convince them. Thus two means were used to persuade and frighten the people into this act of idolatrous worship. This is Satan's mode of operation. Superstition and fear have been his stock in trade in binding many people to the world's false religions. As far as the masses of society are concerned, the devil succeeds. It was so in Babylon and it is equally so today.

"Therefore at that time, when all the people heard the sound of the cornet, flute, harp, sackbut, psaltery, and all kinds of musick, all the people, the nations, and the languages, fell down and worshipped the golden image that Nebuchadnezzar the king had set up" (3:7). The edict was clear—bow or burn! And so the people bowed. The emperor was publicly recognized as the head of state and the head of religion.

I would guess that the sight of his subjects bowing before him swelled the king with sinful pride. If the image in chapter 2 meant that Babylon must eventually give way to Medo-Persia, then to Greece, to Rome, and finally to the kingdom of the Son of God, the image in chapter 3 was Nebuchadnezzar's defiant reply to God. This king would not be satisfied being the head; he must comprise the whole body. If it is good to have the head of gold, why not have the entire body of gold? If the times of the Gentiles can begin with Babylon, why can't they continue with Babylon? At the dedication of his image, Nebuchadnezzar must have felt that Babylon would continue to the end of time. And to think that he acted in the name of religion and under the pretense of piety!

THE DEFIANCE OF THE FAITHFUL THREE (3:8-15)

Wherefore at that time certain Chaldeans came near, and accused the Jews. They spake and said to the king Nebuchadnezzar, O king, live for ever. Thou, O king, hast made a decree, that every man that shall hear the sound of the cornet, flute, harp, sackbut, psaltery, and dulcimer, and all kinds of musick, shall fall down and

*worship the golden image: And whoso falleth not down
and worshippeth, that he should be cast into the midst of
a burning fiery furnace. There are certain Jews whom
thou hast set over the affairs of the province of Babylon,
Shadrach, Meshach, and Abed-nego; these men, O king,
have not regarded thee; they serve not thy gods, nor
worship the golden image which thou hast set up. Then
Nebuchadnezzar in his rage and fury commanded to
bring Shadrach, Meshach, and Abed-nego. Then they
brought these men before the king. Nebuchadnezzar spake
and said unto them, Is it true, O Shadrach, Meshach, and
Abed-nego, do not ye serve my gods, nor worship the
golden image which I have set up? Now if ye be ready
that at what time ye hear the sound of the cornet, flute,
harp, sackbut, psaltery, and dulcimer, and all kinds of
musick, ye fall down and worship the image which I have
made; well: but if ye worship not, ye shall be cast the
same hour into the midst of a burning fiery furnace; and
who is that God that shall deliver you out of my hands?
(Daniel 3:8-15)*

The defiance of Daniel's three friends is not recorded
separately, but it first appears as a report to the king from
certain Chaldeans. From their entire report it might be as-
sumed that envy and jealousy motivated their action. Their
words to the king, "There are certain Jews whom thou
hast set over the affairs of the province of Babylon, Shadrach, Meshach, and Abed-nego; these men, O king, have
not regarded thee: they serve not thy gods, nor worship the
golden image which thou hast set up" (3:12), show their
personal feelings in the matter. Daniel and his friends were
the only Jews in captivity who were appointed to positions
of leadership. We are not to assume that the remainder of
the Jews in captivity bowed before the image, but we must

remember that only those throughout the empire who held some office were summoned to the dedication. They were the representatives of the people, thus they would carry back to them the reports of the dedication and the decrees of the king. In much the same way the pope regiments and controls the millions of Roman Catholics throughout the world by his periodic conclaves with his cardinals. It was the duty of the three Hebrews to be present at the dedication, but, as already has been stated, neither they nor others of their rank had any knowledge that the whole affair was to be a religious one.

The Chaldeans who brought the report to the king knew these three Jews. How could they help but know them? When those very Chaldeans were sentenced to die for their failure to reveal the king's dream, it was the prayers of Daniel and his three Jewish companions that saved them. What ingratitude! One might think that these men would have been eternally grateful to the Jews who were responsible for their being alive. While their charge to the king was accurate, and their approach to him according to protocol, they were motivated by the demon of jealousy. This assumption is correct, else why didn't the Chaldeans return the act of mercy and try to save the three Jews?

Upon hearing the report Nebuchadnezzar went into a rage. His furnace was hot but he was hotter. No doubt he felt justified in his anger because he had promoted these foreigners to positions of importance. And now they had defied his edict. They stood when they should have been bowing down before the image. They had not respected the king's commands nor his gods. Yet, in spite of his anger, the king extended to them the benefit of the doubt and another chance to live. He asked them if the report were true (3:14), and then he followed up with his offer to spare them if they would bow down before his image. Finally he charged them, "But if ye worship not, ye shall be cast the same hour into the midst of a burning fiery furnace; *and who is that God that shall deliver you out of my hands?*" (3:15)

What a change in Nebuchadnezzar's attitude toward the true God! Some twenty years earlier he had said to Daniel, "Of a truth it is, that your God is a God of gods, and a Lord of kings, and a revealer of secrets" (2:47). It hardly seems possible that from the same lips and same heart proceeded the blasphemous challenge, "Who is that God that shall deliver you out of my hands?" The king was feeling his strength in his rage and fury but he was soon to discover his weakness. I somehow feel that Nebuchadnezzar sincerely believed his god was greater than Jehovah.

THE DEFENSE OF THE FAITHFUL THREE (3:16-23)

Shadrach, Meshach, and Abed-nego, answered and said to the king, O Nebuchadnezzar, we are not careful to answer thee in this matter. If it be so, our God whom we serve is able to deliver us from the burning fiery furnace, and He will deliver us out of thine hand, O king. But if not, be it known unto thee, O king, that we will not serve thy gods, nor worship the golden image which thou hast set up. Then was Nebuchadnezzar full of fury, and the form of his visage was changed against Shadrach, Meshach, and Abed-nego: therefore he spake, and commanded that they should heat the furnace one seven times more than it was wont to be heated. And he commanded the most mighty men that were in his army to bind Shadrach, Meshach, and Abed-nego, and to cast them into the burning fiery furnace. Then these men were bound in their coats, their hosen, and their hats, and their other garments, and were cast into the midst of the burning fiery furnace. Therefore because the king's commandment was urgent, and the furnace exceeding hot, the flame of the fire slew those men that took up Shadrach, Meshach, and Abed-nego. And these three men, Shadrach, Meshach, and Abed-nego, fell down bound into the midst of the burning fiery furnace (Daniel 3:16-23).

With calmness and courage the three Jews offered no alibis, nor did they avail themselves of the king's offer of a second chance. There is neither insolence nor arrogance in their reply, only a firm and resolute stand for their mighty and faithful God into whose hands they had committed their bodies and souls. They simply replied, "We see no need to answer you in this matter." But their reply did not stop short with that one sentence; with confidence and trust they assured Nebuchadnezzar that God was able to deliver them from the burning fiery furnace and out of the king's hand.

The "if" in verse 17 should not cause the student of Scripture any difficulty. There was not the slightest casting of doubt upon the omnipotence of God. The faith of the three was too strong and clear to allow for any doubt. If God is not omnipotent He is not God at all. The second "if" in verse 18 makes it clear that there was no questioning God's ability, but rather His will. The three men believed that God was able to deliver them alive, but they took the only proper position. They knew that God could work a miracle on their behalf but they were not certain that in this instance He would. If, for reasons best known to Him, His wise and benevolent plans did not include their deliverance, they could not change their position. They believed that God would be vindicated even if they were permitted to die. They did not so much as ask God to perform a miracle in their behalf, but, like Job who preceded them, they could say, "Though He slay me, yet will I trust Him" (Job 13:15). Under no circumstance were they willing to compromise their convictions or be shaken from their loyalty to God. "Be it known unto thee, O king, that we will not serve thy gods, nor worship the golden image which thou hast set up" (3:18).

In these days of cowardice and compromise, the moral and spiritual courage of Shadrach, Meshach, and Abed-nego will serve as a pattern for God's people everywhere. Rather than submit to the ecumenical religion of their day they were prepared to pay with their lives if necessary. Their love and loyalty to God were of far greater importance than life itself. Nebuchadnezzar might kill their bodies, but God would preserve their souls. Not for one single moment did the three faithful Jews doubt the omnipotence of God. They were in Babylon but they refused to do as the Babylonians did. The Word of the Lord was clear, "Thou shalt not make unto thee any graven image, or any likeness of any thing that is in heaven above, or that is in the earth beneath, or that is in the water under the earth" (Exodus 20:4). So they had a very good reason for not bowing down. In order to obey the Word of God they had to refuse to obey the order of the state. With their confidence in the God of all power, they could boldly say, "I will not fear what man shall do unto me" (Hebrews 13:6). We need such courage and faith today. "Therefore, my beloved brethren, be ye stedfast, unmoveable, always abounding in the work of the Lord, forasmuch as ye know that your labour is not in vain in the Lord" (1 Corinthians 15:58).

No doubt Nebuchadnezzar was greatly surprised when God's faithful few refused to bow down before the image and worship it. Their refusal brought the dedication service to an abrupt and disappointing end, as far as the king was concerned. His uncontrollable temper showed itself when he flew into a rage and shouted an order that the fire in the furnace was to be built up seven times larger and hotter than usual, but the angry monarch's fury only showed his emotional instability. He was determined to vent his fury on those who would dare to disobey him. With the visage of his face having changed into that of a madman, the king ordered a group of his strongest men to bind the three Jews and cast them into the furnace. With the stores of fuel having been thrown into the fire, the young men of God were bound fully clothed and cast into the furnace.

Now we see something of the magnitude of the miraculous. Failing to take into account the larger danger that resulted from the increased intensity of the flames, the executioners were brought to instantaneous death. In their mad rush to carry out the king's order to thrust Shadrach, Meshach, and Abed-nego into the furnace, the flames leaped at them, and even though they succeeded in carrying out their assignment, they themselves died in the flames. One can imagine the excitement and drama as a curious crowd and the proud monarch witnessed those executioners being scorched to death. The very death that was planned for the accused was suffered by the executioners. This, of course, merely adds marvel to the miraculous deliverance of the three children of God. While it might have troubled the king to witness his own men perish in the flames, he was doubtless pleased as he saw the three Jews fall down bound into the midst of the burning fiery furnace.

THE DELIVERANCE OF
THE FAITHFUL THREE (3:24-28)

Then Nebuchadnezzar the king was astonied, and rose up in haste, and spake, and said unto his counsellors, Did

*not we cast three men bound into the midst of the fire?
They answered and said unto the king, True, O king.
He answered and said, Lo, I see four men loose, walking
in the midst of the fire, and they have no hurt; and the
form of the fourth is like the Son of God. Then Nebuchadnezzar came near to the mouth of the burning fiery furnace, and spake, and said, Shadrach, Meshach, and Abed-
nego, ye servants of the most high God, come forth, and
come hither. Then Shadrach, Meshach, and Abed-nego,
came forth of the midst of the fire. And the princes, governors, and captains, and the king's counsellors, being
gathered together, saw these men, upon whose bodies the
fire had no power, nor was an hair of their head singed,
neither were their coats changed, nor the smell of fire had
passed on them. Then Nebuchadnezzar spake, and said,
Blessed be the God of Shadrach, Meshach, and Abed-
nego, who hath sent His angel, and delivered His servants that trusted in Him, and have changed the king's
word, and yielded their bodies, that they might not serve
nor worship any god, except their own God (Daniel 3:
24-28).*

Here is the greater miracle! The faithful three were walking about calmly in the flames *unbound* and *unburned*.
Through the opening in the furnace the king witnessed with
astonishment a demonstration of the power of the only true
God. The flames had burned off the bonds but did not so
much as singe a hair on the heads of God's loyal subjects.
Here was a mighty and miraculous deliverance.

Though seated at a safe distance from the dangerous
flames, the king was viewing the proceedings, when suddenly he leaped to his feet startled and amazed. Summoning
his counselors he asked them how many men had been cast
into the furnace. They answered him that there were three.

"He answered and said, Lo, I see four men loose, walking in the midst of the fire, and they have no hurt; and the aspect of the fourth is like a son of the gods" (verse 25 ASV). He saw a mysterious deity whom he later referred to as an angel of God (verse 28). The sight would have been enough to startle any man. The three men in the flames were unhurt, not lying down, but walking about, and they were not even looking for a way of escape but were perfectly content to remain in the fire. The heathen king was convinced that the young men in the furnace were being preserved from the fire and that some supernatural being now walked with them.

Who was this fourth person appearing to Nebuchadnezzar as one of the gods or an angel? I am fully convinced that He was the Son of God, our Lord Jesus Christ. There seems to be no question about this being a preincarnate manifestation, a theophanic appearance of the Son of God. There are several such theophanies in the Old Testament. That fourth person was He who said, "Lo, I am with you alway, even unto the end of the world" (Matthew 28:20). "In the world ye shall have tribulation: but be of good cheer; I have overcome the world" (John 16:33). In a moment when His devoted followers needed Him, the eternal God descended to earth to be their companion and protector in the flames. What God promised to His ancient people He literally fulfilled in the preservation of Shadrach, Meshach, and Abednego: "When thou walkest through the fire, thou shalt not be burned; neither shall the flame kindle upon thee" (Isaiah 43:2). And so the faithful three are included in God's hall of fame as men "Who through faith . . . Quenched the violence of fire" (Hebrews 11:33-34).

There is a Scripture which says, "For our God is a consuming fire" (Hebrews 12:29, cf., Deuteronomy 4:24). This verse is literally true. The Bible speaks often of the God of the fires and of the fires of God. We have seen:

God's presence in the fire	(Exodus 3:1-4).
God's pathway in the fire	(Exodus 13:21).
God's precepts in the fire	(Exodus 19:16-18, cf., 20:1-17).
God's punishment in the fire	(Genesis 19:23-24; Leviticus 10:2).
God's power in the fire	(1 Kings 18:24).
God's protection in the fire	(Daniel 3:25).
God's prophecy of the fire	(2 Thessalonians 1:6-10; 2 Peter 3:10; Luke 17:29).

Nebuchadnezzar saw the manifestation of God in the fire in God's punishment (3:22), presence (3:25), protection (3:25), and power (3:27). Acknowledging the God of the fire as the "most high God" (3:26), he called to Shadrach, Meshach, and Abed-nego to come out of the fiery furnace. All of the king's cabinet members drew near to witness this astounding miracle. Not even was the smell of fire clinging to the faithful three. The king saw but one course of action. He was forced to acknowledge that "there is no other God that can deliver after this sort" (3:29). In speaking his word of praise for Jehovah, the God of Israel, Nebuchadnezzar testified that this "most high God" had distinguished Himself by displaying a power greater than any other god was capable of.

I cannot pass lightly or hurriedly over the word of testimony that Nebuchadnezzar bore in behalf of God's three choice young men. He said they had *yielded their bodies, that they might not serve nor worship any god, except their own God*" (3:28). By this is meant not merely the risking of their lives, but the giving of themselves (2 Corinthians 8:5), the surrender of God's temple to Him who both created and redeemed the body (1 Corinthians 3:16; 6:19-20; 2 Corinthians 6:16). It would have been impossible for them to communicate with the Babylonians apart from their bodies, therefore any misuse of any part of the body by them could not have produced this grand testimony as to their yielded bodies. They had not sinned with their bodies but rather had placed them at God's disposal. Their bodies were free from sinful practices because they were surrendered to God for pure and righteous purposes.

In our day of prevailing immodesty and promiscuity we need more of this spirit and devotion of our bodies to Him who has purchased us and washed us in His own blood. "I beseech you therefore, brethren, by the mercies of God, that ye present your bodies a living sacrifice, holy, acceptable unto God, which is your reasonable service" (Romans 12:1). There can be no full surrender to Jesus Christ apart from the surrender of the body. The Christian, for example, who boasts or lies or gossips with his tongue is not surrendered to his Lord. Yielding every member of the body is the way of life for us at all times. "Neither yield ye your members as instruments of unrighteousness unto sin: but yield yourselves unto God, as those that are alive from the dead, and your members as instruments of righteousness unto God" (Romans 6:13).

THE DECREE OF NEBUCHADNEZZAR
(3:29-30)

Therefore I make a decree, That every people, nation, and language, which speak any thing amiss against the God of Shadrach, Meshach, and Abed-nego, shall be cut in pieces, and their houses shall be made a dunghill: because there is no other God that can deliver after this sort. Then the king promoted Shadrach, Meshach, and Abed-nego, in the province of Babylon (Daniel 3:29-30).

We are not to assume at this point that Nebuchadnezzar's decree means that he had been converted, that is, that he had a personal experience with God. The testimony of his conversion appears in the next chapter. Here he was merely recognizing that the power of God is greater than that of the Babylonian gods and so he gives priority to Israel's God. At this time it did not occur to the king to acknowledge Him as the only true God and all other gods mere creations of man.

In typical oriental fashion he issued a decree in which penalties were threatened to anyone caught speaking ill against the God of Shadrach, Meshach, and Abed-nego. The king would not deny his own national gods. He merely expressed admiration for the God of these three brave men, but he did not bow to Him or worship Him. His decree was a mere negative one because he was not yet ready to esteem Jehovah as the one and only God. But because of the unusual demonstration of power he had just witnessed, he felt that he owed at least this much recognition to Him. Even if fear inspired his decree, there must have been some sincerity of purpose in his heart. Yet one could wish that he would have gone farther than he did.

"Then the king promoted Shadrach, Meshach, and Abed-nego, in the province of Babylon" (3:30). The faithfulness of the three young men brought to them the rewards of both protection and prosperity. He who honors God will not go unrewarded. There are some worthy lessons to be learned from this chapter, such as the power of God to protect His own and the inability of world power to imperil the safety of God's children when they are dedicated to Him. But not the least of these is a principle stated by a man of God to Eli in the following words, "The LORD saith . . . them that honour Me I will honour, and they that despise Me shall be lightly esteemed" (1 Samuel 2:30). Our Lord said, "Whosoever therefore shall confess Me before men, him will I confess also before My Father which is in heaven. But whosoever shall deny Me before men, him will I also deny before My Father which is in heaven" (Matthew 10:32-33). The enemies of the faithful three sought to destroy them, but God saw to it that they were further promoted and prospered.

Beloved child of God, let us not miss this needed lesson of life. We may be called upon to pass through some trial which seems impossible, but our faithful and all-powerful God desires only to strengthen our faith, enlarge our witness for Jesus Christ, and bring greater triumph to Himself in this world of unbelieving men.

> When through fiery trials thy pathway shall lie;
> My grace all-sufficient shall be thy supply;
> The flames shall not hurt thee, I only design
> Thy dross to consume, and thy gold to refine.

The trial that comes to the child of God is not without design and purpose. In the case of David it was *punitive* (2 Samuel 12:10). Job's trial served as a *proof* (Job 42:5). For Paul it was a *preventive* (2 Corinthians 12:7). Peter tells us it is a *partnership* (1 Peter 4:12-13). For John it was *prophetic* (Revelation 1:9). But in every instance it is *profitable* (Hebrews 12:10).

THE DETAILS OF PROPHECY

We began this series of studies by pointing out the fact that the book of Daniel contains both history and prophecy. At times the prophecy is clearly stated, as is the case in chapter 2. At other times the prophetic preview is in type, as we see how the incidents in Daniel parallel the end times. Here in chapter 3 certain details serve as a prophetic example of certain events which will occur in the closing days of the age after the Church of Christ has been caught up to Heaven. Let us examine some of the historical incidents which serve as types of future events.

Nebuchadnezzar is a type of the Antichrist, the man of sin who will by force unite all religion under one head. His religious system will be Satan's ecumenical church, demanding the worship of all people upon the earth. Any person refusing to conform will do so under penalty of death (Revelation 13:4, 7, 12, 15). There is a close parallel between Daniel 3 and Revelation 13. In both chapters there is a ruling despot and an image to be worshiped. Nebuchadnezzar is a type of the political "beast" who creates an image of himself as an object of state worship. In each instance the image is external, visible, magnificent, and impressive.

The image in Daniel 3 is a type of an image to be erected by the Antichrist and set up in a Jewish temple. Our Lord refers to this image as "the abomination of desolation, spoken of by Daniel the prophet" (Matthew 24:15). Satan will perform a miracle by giving life to the image and causing it to speak (Revelation 13:15). Like Nebuchadnezzar's image, the image of the end time will be the object of wonder and veneration throughout the world. Daniel 3 is related to the beginning of the times of the Gentiles while Revelation 13 marks the end of the times of the Gentiles.

The fiery furnace is a type of the great tribulation, that seven-year period mentioned by Daniel as the seventieth week (Daniel 9:24-27). It will appear to have a good beginning, with promises being made to the Jews and apparent strides toward peace and prosperity. But like the peace and prosperity of Shadrach, Meshach, and Abed-nego in Babylon, which was short-lived, the Jews in the tribulation will pass through a great trial of affliction. Their fiery furnace at that time will be hotter than any previous fiery trials. A more detailed study of that seventieth week awaits us when we examine chapter 9.

The three Hebrew young men are a type of the children of Israel who will be preserved in the great tribulation. All will not be martyred in that day. God will miraculously preserve a remnant through the fiery furnace of the tribulation, a faithful group whom the Antichrist will not be able to exterminate. Neither Nebuchadnezzar nor Hitler could exterminate the Jews by cremation, nor will the Antichrist. The 144,000 sealed ones, twelve thousand of each of the twelve tribes of Israel, will be preserved to go about witnessing the gospel of the kingdom (Revelation 7), and later they will be seen still standing on the other side of the tribulation (Revelation 15:2), brought through the tribulation victorious over the beast, his image, and his mark (666).

The men who threw the three Hebrews into the fiery furnace were themselves destroyed by the flames. Their death is a prophecy in type of the final doom of the Antichrist who persecutes the Jews in the end time and "whom the Lord shall consume with the spirit of His mouth, and shall destroy with the brightness of His coming" (2 Thessalonians 2:8). "And the devil that deceived them was cast into the lake of fire and brimstone, where the beast and the false prophet are, and shall be tormented day and night for ever and ever" (Revelation 20:10). "And the beast was taken, and with him the false prophet that wrought miracles before him, with which he deceived them that had received the mark of the beast, and them that worshipped his image. These both were cast alive into a lake of fire burning with brimstone" (Revelation 19:20). One day God said to Abraham, "I will bless them that bless thee, and curse him that curseth thee: and in thee shall all families of the earth be blessed" (Genesis

12:3). Those who have persecuted the chosen people of God will one day meet their own doom in the lake of fire. History is repeating itself and it will continue to do so until our Lord Jesus Christ returns to earth and sets the world aright. My fellow believers, we can well afford to believe God and wait the day of His righteous vindication.

The Babylon of Daniel 3 will find its last effort being put forth to unite all the world in one religion in Revelation 17. The city of Babylon where Nebuchadnezzar held forth was the site of Nimrod's tower of Babel (Genesis 11:1-9). It presents a prophetic preview of that system and city that is growing in the world today. It is the devil's counterfeit for God's true kingdom. While the ancient city of Babylon was destroyed, the spirit of Babylon lives on. Political and religious Babylonianism will continue to spread its influence and power throughout the earth until the end of the age.

But, blessed be God, the Christian's future is bright with prospect. With the end times coming upon us, the problems in this world become more complex. We do not look for any man's world betterment program to succeed, but we do look "for that blessed hope, and the glorious appearing of the great God and our Saviour Jesus Christ" (Titus 2:13).

CHAPTER FOUR

CHAPTER FOUR

This entire chapter 4 is in a sense autobiographical. Having been related by Nebuchadnezzar, it is his own account of his conversion to God. The details are valid and authentic. The king's personal testimony belongs chronologically at the end of the chapter, because his conversion was the result of those experiences recorded in the chapter. In my study of this portion of the book of Daniel I was led to the conclusion that Nebuchadnezzar had become a truly saved man, therefore I expect to meet him in Heaven. Read this chapter in Daniel with great care, and even though it might read like fiction, keep in mind that it is fact. It is the last view we have of Nebuchadnezzar, and it is a thrilling account of what God did for his soul. His testimony reminds us of the Psalmist when he said, "Come and hear, all ye that fear God, and I will declare what He hath done for my soul" (Psalm 66:16). Here we meet a new Nebuchadnezzar.

THE REGENERATED KING SPEAKS
(4:1-3)

Nebuchadnezzar the king, unto all people, nations, and languages, that dwell in all the earth; Peace be multiplied unto you. I thought it good to shew the signs and wonders that the high God hath wrought toward me. How great are His signs! and how mighty are His wonders! His kingdom is an everlasting kingdom, and His dominion is from generation to generation (Daniel 4:1-3).

These first three verses are a sort of preamble to what follows. It is a statutory declaration by a monarch to all the people in his empire. It went into the records as a Babylonian state document. It is one of the few such state documents to be found in the Word of God, thus from a historic point of view, this chapter in Daniel is an extraordinary one.

The opening statement identifies the author and the people to whom the document is addressed. It has all the marks of a royal edict. Notice the extravagant style in the phrase, "unto all people, nations, and languages, that dwell in all the earth." While Nebuchadnezzar was sincere in wanting his edict proclaimed universally, he surely knew that there were unexplored areas over which Babylon exercised no authority. But it must be said in the king's favor that he attached much importance to his spiritual experience. He wanted all the world to know what God had done for his soul. Whenever God truly saves a man, that new convert becomes a witness. If you have no witness, it is doubtful that you ever experienced a conversion. It seems almost criminal for a child of God to withhold from poor lost sinners the message of salvation. It was no small matter for the renowned and influential Babylonian monarch to renounce his pagan gods and declare his faith in Israel's God. But he did so courageously and in good taste. He began with the words, "Peace be multiplied unto you." He recognized that there were many in his empire who were not at peace with God, and he longed in his heart that they might have that peace which he experienced.

He told the people that he thought it only fair and proper to let them know what God had done for him. "How great are His signs! and how mighty are His wonders!" (verse 3) The king was deeply impressed with his remarkable deliverance and the power of God which wrought it. The God of creation, who is also the God of redemption, is the God of "signs and wonders" (see Deuteronomy 6:22; 7:19; 13:1-2; 26:8). These attributes are embodied in the name used for God, "*the high God.*" He is sovereign over men and nations, for "His kingdom is an everlasting kingdom, and His dominion is from generation to generation."

It was nothing short of a divine miracle that in Babylon, the starting point of human idolatry and pagan worship, a mighty witness for God should go forth. Centuries later the Apostle Paul testified how God "in times past suffered all nations to walk in their own ways. Nevertheless He left not Himself without witness" (Acts 14:16-17). This fourth chapter of Daniel seems all the more remarkable as we realize that the witness for God was not that of a Hebrew prophet but of a Gentile king who was raised in the midst of pagan idolatry. History reveals that from time to time God has raised up a witness for Himself in unlikely places and through unsuspecting sources. Very often the witness has demanded world-wide attention. Even when a nation like Israel, who was made the repository for God's Word, has failed in its witness, God will see to it that His witness goes forth. During Israel's captivity, God sent forth from the imperial palace of Babylon, through the decree of King Nebuchadnezzar, a glowing and glorious testimony to His sovereignty and saving grace.

And now I am constrained to ask if you have been delivered from the bondage and guilt of your sin? Do you know in your own experience of the delivering power of the Most High God? Do you have a witness to tell of the miracle and wonder of regeneration in your life? I beg of you not to turn aside from these questions. To those who are saved there comes the challenge to witness faithfully of Him who has saved us. We all can learn a lesson from Nebuchadnezzar who expressed publicly his gratitude for the salvation given to him by God. We then hear the king tell the whole world about his conversion.

THE RELATING OF THE DREAM (4:4-16)

I Nebuchadnezzar was at rest in mine house, and flourishing in my palace: I saw a dream which made me afraid, and the thoughts upon my bed and the visions of my head troubled me. Therefore made I a decree to bring in all the wise men of Babylon before me, that they might make known unto me the interpretation of the dream. Then came in the magicians, the astrologers, the Chaldeans, and the soothsayers: and I told the dream before them; but they did not make known unto me the interpretation thereof. But at the last Daniel came in before me, whose name was Belteshazzar, according to the name of my god, and in whom is the spirit of the holy gods: and before him I told the dream, saying, O Belteshazzar, master of the magicians, because I know that the spirit of the holy gods is in thee, and no secret troubleth thee, tell me the visions of my dream that I have seen, and the interpretation thereof. Thus were the visions of mine head in my bed; I saw, and behold a tree in the midst of the earth, and the height thereof was great. The tree grew, and was strong, and the height thereof reached unto heaven, and the sight thereof to the end of all the earth:

The leaves thereof were fair, and the fruit thereof much, and in it was meat for all: the beasts of the field had shadow under it, and the fowls of the heaven dwelt in the boughs thereof, and all flesh was fed of it. I saw in the visions of my head upon my bed, and, behold, a watcher and an holy one came down from heaven; He cried aloud, and said thus, Hew down the tree, and cut off his branches, shake off his leaves, and scatter his fruit: let the beasts get away from under it, and the fowls from his branches: Nevertheless leave the stump of his roots in the earth, even with a band of iron and brass, in the tender grass of the field; and let it be wet with the dew of heaven, and let his portion be with the beasts in the grass of the earth: Let his heart be changed from man's, and let a beast's heart be given unto him; and let seven times pass over him (Daniel 4:4-16).

The details to be put into the record by means of a royal edict begin. It all happened after his successful military campaigns were behind him. With no more nations and tribes to conquer, the king was relaxing in his palace amidst the luxuries of a conquering monarch. One can imagine with what pride and arrogance he reflected upon the weaker nations he had conquered.

Let us not lose sight of the fact that this man had heard God's truth, and that he had repeated opportunities to turn to God. His contact with the things of God goes as far back as the captivity, when godly young Jewish men were brought into the royal court to be trained in Babylonian schools. Surely he must have been impressed with the testimony of Daniel and his friends when they refused to eat royal food, and still they were keen and bright and physically fit. Certainly he saw God at work in Daniel when the young Hebrew interpreted the dream image in chapter 2 and predicted the whole course of Gentile history. Finally, as we saw in our study of chapter 3, Nebuchadnezzar witnessed a demonstration of the mighty power of God in the miraculous preservation of the three Hebrew young men in the fiery furnace. All of this impressed the king and brought from him a verbal acknowledgment of Israel's God (3:29). But with all that he had seen and heard, his heart went unchanged. He was a professing believer merely. He was like many who attend our churches today and hear God's Word but refuse to yield their proud and stubborn will to God.

Right here I take courage and find comfort. If a Daniel, with the anointing of God upon his mind and message, could not witness the conversion of Nebuchadnezzar, I am determined to carry on trying to be my human best filled with the Spirit. I trust that we ministers of God will not allow the apathy in people to discourage or dissuade us. We do not know how many of our hearers have turned to God long after we pronounced our benediction. Let us never forget that our benediction does not mean that the Holy Spirit ceases to do His work. I once heard Dr. Vance Havner say that his sermons were like time bombs; some of them went off long after he had preached them. If ever a minister of God discharged his debt to a man, Daniel had discharged his to Nebuchadnezzar.

But now one of Daniel's time bombs was about to go off. With all of the king's power and possessions he was in poverty—poverty of soul. He was like the Laodiceans of our own day who smugly say, "I am rich, and increased with goods, and have need of nothing" (Revelation 3:17). But as he lay upon his bed, surrounded by wealth, he was made aware of his misery, wretchedness, and poverty. Suddenly and unexpectedly he had a dream, the details of which left him frightened and alarmed. Awakened by the dream, he could not dismiss from his mind the horrible reflections of what he had seen. Do you see the whole picture of this man? Before the dream he said he was "at rest." But it was the deceitful rest of a false security. So God sent him the vision to arouse him from his false security.

Nebuchadnezzar was so frightened by the dream that he issued a decree summoning all the scholars, teachers, magicians, and astrologers to come before him at once. This time he did not feign having forgotten the dream, but told them what he had seen and requested of them the interpretation. Had the king forgotten the event recorded in chapter 2? This institution of Babylonian "wise men" was not able to interpret the earlier dream. Why would he bypass Daniel and call in the very men who had failed him before? Typical of the unregenerated man, he turned to the wrong source for help. Those men who were powerless to recall his first dream could not now interpret this one. How apropos this story is to our times! Men become troubled, and in their fear, what do they do? They run to a psychiatrist, or a psychologist, or a lawyer, or a politician, but they will not go to a true servant of God who can lead them to the Word of God. Human nature remains unchanged.

Continuing with his testimony, the king said, "But at the last Daniel came in before me" (4:8). I wonder why Daniel did not come with Babylon's wise men when the king issued his decree summoning them? I am going to venture to answer this question: Daniel had been appointed chief over all the wise men of Babylon after he interpreted the dream in chapter 2 (2:48). Thus he was in a position of authority whereby he could send them before the king while he waited in his own chamber until they exhausted themselves trying to interpret the dream. Of course Daniel knew they would fail. His arrival was timed carefully. At least twenty-five years had passed since their dismal defeat in chapter 2. Daniel knew well their fakery and quackery. So he who was the master of the magicians waited for the right moment to make his appearance: "At the last." After each Babylonian wise man had had his chance and failed, "Daniel came in." At last Nebuchadnezzar was to learn the folly of turning to Satan's emissaries for wisdom. He was about to discover that "It is better to trust in the LORD than to put confidence in man" (Psalm 118:8). "Blessed is the man that walketh not in the counsel of the ungodly" (Psalm 1:1). Omniscience and the revealing of future events belong to God only. History shows that God has chosen holy men guided by the Holy Spirit to reveal and record His message (2 Peter 1:21). "There is a spirit in man: and the inspiration of the Almighty giveth them understanding" (Job 32:8). Daniel was such a man, and Nebuchadnezzar knew it.

There is an interesting observation here in Nebuchadnezzar's use of the name *Daniel*. In relating the details, as a converted man, he said, "But at the last Daniel came in before me, whose name was Belteshazzar, according to the name of my god" (4:8). However, when he addressed Daniel before his conversion he called him "Belteshazzar" (4:9, 18, 19). Here is another of the many evidences for the verbal inspiration of the Scriptures. After Nebuchadnezzar's conversion, which resulted from a severe judgment of God, he would not do or say anything that might grieve God. "Therefore if any man be in Christ, he is a new creature: old things are passed away; behold, all things are become new" (2 Corinthians 5:17).

Verses 10-16 contain the substance of the dream. Nebuchadnezzar related to Daniel how he had seen a great tree, tall and strong. The height of the tree reached to Heaven, and its branches spread throughout all the earth. The significance of the tree in relation to its ecumenical importance is indicated by the fact that it was visible "to the end of all the earth" (4:11), "in it was meat for all . . . and all flesh was fed of it" (4:12). While the tree, in its primary association, represented Nebuchadnezzar and his kingdom of Babylon, we should not lose sight of the fact that the book of Daniel is prophetic as well as historical. In its primary association the tree predicted the fall of Nebuchadnezzar and Babylon, but in its prophetic anticipation the tree depicts the ecumenical outreach of Babylonianism and Gentile power in the last days, and its final overthrow.

The Scriptures offer numerous illustrations of a tree representing a man or a nation, or both as a picture of an earthly kingdom. The blessed man shall be "like a *tree* planted by the rivers of water" (Psalm 1:3). The wicked man of great power is "like a green bay *tree*" (Psalm 37:35). David said, "I am like a green olive *tree* in the house of God" (Psalm 52:8). The Psalmist said, "The righteous shall flourish like the palm *tree*: he shall grow like a cedar in Lebanon" (Psalm 92:12). See also Isaiah 56:3 and Jeremiah 17:8. In Ezekiel 31:3-18 Assyria is likened to a mighty cedar. The mustard tree in Matthew 13:31-32 represents Christendom today. The olive tree represents both Israel and the Gentiles (Romans 11:16-24).

Returning to the relating of the dream by Nebuchadnezzar to Daniel, the king continued, "I saw in the visions of my head upon my bed, and, behold, a watcher and an holy one came down from heaven" (4:13). As he fixed his gaze upon the dream tree, not knowing what to expect next, there was the sudden appearance of an angel from Heaven. There are different ranks of angels who are assigned specific tasks. These vigilant, sleepless creatures keep up an unceasing guard, functioning as agents of God's judgment. One of these angels slew the firstborn in Egypt (Exodus 12:23); another brought the judgment of pestilence in David's day (2 Samuel 24:16). They are called "watchers" because that is their function and ministry. David wrote of them, saying, "Bless the LORD, ye His angels, that excel in strength, that do His commandments, hearkening unto the voice of His word. Bless ye the LORD, all ye His hosts; ye ministers of His, that do His pleasure" (Psalm 103:20-21). They also function as "ministering spirits, sent forth to minister for them who shall be heirs of salvation" (Hebrews 1:14). It is through these unseen intelligent beings that God carries out much of His spiritual program (see 1 Kings 22:19-23).

In verse 14, the angel is both seen and heard by Nebuchadnezzar. As one with authority and assurance, the angel called aloud to unnamed and unseen associates, commanding them to cut down the tree, cut off its branches, shake off the leaves, and scatter the fruit. At this point there is a significant change in the text from the neuter pronoun "it" in verse 12 to the personal pronoun "his" in verse 14. When Nebuchadnezzar described the tree, he said, "in *it* was meat for all: the beasts of the field had shadow under *it* . . . and all flesh was fed of *it*" (4:12). But when the angel issued his order, he said, "Cut off *his* branches, shake off *his* leaves, and scatter *his* fruit . . . and the fowls from *his* branches" (4:14). What the angel said made clear to the king the personification of the tree. It was intended to represent a man, and it was this revelation that frightened Babylon's monarch.

Verses 15 and 16 conclude the telling of the dream by Nebuchadnezzar to Daniel:

> *Nevertheless leave the stump of his roots in the earth, even with a band of iron and brass, in the tender grass of the field; and let it be wet with the dew of heaven, and let his portion be with the beasts in the grass of the earth: Let his heart be changed from man's, and let a beast's heart be given unto him; and let seven times pass over him (4:15-16).*

The tree was not to be completely uprooted and destroyed. The stump and the roots were to be left in the earth. There was the prospect of the tree being revived. Since the subject changed from the tree to the man, there was hope for that man. He would be bound as with a band of iron and brass for seven years, bound by a malady of mental derangement whereby he should regard himself as a beast and behave himself as such a beast would behave. During that period of time, God would accomplish His work in the heart of the man, after which He would restore him to sanity again.

THE REASON FOR THE DREAM (4:17)

This matter is by the decree of the watchers, and the demand by the word of the holy ones: to the intent that the living may know that the most High ruleth in the kingdom of men, and giveth it to whomsoever He will, and setteth up over it the basest of men (Daniel 4:17).

The contents of this verse are most important. They were intended to assure the king that his dream was not meaningless, as so many dreams are. This dream intended to teach a much needed lesson, namely "that the living may know that the most High ruleth in the kingdom of men, and giveth it to whomsoever He will, and setteth up over it the basest of men" (4:17). Nebuchadnezzar and every earthly ruler must know that there is one ruler who is greater than the greatest among men, more powerful than the most powerful among men, and in His hands rest the dividing and disposal of the kingdoms of men. One of the great sins of national leaders is their refusal to take God into their deliberations and decisions. They will not listen to the voice that tells them that God's will must and will prevail. In a democracy a man is voted into office, but in the last analysis men do not set up whomsoever they please. There is a close connection between the earth and its affairs with the spirit world. "The powers that be are ordained of God" (Romans 13:1). The reason for Nebuchadnezzar's dream is obvious: "that the living may know that the most High ruleth in the kingdom of men, and giveth it to whomsoever He will, and setteth up over it the basest of men" (4:17). A man's power is not a sign of his own greatness, but that he has been ordained of God to rule. Let any ruler fail to recognize that his position, power, and possessions are due to the blessing of the Almighty, and God's angels will demand judgment upon him for taking God's glory from Him. Nations have risen and fallen, but man still refuses to believe that God rules and overrules in the kingdoms of earth. The God who sets up a man as ruler can just as easily put him down. The greatest of men are but subordinates to the "only Potentate, the King of kings, and Lord of lords" (1 Timothy 6:15). God's divine demolition squad has brought to nought more than one haughty earthly ruler. International affairs are not mere matters of chance.

Victor Hugo has left to us a bit of interesting history concerning Napoleon and the battle of Waterloo. On the morning of the battle, the little dictator stood gazing upon the field of battle as he described to his commanding officer his strategy for that day's campaign.

"We will put the infantry here, the cavalry there, the artillery here. At the end of the day England will be at the feet of France and Wellington will be prisoner of Napoleon."

After a pause the commanding officer said, "But we must not forget that man proposes but God disposes."

With arrogant pride the little dictator stretched his body to full height and replied, "I want you to understand, sir, that Napoleon proposes and Napoleon disposes."

Hugo went on to write, "From that moment Waterloo was lost, for God sent rain and hail so that the troops of Napoleon could not maneuver as he had planned, and on the night of battle it was Napoleon who was prisoner of Wellington, and France was at the feet of England."

In days like ours, when imperialistic aims are proudly predicted, we all will do well if we heed the teaching of God's Word when it says, "God resisteth the proud, but giveth grace unto the humble" (James 4:6). "Humble yourselves therefore under the mighty hand of God, that He may exalt you in due time" (1 Peter 5:6).

Before continuing on to a consideration of verses 18-26, I am led to pass on to my readers a thought with which Dr. Ironside begins the fourth lecture in his excellent volume, *Lectures on Daniel.* I would not include it here, except for the possibility that some of my readers have not seen this work by the late Dr. Ironside. It has to do with a passage in Job. Elihu said, "For God speaketh once, yea twice, yet man perceiveth it not. In a dream, in a vision of the night, when deep sleep falleth upon men, in slumberings upon the bed; Then He openeth the ears of men, and sealeth their instruction, That He may withdraw man from his purpose, and hide pride from man. He keepeth back his soul from the pit, and his life from perishing by the sword. He is chastened also with pain upon his bed, and the multitude of his bones with strong pain: So that his life abhorreth bread, and his soul dainty meat. His flesh is consumed away, that it cannot be seen; and his bones that were not seen stick out. Yea, his soul draweth near unto the grave, and his life to the destroyers. If there be a messenger with him, an interpreter, one among a thousand, to shew unto man his uprightness:

Then He is gracious unto him, and saith, Deliver him from going down to the pit: I have found a ransom. His flesh shall be fresher than a child's: he shall return to the days of his youth: He shall pray unto God, and He will be favourable unto him: and he shall see His face with joy: for He will render unto man His righteousness. He looketh upon men, and if any say, I have sinned, and perverted that which was right, and it profited me not; He will deliver his soul from going into the pit, and his life shall see the light. Lo, all these things worketh God oftentimes with man, To bring back his soul from the pit, to be enlightened with the light of the living" (Job 33:14-30).

I have quoted the passage in full, not that I believe it has any direct connection with Daniel 4, but because of the remarkable similarity between the two passages. God spoke "once" to Nebuchadnezzar in the dream of the great image, but the king rejected the message and continued in his pride and rebellion of heart. Then God spoke "twice, yet man perceiveth it not." After the dream of the great image, and the vision in the fiery furnace, and finally the second dream in which Nebuchadnezzar saw the great tree, God sent his interpreter Daniel, one among a thousand. This third and final word from Daniel was the solemn pronouncement of how God was going to humiliate the proud and stubborn monarch until he was ready to cry out in sincerity, "I have sinned, and perverted that which was right, and it profited me not." There is a stern and solemn warning here to any and all who pervert the ways of God, for at times God uses drastic means to humble the proud heart.

THE REVELATION IN
THE DREAM (4:18-26)

*This dream I king Nebuchadnezzar have seen. Now
thou, O Belteshazzar, declare the interpretation thereof,
forasmuch as all the wise men of my kingdom are not
able to make known unto me the interpretation: but thou
art able; for the spirit of the holy gods is in thee. Then
Daniel, whose name was Belteshazzar, was astonied for
one hour, and his thoughts troubled him. The king spake,
and said, Belteshazzar, let not the dream, or the interpretation thereof, trouble thee. Belteshazzar answered and
said, My lord, the dream be to them that hate thee, and
the interpretation thereof to thine enemies. The tree that
thou sawest, which grew, and was strong, whose height
reached unto the heaven, and the sight thereof to all the
earth; Whose leaves were fair, and the fruit thereof much,
and in it was meat for all; under which the beasts of the
field dwelt, and upon whose branches the fowls of the
heaven had their habitation: It is thou, O king, that art
grown and become strong: for thy greatness is grown,
and reacheth unto heaven, and thy dominion to the end
of the earth. And whereas the king saw a watcher and an
holy one coming down from heaven, and saying, Hew
the tree down, and destroy it; yet leave the stump of the
roots thereof in the earth, even with a band of iron and
brass, in the tender grass of the field; and let it be wet
with the dew of heaven, and let his portion be with the
beasts of the field, till seven times pass over him; This is
the interpretation, O king, and this is the decree of the
most High, which is come upon my lord the king: That
they shall drive thee from men, and thy dwelling shall be*

*with the beasts of the field, and they shall make thee to
eat grass as oxen, and they shall wet thee with the dew of
heaven, and seven times shall pass over thee, till thou
know that the most High ruleth in the kingdom of men,
and giveth it to whomsoever He will. And whereas they
commanded to leave the stump of the tree roots; thy
kingdom shall be sure unto thee, after that thou shalt have
known that the heavens do rule (Daniel 4:18-26).*

Having told all the details in the dream, the king called
upon Daniel for the interpretation of those details. Admit-
ting once more to the utter failure of the official staff of
dream interpreters in the royal palace, and his confidence
in Daniel's ability to reveal the interpretation, the king
awaited the bad news. We have the feeling that the king
knew at this time that the news was bad for him.

Upon hearing the dream, Daniel became greatly upset.
For one hour he remained silent, dumbfounded. He understood the meaning of the dream, but he dreaded telling it
to the king. It was not that he lacked courage and conviction, for he demonstrated both when called upon to interpret the dream image in chapter 2. But now he must be the
bearer of the terrifying and tragic tidings that would be
coming upon the king himself. One can imagine a whole
chain of thoughts racing through Daniel's mind during that
hour. No man of God ever finds it an easy matter to be the
bearer of evil tidings. During World War II it was my lot
to tell parents that their son was killed in action. Let me
assure you that I delayed my task more than one hour.

Nebuchadnezzar was not slow to discern Daniel's anxiety,
but he wanted to know the truth as quickly as possible. He
broke the long hour of silence with the words, "Belteshazzar,
let not the dream, or the interpretation thereof, trouble
thee" (verse 19). To this Daniel replied, "The dream be to

them that hate thee, and the interpretation thereof to thine enemies." This statement by Daniel I find difficult to interpret. It is possible that Daniel said, "This dream is going to please your enemies, because its fulfillment upon you will cause them to be glad." Then too, it is not impossible that Daniel was saying, "I wish that the calamity which is about to fall upon you would fall upon your enemies instead." Of these two possible interpretations, I favor the first.

Then, reiterating the description of the tree almost exactly as Nebuchadnezzar had described it in his dream, Daniel told to the king the interpretation: "The tree that thou sawest . . . It is thou, O king. . . . They shall drive thee from men, and thy dwelling shall be with the beasts of the field, and they shall make thee to eat grass as oxen, and they shall wet thee with the dew of heaven, and seven times shall pass over thee, till thou know that the most High ruleth in the kingdom of men, and giveth it to whomsoever He will" (4:20, 22, 25). The explanation is authoritative and accurate, the decree of the Most High. What the angels had decreed in the dream was actually the decree of God and therefore not to be trifled with. God was going to accomplish His purpose in Nebuchadnezzar's heart by means of severe punishment upon this wicked monarch. There was no way possible for Nebuchadnezzar to miss the interpretation and application of the dream. Like Nathan's famous words to David, "Thou art the man" (2 Samuel 12:7), so Daniel's pungent and penetrating pronouncement came to Nebuchadnezzar, "It is thou, O king." No doubt Nebuchadnezzar recalled the first dream and saw how the two dreams bore a striking resemblance. As the judgment of God was to strike the dream image, so must it strike the dream tree. And he was that tree. He must be cut down and left in the field "till seven times" or years have passed

(4:23). He was about to be dethroned and debased. Inasmuch as he had behaved as a beast, he would be treated as a beast. The sole nourishment for his body was to be the alfalfa of the fields.

THE REACTION OF DANIEL (4:27)

Wherefore, O king, let my counsel be acceptable unto thee, and break off thy sins by righteousness, and thine iniquities by shewing mercy to the poor; if it may be a lengthening of thy tranquillity (Daniel 4:27).

This one verse stands uniquely alone from the rest of the thirty-six verses in our chapter. What a pity that most commentators have passed it by with little or no comment at all! Actually it is the gospel in this historical narrative. Being a faithful interpreter of God's message, Daniel fearlessly dealt with the matter of sin; "break off thy sins," he said to Nebuchadnezzar. But being the compassionate minister that he was, he appealed to the king to repent. The interpreter turned preacher with an application to his hearer. Daniel offered what he had not been asked to give—sound spiritual counsel. It takes moral courage for a preacher to apply the truth and admonish his hearers as did Daniel. He admonished the king and urged him to correct those wicked abuses associated with his reign. The king had been partial in his administration of justice, but if he would turn to God and do right, he would have imputed to him the righteousness of God. Here Daniel was pleading with the king to surrender his life to God. Such courage and compassion should cause us to hold the highest regard for true servants of the Lord. We can do with more men like Daniel who will "Preach the word; be instant in season, out of season; reprove, rebuke, exhort with all longsuffering and doctrine" (2 Timothy 4:2). In much the same way as did Daniel, Paul proved himself when he stood before Festus and Agrippa (Acts 25—26).

Peter was just such a preacher when he delivered the Pentecostal sermon. Examine carefully that sermon and note three things:

The explanation—"This is that" (Acts 2:16-22)
The proclamation—"Him" (Acts 2:23-35)
The application—"Ye" (Acts 2:36-38)

That is faithfully handling the Word of God, preaching Christ in His fullness, and applying the truth to the hearer. But unlike the hearers on Pentecost, Nebuchadnezzar did not take the prophet's advice. It seems almost incredible that the king would refuse to heed Daniel's pleading, yet that is exactly what he did.

The heart of man has not changed since that historic seventh century. With all the courageous and compassionate preaching of God's Word, men will not turn from their pride and passions to Jesus Christ. The record does not tell us just how Nebuchadnezzar reacted to Daniel's counsel and admonition, but without a doubt the sequel shows that he did not heed it. We must emphasize the fact that Daniel reacted admirably to the prophecy of God and the plight of the king. We do not know if the king was offended, angry, or indifferent at the time, but we do know that Daniel proved himself a faithful minister of God.

THE REBELLION OF NEBUCHADNEZZAR
(4:28-30)

> *All of this came upon the king Nebuchadnezzar. At the end of twelve months he walked in the palace of the kingdom of Babylon. The king spake, and said, Is not this great Babylon, that I have built for the house of the kingdom by the might of my power, and for the honour of my majesty? (Daniel 4:28-30)*

All that is recorded in the chapter before verse 28 is written in the first person. But here there is a change. The section we are about to examine is written in the third person. Is this Nebuchadnezzar speaking? Or is it the record of the historian? Commenting upon such questions, Dr. Leupold writes, "It matters little, as far as we are concerned, whether the king himself reported objectively about himself what others told him had transpired, or whether he let his scribe do it for him." [1] At any rate, the inspired record says, "All of this came upon the king Nebuchadnezzar" (4:28).

The king's reaction to the dream was not good. The prophet's compassionate words of appeal seem to have been wasted upon him. If in his heart he felt any conviction for a time, that eventually wore off. God was gracious and long-suffering in that He waited one full year before executing judgment. The Scripture tells us that God is "Longsuffering to us-ward, not willing that any should perish, but that all should come to repentance" (2 Peter 3:9). I wonder if Nebuchadnezzar would have yielded had he known that at

[1] Leupold, *Daniel*, page 197.

the end of the year God would strike him down? When exactly twelve months had elapsed (4:29), his heart was unchanged. Possibly he thought that Daniel was wrong, or that God had forgotten.

Strutting about his palace, displaying arrogance and pride, the king said, "Is not this great Babylon, that I have built for the house of the kingdom by the might of my power, and for the honour of my majesty?" (4:30) God gave him time to humble himself, but during that time he only hardened his heart and turned from the divine warning. It is true that Babylon had expanded and become the most impressive nation on the earth. The city was glorious. Nebuchadnezzar did build it, but his objective was the glorification of his own name. This is where God's long-suffering terminated and His patience ran out. The haughty king refused to learn that he was indebted to the Most High God for his exalted position of a world leader. Moreover he treated the kindness and mercy of God with contempt. When God gives a man time to repent, and that man uses the time to harden his heart against God's pleadings and warnings, judgment is certain. "Because sentence against an evil work is not executed speedily, therefore the heart of the sons of men is fully set in them to do evil" (Ecclesiastes 8:11). "He, that being often reproved hardeneth his neck, shall suddenly be destroyed, and that without remedy" (Proverbs 29:1). Beware how you treat the patience and long-suffering of God! If He has been calling you to repent, I urge upon you not to trifle.

THE RETRIBUTION OF
THE MOST HIGH GOD (4:31-33)

While the word was in the king's mouth, there fell a voice from heaven, saying, O king Nebuchadnezzar, to thee it is spoken; The kingdom is departed from thee. And they shall drive thee from men, and thy dwelling shall be with the beasts of the field: they shall make thee to eat grass as oxen, and seven times shall pass over thee, until thou know that the most High ruleth in the kingdom of men, and giveth it to whomsoever He will. The same hour was the thing fulfilled upon Nebuchadnezzar: and he was driven from men, and did eat grass as oxen, and his body was wet with the dew of heaven, till his hairs were grown like eagles' feathers, and his nails like birds' claws (Daniel 4:31-33).

Now the time of respite for Nebuchadnezzar was past. While he was boasting, "The same hour was the thing fulfilled upon Nebuchadnezzar." "While the word was in the king's mouth," before he finished his boast that *he* built Babylon for the glory of *his* own name, "there fell a voice from heaven." A man was boasting on earth and God interrupted him with a voice from Heaven. Yes, the words from Heaven "fell" upon the ungodly and proud heart like a bomb. He must stand mute and listen to his sentence being pronounced. And there can be no mistaking the one to whom the voice of God was speaking. "O king Nebuchadnezzar, to thee it is spoken" (4:31). When God speaks, it is done. In this connection examine our Lord's parable of the certain rich man who proudly boasted in his possessions, and to whom God said, "Thou fool, this night thy soul shall be required of thee" (Luke 12:16-21). In a similar way God spoke to Nebuchadnezzar.

As soon as the voice ceased speaking, the king became irrational. A form of mental derangement called lycanthropy seized him, a disease whereby a man regards himself to be other than a man. If he thinks himself to be a beast, then to all intents and purposes he behaves like that beast. Nebuchadnezzar thought himself to be an ox, and since he behaved like an ox he was treated as an ox. In our day there are those who would label such behavior as demon possession. However, let our attention be drawn to the fact that in the case of Babylon's king it was the direct judgment of God. So pronounced was his demented state that he was led outside the palace, yet within the confines of the royal grounds, where he ate grass like an ox. His nails grew and took on the appearance of birds' claws. His uncombed and uncut hair grew and became matted and took on the appearance of eagles' feathers (4:33).

I look upon this historical incident as one of the most solemn and sobering judgments that God ever pronounced upon a man. Whenever a man defies God and deifies himself, that man can expect judgment, because the pride of man is an object of God's hatred. "These six things doth the LORD hate: yea, seven are an abomination unto Him: A *proud look*, a lying tongue, and hands that shed innocent blood, An heart that deviseth wicked imaginations, feet that be swift in running to mischief, A false witness that speaketh lies, and he that soweth discord among brethren" (Proverbs 6:16-19). Take note that pride leads this caravan of sins that God hates. When God entrusts a man with the government of His own earth, He holds him accountable and compensates him accordingly. When the divine ax is laid at the root of a tree, great is the fall of that tree. God only exercises sovereign authority in Heaven and earth. It is most informative to read how Isaiah, in his pronouncement against the king of Babylon, and against Satan, charges them with the sin of insidious pride and ambition in their attempt to be like the "most High" (Isaiah 14:4-14). God's decree to all who attempt to dethrone Him and enthrone themselves is summed up in the words, "Yet thou shalt be brought down." Indeed the proud king had been brought down, reduced to the level of a beast. Minutes before his fall he wore the royal robes of a ruling monarch walking about in his magnificent palace; then he was crawling on all fours in an open field, eating grass like an ox. The retribution of the Most High is inevitable.

THE RESTORATION
OF NEBUCHADNEZZAR (4:34-37)

And at the end of the days I Nebuchadnezzar lifted up mine eyes unto heaven, and mine understanding returned unto me, and I blessed the most High, and I praised and honoured Him that liveth for ever, whose dominion is an everlasting dominion, and His kingdom is from generation to generation: And all the inhabitants of the earth are reputed as nothing: and He doeth according to His will in the army of heaven, and among the inhabitants of the earth: and none can stay His hand, or say unto Him, What doest Thou? At the same time my reason returned unto me; and for the glory of my kingdom, mine honour and brightness returned unto me; and my counsellors and my lords sought unto me; and I was established in my kingdom, and excellent majesty was added unto me. Now I Nebuchadnezzar praise and extol and honour the King of heaven, all whose works are truth, and His ways judgment: and those that walk in pride He is able to abase (Daniel 4:34-37).

These verses are remarkable for their message of hope and encouragement. Here is the king's own personal testimony of his conversion to the Most High God. It happened "at the end of the days," that is, at the end of the divinely appointed period of seven years (verse 16), the duration of the king's dementia. It occurred when he lifted up his eyes to Heaven, when he was ready to surrender his proud will to the Most High. The upward look to God always marks the return to reason. All beasts look down, but man was made to look up. When sin entered the heart of man his gaze was diverted from Heaven to earth. Now God says, "Look unto Me, and be ye saved, all the ends of the earth: for I am God, and there is none else" (Isaiah 45:22). In the wilderness the Israelites discovered that there was life for a look (Numbers 21:5-9). Every sinner who has turned to God in faith has learned that He who hates and judges sin is ready and willing to receive and save sinners. It took seven long and humiliating years for Nebuchadnezzar to learn the needed lesson, but at last he learned it well. Do not miss the spiritual, moral, and ethical instruction in this story. The proud heart that refuses to bow to Jesus Christ the Saviour for redemption, must one day bow to Him as Sovereign for His just retribution.

The first evidence of the king's changed heart is seen in the fact that he praised and honored the Most High as the sovereign ruler in Heaven and on earth. This hardly seems like mere lip service, but rather the language of a man who has known the work of divine grace in his soul. He was not now the Nebuchadnezzar of old. His arrogancy and his pride in himself had been replaced with adoration and praise for God. There is no lesson more sublime in our chapter than that every erring man can look to God and be saved. When the transformation is complete, that regenerated soul will say, "Worthy is the Lamb that was slain to receive power, and riches, and wisdom, and strength, and honour, and glory, and blessing. And every creature which is in heaven, and on the earth, and under the earth, and such as are in the sea, and all that are in them, heard I saying, Blessing, and honour, and glory, and power, be unto Him that sitteth upon the throne, and unto the Lamb for ever and ever" (Revelation 5:12-13). We feel inclined to differ with Calvin, who doubted whether the king's experience led to his conversion.

Continuing his praise of the God who redeemed him, the king added, "And all the inhabitants of the earth are reputed as nothing: and He doeth according to His will in the army of heaven, and among the inhabitants of the earth: and none can stay His hand, or say unto Him, What doest Thou?" (verse 35) So thorough was the work of grace in his life that he saw all the inhabitants of the earth, when contrasted alongside of God, accounted as nothing. He said that God will ultimately have His way among the angelic hosts of Heaven and with all that dwell upon the earth. No created being can question His acts nor limit His actions. He gave a concise and clear testimony to the absolute power and authority of Almighty God.

Verse 36 contains that phase of the king's testimony which points to the blessings he enjoyed in his later years. His reason was restored, his throne was given to him again, and unprecedented honor and greatness were bestowed upon him. He achieved greater fame than ever. He gained the respect of the most distinguished men in the Babylonian court. Except for the seven years of insanity and debasement, the king seems to have suffered no ill effects politically. His experience was similar to that of Job, of whom it is written, "So the LORD blessed the latter end of Job more than his beginning" (Job 42:12). Thus it was with Nebuchadnezzar after he had humbled himself before God: "excellent majesty [or greatness] was added unto me." Had he acknowledged the supremacy and greatness of God upon hearing Daniel's compassionate appeal, he would have been spared those seven years of insanity accompanied by his dethronement and disgrace. When his eyes were opened at last, he saw that the changing thrones, with their representative kings and kingdoms, were not mere matters of chance, but that behind all world affairs there is working the eternal King and an everlasting kingdom.

"Now I Nebuchadnezzar praise and extol and honour the King of heaven, all whose works are truth, and His ways judgment: and those that walk in pride He is able to abase" (4:37). It is not possible to overstate the value and importance of the lesson learned by the first great monarch of Gentile times. It is the key to all history and prophecy. It applies to all walks of life: "The most High ruleth in the kingdom of men, and giveth it to whomsoever He will. . . . and those that walk in pride He is able to abase."

This is the last we read in the Scriptures of Nebuchadnezzar. After his restoration and return to the throne of Babylon, he lived about one year. His son Evil-merodach, who reportedly occupied the throne during his years of insanity, succeeded him as Babylon's next ruling monarch.

"Thus saith the LORD, Let not the wise man glory in his wisdom, neither let the mighty man glory in his might, let not the rich man glory in his riches: But let him that glorieth glory in this, that he understandeth and knoweth Me, that I am the LORD which exercise lovingkindness, judgment, and righteousness, in the earth: for in these things I delight, saith the LORD" (Jeremiah 9:23-24).

THE RELATION OF THE DREAM TREE TO PROPHECY

The book of Daniel is not a collection of twelve disconnected and unrelated chapters. In addition to the historical details, and the moral and spiritual lessons to be applied to us all, the book has its clear prophetic aspect, as stated by our Lord in Matthew 24:15. We saw this fact in the dream image in chapter 2, where the picture was presented showing the course of history from Babylon to the last Gentile world power which will be overthrown when the Lord Jesus Christ returns to earth to set up His everlasting kingdom. The main purpose of Daniel, then, is to present the times of the Gentiles, tracing the course of human government from the days of the kingdom of Babylon to our Lord's second coming.

The seven years of Nebuchadnezzar's madness reflect, in type at least, another seven-year period yet future. It is that seventieth "week" (Daniel 9:24-27), the period of seven years when the last great Gentile ruler will control the nations of the earth in his insane madness. This is all typical and prophetic of the reign of the Antichrist between the rapture of the Church and Christ's second coming to the earth. Just as Nebuchadnezzar and Babylon succeeded in conquering the then known world, providing food and shelter for all (Daniel 4:11-12), so the ecumenical Babylon of the last days, under the Antichrist, will control all buying and selling as well as all religious activity (Revelation 13).

Today this one-world government is in the making, promising to all races a great society of man-made prosperity and peace, the cessation of poverty and war. As in the case of Nebuchadnezzar, the pride of man will reach its zenith, and then shall the Lord Jesus come and lay the ax to the tree. We believe that the time for the cutting down of this ecumenical tree is getting nearer. When proud man reaches the pinnacle of his own effort and achievement, the Lord will cut him down. The seeming beauty, protection, shade, rest, and food of the ecumenical tree of the last days will be short-lived.

My concluding word on this chapter in Daniel should be an encouraging one to every man. Just as there was hope for the personal conversion of Nebuchadnezzar, so there is hope to you who read these lines. If you have not experienced a genuine conversion to God through personal faith in the Lord Jesus Christ, then I beseech you to humble yourself, look to Him who alone is able to save you.

CHAPTER FIVE

CHAPTER FIVE

In 1868 Dr. Daniel March gave to the English-speaking world his fine book entitled, *Night Scenes in the Bible*. It provides interesting, informative, and instructive reading. As one would expect, the author includes a chapter on "The Night Feast of Belshazzar." That night was the night of prophetic fulfillment when God removed the head of gold from Nebuchadnezzar's dream image. That night God kept His Word, as He always does, and the record still stands as a solemn warning to any and all who attempt to defy the Almighty. Here is the last sobering scene of the downfall of a man's dynasty, the night in which the proud heart of a king was abased, when the breast and arms of silver replaced the head of gold.

This portion of the book of Daniel has been a target for the critics of the Bible, the controversy revolving around Belshazzar. Even the late Dean Farrar said that there was no such king in Babylon named Belshazzar, that Nabonidus was the last Chaldean to occupy a throne in Babylon. Other critics have attacked this portion of Scripture because Nebuchadnezzar is called the father of Belshazzar (5:2, 11, 18, 22). These objections from the critics appeared for a time to be valid but every Christian knew that, inasmuch as Daniel had written his book by divine inspiration, his record would of necessity be historically correct. The Christian need never fear that secular history will ever disprove the records in the Holy Scriptures. However, just for the critics' books, there is ample collated extant material which shows unreservedly that tablets and clay cylinders have been discovered in the ruins of Chaldea on which the name of Belshazzar was inscribed as the eldest son of Nabonidus. Those who need any confirmation of God's Word can check on the translation work of Sir Herbert Rawlinson done in 1854.

As to the matter of the father-son relationship between Nebuchadnezzar and Belshazzar mentioned in Daniel 5, there is no real problem. Robert Dick Wilson, that able scholar who answered so admirably Dean Farrar, has shown that among the Arabs and Babylonians the word "son" was used in not less than twelve ways, including "grandson" and "adopted son," and that the word "father" had no fewer than seven different uses.[1] The word "father" was used for any ancestor, for one's father, grandfather, great-grandfather, great-great-grandfather, and even back beyond that. However, to facilitate understanding or confirmation, I present in order the kings of Babylon, as I understand that order after consulting the best-known and most reliable sources:

1. Nebuchadnezzar died 561 B.C.

2. Evil-merodach, Nebuchadnezzar's son, succeeded him (2 Kings 25:27-30; Jeremiah 52:31-34).

3. Neriglissar (Nergal-sharezer), son-in-law of Nebuchadnezzar, murdered his brother-in-law Evil-merodach.

4. Laborosoarchod, an imbecile son of Neriglissar, reigned less than one year.

5. Nabonidus (Nabonnaid), another son-in-law of Nebuchadnezzar, who married the widow of Neriglissar.

6. Belshazzar was the son of Nabonidus. It is not known

[1] Robert Dick Wilson, *Studies in the Book of Daniel.*

for certain if he was the son of Nabonidus by birth or by adoption. Since Nabonidus married the widowed daughter of Nebuchadnezzar, it is possible that Belshazzar had already been born at the time of the marriage. A clay cylinder found by Rawlinson in the ruins of ancient Chaldea had inscribed on it the fact that Belshazzar was the eldest son of Nabonidus.

Nabonidus, who spent much of his time away from his kingdom seeking other conquests, appointed his son Belshazzar to remain at Babylon as coruler, or coregent. Since Belshazzar shared the throne with his father, and was ruling when the Persian general besieged the royal city, the accuracy of Daniel's record is beyond dispute. Actually Belshazzar was the *second ruler* in the kingdom, which accounts for his offering to the one interpreting the handwriting on the wall the position of "*third ruler* in the kingdom" (5:7). We can be sure that the Bible will vindicate itself every time.

THE FAME OF BABYLON

Babylon was founded by Nimrod, the great-grandson of Noah (Genesis 10:8-10). Surviving a series of conflicts, it became one of the most magnificent and luxurious cities in the known world. Superbly constructed, it spread over an area of fifteen square miles, the Euphrates River flowing diagonally across the city. The famous historian Herodotus said the city was surrounded by a wall 350 feet high and 87 feet thick, wide enough for six chariots to drive abreast. Around the top of the wall were 250 watchtowers placed in strategic locations. Outside the huge wall was a large ditch, or moat, which surrounded the city and was kept filled with water from the Euphrates River. The large ditch was meant to serve as an additional protection against attacking enemies, for any attacking army would have to cross this body of water first before approaching the great wall. The cost of constructing this military defense was estimated to be in excess of one billion dollars. When we consider the value of a billion dollars in those days, plus the fact that it was all built with slave labor, one can imagine something of the wonder and magnificence of this famous city.

But in addition to being a bastion for protection, Babylon was a place of beauty. The famous hanging gardens of Babylon are on record yet today as one of the seven wonders of the world. Arranged in an area 400 feet square, and raised in perfectly-cut terraces one above the other, they soared to a height of 350 feet. Viewers could make their way to the top by means of stairways which were 10 feet wide. Each terrace was covered with a large stone slab, topped with a thick layer of asphalt, two courses of brick cemented together, and finally, plates of lead to prevent any leakage of water. On top of all this was an abundance of rich, fertile earth planted with vines, flowers, shrubs, and trees. From a distance these hanging gardens gave the appearance of a beautiful mountainside, when viewed from the level plains of the valley. The estimated cost to build this thing of beauty ran into hundreds of millions of dollars.

The tower of Babel with its temples of worship presented an imposing sight. The tower itself sat on a base 300 feet in breadth and rose to a height of 300 feet. The one chapel on the top contained an image alone reported to be worth $17,500,000, and sacred vessels, used in worshiping Babylonian gods, estimated at a value of $200,000,000. In addition to this wealth and grandeur the temple contained the most elaborate and expensive furniture ever to adorn any place of worship. Every student should read a good history and a reliable encyclopedia on the city of Babylon, and he will be convinced that this ancient city surpassed anything that man has built on earth in its military fortifications, its beauty and wealth, its religious pomp and extravagance. Nebuchadnezzar indeed had been an ambitious builder, and his own words fit well his accomplishments when he said, "Is not this great Babylon, that I have built?" (Daniel 4:30)

THE FEAST OF BELSHAZZAR (5:1)

Belshazzar the king made a great feast to a thousand of his lords, and drank wine before the thousand (Daniel 5:1).

Lavish feasts were not uncommon in the kingdoms and empires of the old world. The Bible describes several, as for example the feast given by Ahasuerus, king of Persia (Esther 1). But the feast of Belshazzar stands out in the records as one of the most unusual of all time. As a rule the monarchs dined alone, but on special occasions and at state functions a king has been known to provide food and drink for as many as fifteen thousand guests. Belshazzar invited one thousand of his leaders to his feast. From the context it appears that the banquet was arranged in honor of one of the Babylonian gods.

It was in the year 538 B.C., about twenty-three years after the death of Nebuchadnezzar. Daniel was not instructed to write of his own whereabouts during that time, but we do know from this chapter that God had preserved and protected him through the passing years. The aging prophet of

God was not present at the king's banquet, but he was no doubt in his private quarters writing under the inspiration and guidance of the Holy Spirit.

The feast was not that kind of an affair at which a man of God would choose to be present. The character of the feast is seen in the behavior of those in attendance. It was a night's menu of wine, women, and song, an affair wanting in piety and reverence, to say the least. Historians tell us that such orgies were known for their licentiousness and idolatrous worship. Drunkenness, idolatry, and base sensuality are often closely related. From the Biblical context one might conclude that Belshazzar's feast had turned into a drinking bout. However, liquor and licentiousness are weak props for any person.

At the same time that this great festival day was being celebrated in the palace, Cyrus the Persian and his army were outside the gates of the city of Babylon, planning their strategy to besiege the city. Belshazzar certainly knew this. Was his feast then in defiance of the Persian forces? Was his confidence in the mighty walls surrounding the city? Certainly the guards in the two hundred and fifty watchtowers knew every move of the Persian forces. How powerful and protected Belshazzar must have felt! But the holding of such a feast at a critical hour like this seems unbelievable.

THE FOLLY OF BELSHAZZAR (5:2-4)

Belshazzar, whiles he tasted the wine, commanded to bring the golden and silver vessels which his father Nebuchadnezzar had taken out of the temple which was in

Jerusalem; that the king, and his princes, his wives, and his concubines, might drink therein. Then they brought the golden vessels that were taken out of the temple of the house of God which was at Jerusalem; and the king, and his princes, his wives, and his concubines, drank in them. They drank wine, and praised the gods of gold, and of silver, of brass, of iron, of wood, and of stone (Daniel 5:2-4).

Very little is recorded in the Bible about Belshazzar. His reign was brief and his deeds were hardly worth reporting. He is best known for the ignoble and insolent act committed while under the influence of alcohol. This demon of drink has continued to dig at all the foundations of civilization, destroying the moral fiber of nations. People outdo themselves in wickedness when they are overpowered by a pseudo boldness and the absence of restraint produced by the alcohol demon. One of the perils of strong drink is that it too often carries away the drinker to do and say foolish and fatal things, the hidden depths of iniquity being stirred up within him. The presence of wives and concubines was generally not practiced at such banquets, but the fact that Belshazzar in his drunken state sent for the women to be brought in leaves the reader to fill in the rest. (Esther chapter 1 and Matthew 14:1-12 should be read in this connection.)

But the height of Belshazzar's folly was the climax of his impiety when he "commanded to bring the golden and silver vessels which his father Nebuchadnezzar had taken out of the temple which was in Jerusalem; that the king, and his princes, his wives, and his concubines, might drink therein" (5:2). These holy vessels were taken by Nebuchadnezzar as a part of the spoils when he overthrew Jerusalem and plundered the holy city. When that drunken crowd desecrated those consecrated vessels, they were guilty of unparalleled sacrilege. Their act was one of contemptuous profanity; it was the acme of wickedness, the apogee of wantonness. Belshazzar's folly is marked by intemperance, impropriety, impiety, and idolatry. These four go hand-in-hand. (See 2 Kings 24:13 and 25:15.)

Man is intuitively religious and is therefore a worshiper. If his heart is not yielded to God in true worship, he will be dominated by Satan in idolatrous worship. There are as many gods in this world as there are people to worship them. A missionary to India reported that in India alone there are more than three hundred million gods. I do not know how many gods the Babylonians claimed, but we do know that the six mentioned here are representative of man-made deities throughout the earth. In his fine book, *Voices from Babylon*, Dr. Seiss wrote, "Not only their ill-timed merriment, their trampling on the customary proprieties, and their drunkenness, but even their foolhardy and blasphemous insult to the Most High God, is veiled over, cloaked up with a pretense of devotion. This was as far as it was possible for human daring to go. It was more than the powers of Heaven could quietly endure." The moment of doom had come. The Most High God is merciful and gracious, slow to anger, but even with the God of compassion there must come the day of judgment.

If ever a man needed the God of Heaven Belshazzar was that man. But the only God who could help him at that hour was the God he was defying and whose name he was defiling. When God had announced through His prophet the rise of Nebuchadnezzar to power, He had also declared that in the days of Nebuchadnezzar's grandson doom would fall upon Babylon (Jeremiah 27:7). Belshazzar was that grandson, and now the hour had arrived when judgment must strike. Jeremiah was given an additional prophecy which seems to have application to this night feast and folly of Belshazzar. God had said through His servant, "In their heat I will make their feasts, and I will make them drunken, that they may rejoice, and sleep a perpetual sleep, and not wake, saith the LORD. I will bring them down like lambs to the slaughter, like rams with he goats. . . . And I will make drunk her princes, and her wise men, her captains, and her rulers, and her mighty men: and they shall sleep a perpetual sleep, and not wake, saith the King, whose name is the LORD of hosts" (Jeremiah 51:39-40, 57). Here is the solemn prediction from Jehovah Himself that, inasmuch as Babylon would defy His repeated warnings, He would shut up the nation to her sins and to sin's inevitable consequences.

Such desecration of the vessels of the Most High God is typical of Babylonianism. The holy things of God, consecrated by God for His own praise and glory, are being desecrated on a larger scale today than ever before. Such desecration will increase until the man of sin stretches forth his hand to touch God's holy Temple and His covenant people, Israel. Babylon the great, the mother of harlots, will show herself glamorously in the last days, "arrayed in purple and scarlet colour, and decked with gold and precious stones and pearls and having a golden cup in her hand full of abominations and filthiness of her fornication" (Revelation 17:4-6). The climax of the age will be marked by an amalgamated federation of religious groups set forth in Revelation 17 and 18 under the figure of a drunken harlot. This apostate religio-political machine, the largest organized church in world history, will bear the name of Christ, but in reality it will be the masterpiece of Satan. Babylon, the mother of harlots, will come to certain doom. All of this is foreshadowed in Daniel 5.

THE FINGERS OF GOD (5:5)

In the same hour came forth fingers of a man's hand, and wrote over against the candlestick upon the plaister of the wall of the king's palace: and the king saw the part of the hand that wrote (Daniel 5:5).

At the height of Belshazzar's awful blasphemy and defiance of God, when his cup of iniquity was full, there came forth in full view of that inebriated crowd a weird phenomenon. Out of the sleeve of the night there appeared the fingers of a man's hand writing strange words across the plaster of the wall in the king's palace. The fingers suggested the presence of some personality, but the sight of the fingers merely may have served to solemnize the whole incident. Suddenly the disgusting revelry ceased, and all eyes were riveted upon the wall. The lampstand of Jehovah, being at that very hour desecrated by Belshazzar, was now being used to illuminate the handwriting on the wall so that all could read the words. That which was written was no mere optical illusion, nor was it a prank being played on the king by some of the revelry makers, nor was anyone having a hallucination.

The fingers which wrote the message on the wall were not the fingers of an ordinary man. Those fingers had written before and they would write again. The same fingers had spelled out the doom of another mighty leader who dared to defy God. When the Lord sent plagues upon Egypt, the magicians admitted to Pharaoh, "This is the finger of God" (Exodus 8:19). Not long afterward, God gave to Moses at Sinai the two tables of testimony, His own holy law, "written with the finger of God" (Exodus 31:18). It was that same finger that cast out demons (Luke 11:20), that wrote on the ground to expose the self-righteous scribes and Pharisees (John 8:1-9, cf., Jeremiah 17:13). Those fingers are the fingers of God, which give God's revelation to man (Matthew 12:28, cf., Luke 11:20).

One day those fingers wrote the following words, "I am the LORD: that is My name: and My glory will I not give to another, neither My praise to graven images" (Isaiah 42:8). Belshazzar was about to learn this truth the hard way. Though his brain was befogged with wine, the handwriting on the wall struck terror to his heart. If his banquet was designed to be a morale builder, it had completely failed, leaving the king in frustration.

THE FEAR OF BELSHAZZAR (5:6-9)

Then the king's countenance was changed, and his thoughts troubled him, so that the joints of his loins were loosed, and his knees smote one against another. The king cried aloud to bring in the astrologers, the Chaldeans, and the soothsayers. And the king spake, and said to the wise men of Babylon, Whosoever shall read this writing, and shew me the interpretation thereof, shall be clothed with scarlet, and have a chain of gold about his neck, and shall be the third ruler in the kingdom. Then came in all the king's wise men: but they could not read the writing, nor make known to the king the interpretation thereof. Then was king Belshazzar greatly troubled, and his countenance was changed in him, and his lords were astonied (Daniel 5:6-9).

The reader of Daniel's record now has his attention diverted from the fingers to the frightened monarch. The handwriting had struck terror to Belshazzar's heart. His face blanched, his lips trembled, his knees smote together. Never did a drunken man sober so quickly. Shouting at his official interpreters so as to hide his fear and trembling, he promised them promotion and honor if they would interpret the frightening words upon the wall. It was plain to all present that painful thoughts were disturbing him. What a pitiful sight! Only a few moments earlier this proud monarch had dared to defy the Almighty.

Belshazzar was never more sincere than when he called for the Chaldeans, the astrologers, and the soothsayers. These enchanters came as usual, but they were just as helpless to interpret the message from God as they were on previous occasions. They knew what the words on the wall were, but they could not read them understandingly. Only the man of God can interpret the Word of God. The tongue of the unregenerate man is powerless to tell the meaning of Heaven's message. The world through its wisdom cannot know God (1 Corinthians 1:21). The true messenger of God, who gets his message from God, must present himself as Paul did when he said, "And my speech and my preaching was not with enticing words of man's wisdom, but in demonstration of the Spirit and of power: That your faith should not stand in the wisdom of men, but in the power of God" (1 Corinthians 2:4-5). When it became apparent that there was no man among the Chaldeans who could make known the meaning of the words on the wall, the king's confusion and consternation increased.

How perfectly comforting it is to the trusting child of God to observe the utter weakness of human wisdom when the Lord Himself exposes that weakness. It is now the third time that those quacks were exposed for their fakery. In chapter 2 they were unable to tell Nebuchadnezzar his dream. In chapter 4 they could not interpret Nebuchadnezzar's second dream. Again in chapter 5 they were powerless to give the meaning of the handwriting on the wall. It seems that Belshazzar would have profited from Nebuchadnezzar's experience with the wise men of Babylon. But most of us are slow to learn. World leaders today turn to every known source of human wisdom, but they will not turn to God and His Word. Even if those servants of lying demons had known the answer, they no doubt would have lacked the necessary courage to tell the king the truth. I have the feeling that they might have lied and have told Belshazzar that it was a good omen.

Belshazzar had every cause to fear. That night he saw only a few of the divine fingers, and the Bible says, "It is a fearful thing to fall into the hands of the living God" (Hebrews 10:31). The mere sight of the fingers frightened him, but he was yet to feel the full weight of God's hand in judgment. The God of Heaven is merciful, slow to anger, and longsuffering, not willing that any should perish, but that all should come to repentance (2 Peter 3:9). But there must come an end to His tolerating of the unholy and wicked deeds of any man.

THE FAME OF DANIEL (5:10-16)

Now the queen, by reason of the words of the king and his lords, came into the banquet house: and the queen spake and said, O king, live for ever: let not thy thoughts trouble thee, nor let thy countenance be changed: There is a man in thy kingdom, in whom is the spirit of the holy

*gods; and in the days of thy father light and understanding
and wisdom, like the wisdom of the gods, was found in
him; whom the king Nebuchadnezzar thy father, the king,
I say, thy father, made master of the magicians, astrologers, Chaldeans, and soothsayers; Forasmuch as an
excellent spirit, and knowledge, and understanding, interpreting of dreams, and shewing of hard sentences, and
dissolving of doubts, were found in the same Daniel, whom
the king named Belteshazzar: now let Daniel be called,
and he will shew the interpretation. Then was Daniel
brought in before the king. And the king spake and said
unto Daniel, Art thou that Daniel, which art of the children of the captivity of Judah, whom the king my father
brought out of Jewry? I have even heard of thee, that the
spirit of the gods is in thee, and that light and understanding and excellent wisdom is found in thee. And now
the wise men, the astrologers, have been brought in before
me, that they should read this writing, and make known
unto me the interpretation thereof: but they could not shew
the interpretation of the thing: And I have heard of thee,
that thou canst make interpretations, and dissolve doubts:
now if thou canst read the writing, and make known to
me the interpretation thereof, thou shalt be clothed with
scarlet, and have a chain of gold about thy neck, and
shalt be the third ruler in the kingdom (Daniel 5:10-16).*

At this point in the sacred narrative the queen mother
appeared in the banquet room. It seems reasonable to conclude, from verse 2, that this woman was not the wife of
Belshazzar, but that she may have been the widow of Nebuchadnezzar. Her appearance seems to have been at the
request of the king and his lords (5:10). We are not told why
she was not present when the feast began. Possibly she
stayed away from it all by her own choice as a protest

against those practices she could not condone. On the other hand, Belshazzar may have been responsible for her absence from the banquet hall. Whether she was the widow or the daughter of Nebuchadnezzar, she knew of Jehovah and the late king's conversion to Him, and it is not impossible that she too had been converted.

Upon entering the banquet hall the queen mother called Belshazzar's attention to the fact that there was a man in the kingdom who could interpret the handwriting on the wall. She gave his name, listed his gifts and ability, and told just enough of his past to inform Belshazzar of the honored place Daniel held in Nebuchadnezzar's kingdom. Here indeed is a display of sound judgment on the part of the queen mother.

Daniel was now an old man, but God still had a work for His servant to perform. No longer was he that youthful lad of the early days of the captivity, but a seasoned, mature man of God, between eighty and ninety years of age, richer in spiritual experience for his years. There is no record as to where or how Daniel spent those intervening years. It is possible that upon the death of Nebuchadnezzar Daniel had been removed from his official position and retired to private life. In view of the miracles associated with Daniel and his three friends, it hardly seems possible that he was forgotten. It is more reasonable to assume that with the rise of a new regime Daniel was demoted and placed in obscurity. Men are known to forget what it is convenient to forget. Whatever the reason for Daniel's obscurity, we must be careful that we do not read into the record that which is not there.

Daniel was brought into the banquet hall before the king. What a striking figure the venerable old gentleman made as he stood before that drunken crowd! Courage and confidence were shining forth from his godly face. The king was the first to speak. He ascribed more to Daniel than he could to all of Babylon's wise men put together. Verse 13 does not necessarily mean that Belshazzar did not know Daniel personally. It is possible that there is no interrogation here, but that the king is saying, "So thou art Daniel!" After reiterating what the queen mother had said about Daniel, Belshazzar offered to Daniel great honor and gifts if he would read the writing with understanding. It is safe to conclude that Belshazzar was not interested in Daniel's God, nor did he have any sense of his own spiritual need. It was his present dilemma that compelled him to listen to Daniel. Some men in their extremity will accept help from anyone. Belshazzar had reached his extremity. He was within twenty-four hours of death and hell. His cup of iniquity was full and his doom was sealed.

THE FAITHFULNESS OF DANIEL (5:17-24)

Then Daniel answered and said before the king, Let thy gifts be to thyself, and give thy rewards to another; yet I will read the writing unto the king, and make known to him the interpretation. O thou king, the most high God gave Nebuchadnezzar thy father a kingdom, and majesty, and glory, and honour: And for the majesty that He gave him, all people, nations, and languages, trembled and feared before him: whom he would he slew; and whom he would he kept alive; and whom he would he set up; and whom he would he put down. But when his heart was lifted up, and his mind hardened in pride, he was deposed from his kingly throne, and they took his glory from him:

*And he was driven from the sons of men; and his heart
was made like the beasts, and his dwelling was with the
wild asses: they fed him with grass like oxen, and his
body was wet with the dew of heaven; till he knew that the
most high God ruled in the kingdom of men, and that
He appointeth over it whomsoever He will. And thou his
son, O Belshazzar, hast not humbled thine heart, though
thou knewest all this; But hast lifted up thyself against
the Lord of heaven; and they have brought the vessels of
His house before thee, and thou, and thy lords, thy wives,
and thy concubines, have drunk wine in them; and thou
hast praised the gods of silver, and gold, of brass, iron,
wood, and stone, which see not, nor hear, nor know: and
the God in whose hand thy breath is, and whose are all
thy ways, hast thou not glorified: Then was the part of the
hand sent from Him; and this writing was written (Daniel
5:17-24).*

The aged Daniel stood listening to the king's offer. But
God's true servant could not be bought at any price. No
mercenary minister, this man of God! The Balaams have
their price and they prostitute their office and message for
personal gain, but Daniel was not one of them. Having been
delivered from covetousness, he refused to be dissuaded by
the king's offer. Why should he be enticed by the temporal
tinsel of this world's power and possessions? For fourscore
years Daniel had trusted and proved the Most High God.
Now he could well afford to be contemptuous of Belshazzar's offer. Actually, Belshazzar did not have anything to
give to Daniel, for Daniel knew that in that very night the
great kingdom of Babylon would be lost and Belshazzar
himself would be dead. Daniel would not stoop to the
mercenary tactics of the men of Babylon (cf., Genesis 14:21-
23; 2 Kings 5:15-16; Acts 8:18-20). The true servant of the

Lord will not prostitute divine truth for personal gain. The deplorable practice of offering "gifts" for services in return has contributed to corruption in business and government. Many an honest and sincere man has been led to do wrong through the "gift" approach. Daniel would have no part of it. He replied to the king, "Let thy gifts be to thyself, and give thy rewards to another" (5:17). There is no flattery in Daniel's reply; nor is there disrespect. If the king's approach is wrong in God's sight, it must of necessity be wrong in Daniel's eyes.

"Yet I will read the writing unto the king, and make known to him the interpretation" (5:17). No offer of a gift, regardless of its size or worth, could change the course of Daniel's conduct. Like Moses (Numbers 16:15), and Samuel (1 Samuel 12:3), and Paul (Acts 20:33), and every true servant of God (1 Timothy 3:3; 1 Peter 5:2), the mercenary spirit does not govern the life and labors of God's minister. He is faithful to his task and to the truth even if no remuneration is forthcoming. Belshazzar was deliberately outraging God by defying divine truth and defiling the holy vessels, therefore Daniel could only look with disgust upon the proffered gifts. Yet the servant of the Lord was true to his calling. He had a duty and responsibility to the Word of God written upon the wall. He must be faithful, fearing no man, not even the king.

In verses 18-21 Daniel reminded Belshazzar of the pride of Nebuchadnezzar and the subsequent judgment of God upon him. This prophet of God was neither inflated by the king's flattery nor influenced by his offer. He told the whole truth with unmistakable clarity. The sermon was pointed and pungent. It was a historical review of Nebuchadnezzar's progress (verse 18), power (19), pride (20), and punishment (21). The preaching was not lacking and the preacher was not found wanting. Daniel's ministry here was a remarkable demonstration of faithfulness. I detect in all of this background material about Nebuchadnezzar, his progress and power as well as his pride, an attempt on Daniel's part to show to Belshazzar that there was at least some accomplishment by Nebuchadnezzar which occasioned his pride, an accomplishment which, by contrast, Belshazzar could hardly advance. The whole point of Daniel's message was that Nebuchadnezzar, with the greatness and power which were rightly his, might have felt justified in being proud, but with all his achievements God punished him because of his pride. On the other hand, Belshazzar, who had not yet won his wings, had no justifiable cause to be proud.

Then Daniel drove home the application in a fearless and forthright manner: "And thou his son, O Belshazzar, hast not humbled thine heart, though thou knewest all this; But hast lifted up thyself against the Lord of heaven" (5:22-23). Daniel was telling him that his sin was much greater than Nebuchadnezzar's because he (Belshazzar) knew better. "Thou knewest," declared Daniel in his plain-spoken indictment. The king had sinned against ample knowledge, and since the greater knowledge calls forth a more severe judgment, Belshazzar knew that his doom was imminent. All sin is sin, but guilt and punishment are proportionate to knowledge. The Apostle Paul wrote, "And even as they did not like to retain God in their knowledge, God gave them over" (Romans 1:28). "Because that, when they knew God, they glorified Him not as God" (Romans 1:21). Peter spoke of those who "willingly are ignorant" (2 Peter 3:5), that is, the truth escapes them only because they want it to. (See 2 Thessalonians 1:7-8.) G. H. Lang in his book, *The Histories and Prophecies of Daniel,* entitles this fifth chapter, "Though Thou Knewest." In it he writes, "Men are responsible to take to heart the lessons of the dealings of God with others. Belshazzar knew right well how God had humbled his grandfather, and yet dared to defy the Most High. Knowing of those events he could scarcely *not* have known of Daniel. It is upon this just principle that God judges." Let me remind my brothers and sisters in Christ, and all who are yet not saved, that we expose ourselves to greater retribution when we sin against light. I am reminded of our Lord's words in the parable of the talents, where the employer said to his slothful servant who misused the talent, "Thou knewest. . . . Thou oughtest therefore" (Matthew 25: 26-27).

Daniel's words in verse 23 doubtless called for remarkable courage. He was telling Belshazzar that he had been worshiping dumb gods "which see not, nor hear, nor know: and the God in whose hand thy breath is, and whose are all thy ways, hast thou not glorified." With authority and incisiveness Daniel struck at the very root of the problem, namely Belshazzar's religion. The king had been worshiping dumb gods of man's fashioning, and his religion had led him into shameful idolatry and moral lawlessness. On the other hand, he had insulted the one true God to whom he owed his very existence. The words, "the God in whose hand thy breath is," form a most revealing and remarkable statement. They remind us that no man holds a lease on life. Our times are in the hands of Him who created us—"In whose hand is the soul of every living thing, and the breath of all mankind" (Job 12:10). "Thus saith God the LORD, He that created the heavens, and stretched them out; He that spread forth the earth, and that which cometh out of it; He that giveth breath unto the people upon it, and spirit to them that walk therein" (Isaiah 42:5). These verses from God's Word should remind every man how utterly dependent upon God we all are for our very existence. But poor, proud Belshazzar had utterly denied this great truth.

"Then was the part of the hand sent from Him; and this writing was written" (5:24). This statement concluded the preliminary explanation necessary to the interpretation of the handwriting. All that Daniel said to Belshazzar to this point was preparation for the final and fatal word. By this time the king must have sensed that nothing could avert the judgment of the Most High upon him and his kingdom. The case had been tried, the facts had been presented, and now Belshazzar stood arraigned before the tribunal of God. It would not be necessary to call any additional witnesses. The criminal stood mute awaiting his sentence. Actually the sentence had already been given in the handwriting on the wall. Having been written in the Chaldean language, the wise men of Babylon understood the words, but the interpretation and application of those words they were not able to unfold. This they were now to hear.

THE FALL OF BABYLON (5:25-31)

And this is the writing that was written, MENE, MENE, TEKEL, UPHARSIN. This is the interpretation of the thing: MENE; God hath numbered thy kingdom, and finished it. TEKEL; Thou art weighed in the balances, and art found wanting. PERES; Thy kingdom is divided, and given to the Medes and Persians. Then commanded Belshazzar, and they clothed Daniel with scarlet, and put a chain of gold about his neck, and made a proclamation concerning him, that he should be the third ruler in the kingdom. In that night was Belshazzar the king of the Chaldeans slain. And Darius the Median took the kingdom, being about threescore and two years old (Daniel 5:25-31).

The message on the wall was brief, yet every word carried a note of unquestioned authority. There were only four words in all—"Mene, Mene, Tekel, Upharsin." Actually there are just three different words inasmuch as the first word (*Mene*) is repeated. Now all persons present knew that the words meant "number, weight, division," or in their verb form, "numbered, weighed, divided." But only Daniel knew their divine significance.

Mene. "This is the interpretation of the thing: MENE; God hath numbered thy kingdom, and finished it" (5:26). To "number" the kingdom means to fix or limit its duration as to time, as in Leviticus 15:13, 28; 23:16; and Psalm 90:12. Here in Daniel it means that God had fixed the duration of Babylon as a ruling empire and the day of her destruction had come. The repetition of the word could well be for emphasis, to press and impress upon Belshazzar that there would be no extension of time. His number was up! The word *Mene* denotes calculation. God's decisions are not carelessly arrived at, but they are carefully calculated. The duration of the kingdoms of men are perfectly timed and not left to chance, because God "removeth kings, and setteth up kings. . . . the most High ruleth in the kingdom of men, and giveth it to whomsoever He will, and setteth up over it the basest of men" (2:21; 4:17). Belshazzar had been one of the basest of men, and now his days were numbered and his kingdom was doomed. The times of the Gentiles are reckoned out by God. He knows exactly how long it will be until Christ comes.

"*Tekel;* Thou art weighed in the balances, and art found wanting" (5:27). The scales of God weigh accurately, and because God deals with exactness He deals in justice. None but God is competent to weigh every man's life with perfect accuracy, because He only is omniscient and righteous. "The LORD is a God of knowledge, and by Him actions are weighed" (1 Samuel 2:3). Job said, "Let me be weighed in an even balance, that God may know mine integrity" (Job 31:6). Job needed not to fear lest he might not be weighed on accurate scales. "Shall not the Judge of all the earth do right?" (Genesis 18:25) We all may be sure that He will. Belshazzar did not weigh enough on the scales of divine justice, thus he did not measure up to the divine specifications. Both the king and his kingdom were destined to destruction. "Surely men of low degree are vanity, and men of high degree are a lie: to be laid in the balance, they are altogether lighter than vanity" (Psalm 62:9). "All the ways of a man are clean in his own eyes; but the LORD weigheth the spirits" (Proverbs 16:2). On the perfect scales of God Belshazzar did not weigh enough to escape divine judgment. How much do you and I weigh? Let each be reminded that the scale can be turned by a wrong spirit within a man. Our Lord warned that a lustful desire in the heart is equal to adultery (Matthew 5:28). Hatred in the heart is the equivalent of murder (1 John 3:15). Therefore "Keep thy heart with all diligence; for out of it are the issues of life" (Proverbs 4:23).

Upharsin. "PERES; Thy kingdom is divided, and given to the Medes and Persians" (5:28). The average reader asks, and rightly so, why the word *Upharsin* (verse 25) is changed to *Peres* (verse 28). Some scholars who know the languages tell us that *Pharsin* is the plural form of *Peres,* the *U* of the original form being the customary conjunction "and." Dr. Leupold says, "The two forms here suggest a double meaning. The verb *peras* as such means 'break or divide.' If we then render *peres* 'divided' (A.V.), that means, of course, 'broken up' into its constituent parts; and so we have trans-

lated 'broken.' But *paras* as such also means the *'Persian';*
parsin or *pharsin* is merely a plural, *'Persians.'* It is given to
Daniel to discern that this means that the kingdom is to be
'given to the Medes and Persians' after it has been broken
up.

"This sequence: 'Medes' first, then 'Persians,' indicates
a point of historical accuracy that fits in beautifully with
the idea of Daniel's authorship of the book. The supremacy
in this dual kingdom remained but a short time with the
Medes and that while Daniel was still on the scene, and
then passed permanently to the Persians, a fine point that
a writer who lived in the Maccabean age would hardly have
thought of recording. Yet the form *upharsin,* 'Persians,'
gives the emphasis to the much longer Persian supremacy.

"Though this interpretation is convincing, and though
no man apparently doubted it when Daniel spoke it, yet it
is like divine revelation generally in this respect, that no
man can discern it by himself, but after it is given it is found
to be simple and clear."[2]

While Daniel was giving the interpretation, the Medes and
the Persians were already on Babylonian soil, and the inebriated Babylonians were helpless to stop their advance.
The Most High God was ruling in the kingdom of men.
The head of gold was about to be removed from the body
of Gentile world power. "In that night" (5:30) judgment
struck very swiftly. Certainly Belshazzar could not have
expected the end to come so soon and suddenly. But even
while Daniel was interpreting the writing, God had already
given the kingdom to the Medes and Persians, "in that
night." Empires do not stand by human might, man-made
machines, and missiles. There is not a wall high enough nor
thick enough to prevent a nation from falling when God

[2] Leupold, *Daniel,* page 235.

pronounces that nation's doom. Now I know that the scoffers will jeer at what I have just said, but the true fact of it remains, and it is corroborated by history. Possibly there were scoffers in Belshazzar's palace who laughed "that night" as Daniel interpreted the writing, but the fact remains that on "that night" Babylon went down in defeat.

The king kept his promise of bestowing the reward (verse 29, cf., verse 16). Whether Belshazzar fully believed Daniel or not we cannot be absolutely certain. Possibly he still felt that his kingdom might be spared, but I doubt this. At any rate, that was Babylon's last night. The kingdom of the head of gold had passed to that of the arms and breast of silver.

There is a last night for every nation and there is a last night for every individual person. Every nation and every man is held accountable to God, and the Almighty holds an indictment against any and all who defy divine light and desecrate holy things. Babylonian pride and confusion are seen on every hand today. There is a handwriting against every man. But our Lord Jesus Christ has made salvation possible for every man, "Blotting out the handwriting of ordinances that was against us, which was contrary to us, and took it out of the way, nailing it to His cross" (Colossians 2:14). And now all who put their trust in Him are saved from the awful night of eternal banishment from the presence of God. But for the proud in heart who refuse to recognize the Most High God, there "is reserved the blackness of darkness for ever" (Jude 13).

THE FOREVIEW OF THE FUTURE

We have been reminded in our study thus far that Babylon represents more than the actual Chaldean Empire of the time of Nebuchadnezzar. In its final form Babylon represents the great religio-political system of the last days. This final Babylon is rising rapidly, as is witnessed in the modern ecumenical movement and in our Lord's description of the Laodicean church in the last days (Revelation 3:17). Religious leaders boast about the great progress being made through the union of large denominations, the World Council of Churches, and the Vatican's ecumenical church. But underneath it all one sees an impiety and infidelity greater than that which flourished in Belshazzar's banquet room.

Today there is the mad pursuit of worldly pleasure, the craze for sports, uncontrolled eating and drinking, and a false sense of security which has been built upon a fake prosperity. "This know also, that in the last days perilous times shall come. For men shall be lovers of their own selves, covetous, boasters, proud, blasphemers, disobedient to parents, unthankful, unholy" (2 Timothy 3:1-2). Just as the downfall of Babylon meant the end of that great civilization, so the end of the age will be marked by the end of Gentile world powers. The doom of Babylon foreshadows the doom of "BABYLON THE GREAT, THE MOTHER OF HARLOTS AND ABOMINATIONS OF THE EARTH" (Revelation 17:5). Men today laugh when we tell them that our modern civilization is doomed, but I am certain that Belshazzar never conceived in his mind the possibility of his mighty empire being overthrown. Read Daniel 5:4, 23, and then read Revelation 9:20, where it is stated plainly that in the end time, before the final overthrow of the Gentile world powers, the same kind of idols will be worshiped, namely "idols of gold, and silver, and brass, and stone, and of wood."

Belshazzar was an individual, an historical figure, but he is also the exponent of the ungodly world leader at the end of the age. He represents the Antichrist, that most ungodly braggart of all time who will hurl his defiance at the Almighty, seeking even to dethrone God while at the same time trying to enthrone himself. But he will be cut off in the midst of his blasphemous career (2 Thessalonians 2:3-7). The writing is not on a wall but indelibly inscribed in the Scriptures by that same hand.

The spirit of Babylonianism has never changed, nor will it ever change. It has followed a pattern from its inception beginning with Nimrod, and it will continue to live on until the return of our Lord Jesus Christ to the earth, which will occasion the judgment of Almighty God. The solution of this world's ills lies in this one great event, the coming again of God's Son from Heaven, the stone cut out without hands.

CHAPTER SIX

CHAPTER SIX

There is probably no chapter in the entire book of Daniel which is more familiar than the sixth chapter, which records the casting of Daniel into the den of lions. Yet I never cease to marvel at the new insight and fresh lessons received each time I read it. If this is your first encounter with this historical incident, or if you have read it a hundred times before, receive it with an open mind. Though Daniel spent only one night of his long life in the lions' den, the lessons in this chapter are too numerous and meaningful to rush through hurriedly.

This chapter concludes the strictly historical section of the book of Daniel. Actually, the history in the first six chapters of the book contains prophecy, and those prophecies in the historical portion, as well as the history in the prophetical section of the book, prove that the predictions of Daniel, revealed to him by God, were true and accurate.

The penman of the Epistle to the Hebrews wrote of those "Who through faith . . . stopped the mouths of lions" (Hebrews 11:33). This reference doubtless includes Samson (Judges 14:5-6) and David (1 Samuel 17:34-35) as well as Daniel. David wrote: "My soul is among lions. . . . My heart is fixed" (Psalm 57:4, 7), and "Break their teeth, O God, in their mouth: break out the great teeth of the young lions, O LORD" (Psalm 58:6). More will be discussed on the lion experience as we pursue the exposition of the text.

As the whereabouts of Daniel has been questioned in chapter 3, when his three Hebrew friends were cast into the fiery furnace, so there is a question as to the whereabouts of the three friends in this chapter. It has been suggested that, because of the position of importance held by Daniel, he was possibly in some other part of the empire on official business. The Bible is silent as to this. However, we may be certain that, wherever he was, he remained faithful to Jehovah and did not bow down to Nebuchadnezzar's image. As to the three Hebrew friends of Daniel in chapter six, again we must remember that where Scripture is silent on such matters we will do wisely if we will not speculate. We merely suggest that, because of the lapse of time here, it is not impossible that the three were not living. At this point in the narrative, Daniel was between eighty and ninety years of age.

THE PRIMACY OF DANIEL (6:1-3)

It pleased Darius to set over the kingdom an hundred and twenty princes, which should be over the whole kingdom; And over these three presidents; of whom Daniel was first: that the princes might give accounts unto them, and the king should have no damage. Then this Daniel was preferred above the presidents and princes, because an excellent spirit was in him; and the king thought to set him over the whole realm (Daniel 6:1-3).

This chapter opens where chapter 5 closed, with Babylon, the head of gold, having been replaced by the Medo-Persian

Empire, represented by the breast and arms of silver. As
Darius ascended the throne of the new empire in 538 B.C.,
Daniel, who had bridged the gap between these first two
Gentile world powers, was still keen and hearty despite his
years. This prophet of God had witnessed the rise of two of
those kingdoms which he predicted in chapter 2. The head
of gold had been removed and time was marching on, but
the old prophet was still alive. Moreover he remained un-
spotted in the midst of luxury, lust, and licentiousness. His
headquarters were in a palace, but a palace that was half
pigsty. It is remarkable that a man should keep himself
spotless in the midst of government officials who were sensual, sinful, and self-seeking. His purity was even more pronounced by reason of the impurity that surrounded him.

The inferiority of this second kingdom of silver to the
first kingdom of gold is at once noticeable. Nebuchadnezzar's rule in Babylon was one of absolute monarchy. It
was autocratic. He refused to share authority with anyone,
being sole dictator in his kingdom. Whom he would he put
to death, and whom he would he kept alive. But under King
Darius there was a change. This second world empire was
not an absolute monarchy. King Darius had the government in his kingdom well organized, setting over it one
hundred and twenty princes, and over these three presidents, of whom Daniel was appointed first or chief, having
both seniority and superiority over the others. The reason
for the king's choice of Daniel was "because an excellent
spirit was in him," meaning, I take it, that Daniel was filled
with and led by the Holy Spirit.

The reasons for the tightly knit organization with Daniel
as its head are suggested in the words, "that the princes might
give accounts unto them [the three presidents], and the king
should have no damage" (6:2). King Darius knew that the
men in his government would stoop to graft and dishonesty

as they administered the affairs of the empire, but he knew also that Daniel was a man of honesty and integrity and therefore would not tolerate corruption in the government. Because of this the king "set him over the whole realm," second in authority only to that of the king himself. The primary objective of the appointment, then, was that the king might not suffer loss. Darius was not slow to recognize Daniel's worth, for God's servant was a man who could be trusted. Thus Daniel was preferred (or distinguished) above the presidents and satraps. This venerable old man, a veteran of some sixty years in public office, qualified himself for his new position. The equipment and enablement God gives to His devoted servants always wear well for a complete lifetime.

THE PLOT AGAINST DANIEL (6:4-9)

Then the presidents and princes sought to find occasion against Daniel concerning the kingdom; but they could find none occasion nor fault; forasmuch as he was faithful, neither was there any error or fault found in him. Then said these men, We shall not find any occasion against this Daniel, except we find it against him concerning the law of his God. Then these presidents and princes assembled together to the king, and said thus unto him, King Darius, live for ever. All the presidents of the kingdom, the governors, and the princes, the counsellors, and the captains, have consulted together to establish a royal statute, and to make a firm decree, that whosoever shall ask a petition of any God or man for thirty days, save of thee, O king, he shall be cast into the den of lions.

Now, O king, establish the decree, and sign the writing, that it be not changed, according to the law of the Medes and Persians, which altereth not. Wherefore king Darius signed the writing and the decree (Daniel 6:4-9).

The promotion and primacy of Daniel marked the beginning of some real trouble for this godly old sage. The twin sins of envy and jealousy, stirred by the devil in the hearts of the other members of the king's cabinet, aroused those men to plot evil against Daniel. Their anticipated gain through graft and other dishonorable means would be in jeopardy as long as Daniel held the number one post in the king's cabinet. Then, too, they could not stand having this foreigner, and a Hebrew at that, in the position of superiority over them. They proceeded with their wicked plot in spite of their acknowledgment that Daniel was without fault or error. They said, "We shall not find any occasion against this Daniel, except we find it against him concerning the law of his God" (6:5).

This indeed is the ideal in a man of God. He cannot be charged with dishonesty or inefficiency, disloyalty or inadequacy. Daniel was like Paul who said, "And herein do I exercise myself, to have always a conscience void of offence toward God, and toward men" (Acts 24:16). Whenever you find a man of God who is living a consistent life of godliness in the world, and the enemies of God become aware of the marked difference, the man of the world will resent that man of God. It was so with both Paul and Daniel. Thank God for men such as these who "have a good report of them which are without" (1 Timothy 3:7), and who are "blameless and harmless, the sons of God, without rebuke, in the midst of a crooked and perverse nation" (Philippians 2:15). Whether in Daniel's day, Paul's day, or our day, the child of God should so carry himself that any charges leveled at him by wicked men will be a lie.

Dr. Walter L. Wilson told how a good and godly Christian gentleman was confronted by a man who berated him and accused him of things which were false. The saint of God stood patiently until his accuser had finished, after which he bowed his head and prayed, "Father, I thank Thee that these accusations against me are not true."

The puny politicians in Darius' cabinet, those presidents and princes, agreed that, if they were successfully to dispose of Daniel, they would have to trump up a religious charge against him. Inasmuch as Daniel "was faithful, neither was there any error or fault found in him," the plotters against Daniel were ready to come before the king with their nefarious scheme fully hatched out. When the assembly had convened, their spokesman began with the customary form of salute, "King Darius, live for ever" (verse 6). Leupold points out that the "for ever" implies no more than "for a good long while." Whatever plan they agreed upon, they must never let Darius know that Daniel was their target.

They commenced with a *falsehood.* "All the presidents of the kingdom, the governors, and the princes, the counsellors, and the captains, have consulted together to establish a royal statute" (6:7). As they saw it, the first matter about which the king must be deceived is the complete unity of *all* the men in office. But in so presenting their case to King Darius they lied. What dishonesty and trickery! They said "all" the presidents had consulted together. This was untrue because they had not consulted with Daniel in their proposal. The words of our Lord to the religious plotters of His day would certainly apply to Daniel's foes: "Ye are of your father the devil, and the lusts of your father ye will do. He was a murderer from the beginning, and abode not in the truth, because there is no truth in him. When he speaketh a lie, he speaketh of his own: for he is a liar, and the father of it" (John 8:44).

Next, they resorted to *flattery*. "Whosoever shall ask a petition of any God or man for thirty days, save of thee, O king, he shall be cast into the den of lions" (6:7). Here they were flattering the king by suggesting that all prayers be made to him, thereby honoring him as their god. It was not uncommon for the subjects of a kingdom to look upon their king or emperor as a deity. So then it was not unnatural for Darius to accept the honor in good faith believing that his men truly revered and respected him. They made their wicked device appear as though nothing but sincere loyalty was behind their project. Why should the king have any suspicion of deceit or disloyalty? The Pharaohs and Ptolemies were called gods and worshiped as such. The proposal of the king's men would mean no more than the worship of Nebuchadnezzar's image meant in chapter 3. But it was all a cleverly devised plot of Satan to deify a man.

Why would the plotters make prayer their main emphasis? They knew that it was Daniel's custom to pray at certain times every day (6:10, cf., Psalm 55:17). Then, too, prayer was a chief factor in the Persian religion. To omit prayer would mean the collapse of everything. Thus we can understand why the enemies of Daniel concentrated on the matter of prayer. The whole device had a pious and religious cloak about it.

Having impressed the king with the idea that they were motivated by his dignity and honor, they strongly urged him to draw up the decree officially and then to seal it so that it might not be changed at any time until the date of expiration. "The law of the Medes and Persians, which altereth not" was a Persian conviction of long standing based on the idea that, since the king represented the gods, their decrees should remain irrevocable. Even if a king passed the death sentence upon one of his subjects, and later evidence led him to the conclusion that he erred in passing the sentence, he was unable to reverse his decision. All of this was taken into account when the plotters drew up their wicked scheme to get rid of Daniel. So when Darius sealed the decree, even he could do nothing about changing it, but actually bound himself to it. "Wherefore king Darius signed the writing and the decree" (6:9). There is further reference to this Persian practice in Esther 1:19 and 8:8. In both instances the seal guaranteed the validity of the decree.

As the presidents and princes left the king's presence, they doubtless felt that their scheme was a success, and soon Daniel would be dead. But they failed to see that they were not attacking an ordinary man but the chosen and anointed servant of the Most High God, who said, "Touch not Mine anointed, and do My prophets no harm" (1 Chronicles 16:22). The law of the Medes and Persians might not be subject to change, but those wicked men had yet to reckon with the mighty Lawgiver.

THE PRAYER LIFE OF DANIEL (6:10-11)

Now when Daniel knew that the writing was signed, he went into his house; and his windows being open in his chamber toward Jerusalem, he kneeled upon his knees three times a day, and prayed, and gave thanks before his God, as he did aforetime. Then these men assembled, and found Daniel praying and making supplication before his God (Daniel 6:10-11).

Though there is but one verse in this entire chapter 6 dealing with the prayer habit of Daniel, that verse provides a key to an understanding of the man and of the miracle performed here by God in Daniel's behalf. There are at least three instances in the book of Daniel where we find him praying: in chapters 2, 6, and 9. We shall devote more time to a study of his prayer in chapter 9, which is indeed one of the classic chapters in the entire Bible on the subject of prayer.

Knowing nothing of the new decree which banned praying to Jehovah, until after it had been issued, Daniel was now faced with an important decision. If ever there were a time when he needed to pray, this was that time. What should he do? The first matter he had to decide was where his loyalty lay. He must choose between loyalty to God or loyalty to the king. Here we need to recall that it was on the basis of "the law of his God" (6:5) that his enemies plotted against him. Our Lord said, "Render therefore unto Caesar the things which be Caesar's, and unto God the things which be God's (Luke 20:25). The Apostle Paul wrote, "Let every soul be subject unto the higher powers. For there is no power but of God: the powers that be are ordained of God" (Romans 13:1). The Apostle Peter added, "Submit yourselves to every ordinance of man for the Lord's sake: whether it be to the king, as supreme; Or unto governors" (1 Peter 2:13). The child of God must bear in mind that the law of God supersedes the law of man. Whenever man's law runs counter to God's law, the child of God has but one choice. It was voiced by Peter when he said, "We ought to obey God rather than men" (Acts 5:29).

Now some of us might reason, could not Daniel have gone to his room, closed and locked the door, shut the windows, drawn the shades, and prayed silently to God? I confess that I might be tempted to do just that. But Daniel was made of finer stuff. Note carefully the text says, "he went into his house; and *his windows being open in his chamber toward Jerusalem*" (6:10). He did not open his window so as deliberately to defy the king's decree. His window was open and there was a reason why it was open. By keeping his window open toward Jerusalem at all times for prayer, Daniel was obeying God's instruction. When Solomon dedicated the Temple, he anticipated a day when the people might be taken captive to another land, and said, "If they sin against Thee, (for there is no man which sinneth not,) and Thou be angry with them, and deliver them over before their enemies, and they carry them away captives unto a land far off or near; Yet if they bethink themselves in the land whither they are carried captive, and turn and pray unto Thee in the land of their captivity, saying, We have sinned, we have done amiss, and have dealt wickedly; If they return to Thee with all their heart and with all their soul in the land of their captivity, whither they have carried them captives, *and pray toward their land*, which Thou gavest unto their fathers, and toward the city which Thou hast chosen, and toward the house which I have built for Thy name: Then hear Thou from the heavens, even from Thy dwelling place, their prayer and their supplications, and maintain their cause, and forgive Thy people which have sinned against Thee" (2 Chronicles 6:36-39; see also 1 Kings 8:44-48).

In Old Testament times Jerusalem was the holy city and the proper place for Jews to worship. If ever they were away from this divinely appointed center of worship, they were to pray facing in that direction. Ever since Daniel had been taken captive to Babylon some sixty years before, this had been his daily habit. He had done so by divine instruction, and now that his life was in danger he must maintain loyalty to his God. Today we are under grace, and no one place on earth is preferred above another (John 4:21-24), but with Daniel there was but one choice. He did not deliberately open his window wider; he merely did that which he was accustomed to do at all times. He could not now allow the king's decree to come between him and his God. He knew what the decree said and he understood clearly the consequences if he disobeyed. Daniel had respect and regard for the king, but he could not afford to cut himself off from the source of God's power and protection. He would resort to no cunning or carnality. His weapon must be a spiritual one. Let us learn the lesson that the finest of God's servants must maintain regular and fixed prayer habits in order to continue steadfast in devotion to the Lord. A godly man will pursue a godly course even though the world be against him.

Knowing he was courting disaster, "he kneeled upon his knees three times a day, and prayed, and gave thanks before his God, as he did aforetime" (6:10). In connection with Daniel's decision, I like Peter's words, "Wherefore let them that suffer according to the will of God commit the keeping of their souls to Him in well doing, as unto a faithful Creator" (1 Peter 4:19). Daniel did what was right according to his knowledge of the will of God, thereby placing himself in the safe keeping of God.

Inasmuch as the text says, "he kneeled upon his knees," I am led to say a few words about Daniel's posture in prayer. I know how possible it is for one to make a fetish of the posture in prayer, and yet I am somehow of the persuasion that this is the position best suited to prayer, especially private prayer. Luke reminds us that in the garden our Lord "*kneeled* down, and prayed" (Luke 22:41). The first recorded martyr of the Christian Church, when in his dying moments, "*kneeled* down" (Acts 7:60). When Peter came to where the dead body of Dorcas lay, he "*kneeled* down, and prayed" (Acts 9:40). When Paul gathered with the Ephesian elders on the dock at Miletus, "he *kneeled* down, and prayed with them all" (Acts 20:36). Then as he concluded his visit to Tyre, Luke says, "we *kneeled* down on the shore, and prayed" (Acts 21:5). Our Lord said, "And when thou prayest, thou shalt not be as the hypocrites are: for they love to pray standing in the synagogues and in the corners of the streets, that they may be seen of men" (Matthew 6:5). (See also Luke 18:11.) I am not suggesting that prayer, in order to be effectual, must be offered on one's knees. I have met some bedridden saints who engaged in daily intercessory prayer. But what a blessed sight it must have been to see the aged prophet of God kneeling in sweet communion with his Lord!

Shadrach, Meshach, and Abed-nego were standing when everyone else in the empire was kneeling before Nebuchadnezzar's image, and God honored them because they would not kneel. Now the people in Darius' empire were standing before a man, but God was about to honor one lonely saint who was kneeling before Him. Daniel's heart was filled with praise, because he "gave thanks" (6:10). Don't miss this seemingly small detail. It is important! Too frequently our prayers lack the note of thanksgiving. How can a man give thanks when he is looking death squarely in the face? The answer is a simple one. Daniel had been thanking God three times daily most of his lifetime, thus he was never without a cause for praising the Giver of every gift. The Scripture exhorts the believer, "In every thing give thanks: for this is the will of God in Christ Jesus concerning you" (1 Thessalonians 5:18). Again, "Be careful for nothing; but in every thing by prayer and supplication with thanksgiving let your requests be made known unto God. And the peace of God, which passeth all understanding, shall keep your hearts and minds through Christ Jesus" (Philippians 4:6-7). In difficult circumstances what course shall the godly take? Look up and thank God for every blessing. Daniel was a man who possessed the rare combination of courage and gratitude.

It is easier to thank God for past blessings than to thank Him before the answer to our prayer comes. But in the heart of the man of God the element of praise is never absent, even under the pressure of impending danger. We are spiritually poor if we fail to find our place on our knees before the Lord, praising Him, even in the midst of life's sorest trials.

THE POWERLESS KING DARIUS (6:12-17)

Then they came near, and spake before the king concerning the king's decree; Hast thou not signed a decree, that every man that shall ask a petition of any God or man within thirty days, save of thee, O king, shall be cast into the den of lions? The king answered and said, The thing is true, according to the law of the Medes and Persians, which altereth not. Then answered they and said before the king, That Daniel, which is of the children of the captivity of Judah, regardeth not thee, O king, nor the decree that thou hast signed, but maketh his petition three times a day. Then the king, when he heard these words, was sore displeased with himself, and set his heart on Daniel to deliver him: and he laboured till the going down of the sun to deliver him. Then these men assembled unto the king, and said unto the king, Know, O king, that the law of the Medes and Persians is, That no decree nor statute which the king establisheth may be changed. Then the king commanded, and they brought Daniel, and cast him into the den of lions. Now the king spake and said unto Daniel, Thy God whom thou servest continually, He will deliver thee. And a stone was brought, and laid upon the mouth of the den; and the king sealed it with his own signet, and with the signet of his lords; that the purpose might not be changed concerning Daniel (Daniel 6:12-17).

Because Daniel refused to hide his prayer habits he was quickly found out. The plotters had arranged for spies to assemble beneath his window, assured that Daniel would pray to the God of Heaven. And they witnessed just that! They were doubtless jubilant that their scheme was working out as they had hoped, but Daniel kept on praying as was his custom. These wicked men had sprung their trap, confident that both Darius and Daniel were their helpless victims. They had the king where they wanted him, and they had Daniel where they wanted him. Envy ever hates the excellency to which it cannot attain.

From beneath Daniel's window the spies hastened to the palace into the presence of Darius to remind him of the decree, to which he gave assent, adding that it was "according to the law of the Medes and Persians, which altereth not" (6:12). Whereupon they went into action and said to Darius, "That Daniel, which is of the children of the captivity of Judah, regardeth not thee, O king, nor the decree that thou hast signed, but maketh his petition three times a day" (6:13). The king knew at once that he had been tricked, but it was too late. The fake flattery of the presidents and princes had done its effective work; and the pride of Darius had made him blind to his better judgment. Realizing that he had been made the dupe of their duplicity, the king was sorely vexed within himself. Even though he held Daniel in high esteem, Darius realized that he was powerless to save the old prophet of God. The king's men, knowing this, belabored him with those words, "Know, O king, that the law of the Medes and Persians is, That no decree nor statute which the king establisheth may be changed" (6:15). The royal edict was irrevocable and everyone concerned knew it.

Daniel was condemned by the law of man, but there was yet a mightier law to be reckoned with. Maybe the law of the Medes and Persians could not be altered, but God has laws of His own, "with God all things are possible" (Mark 10:27). When the Jews sought to put Jesus to death, they said, "We have a law, and by our law He ought to die" (John 19:7), and He did die, but that law of man was superseded by authority and power greater than that of any and all men, namely "the power of His resurrection" (Philippians 3:10). So let the law of the Medes and Persians be carried out, and see what God will do. That law of the state had authority even over kings, for "he [Darius] laboured till the going down of the sun to deliver him" (6:14), but to no avail.

Darius had no choice but to have Daniel brought before him and pronounce the sentence. This he did, and then added the words, "Thy God whom thou servest continually, He will deliver thee" (6:16). Though Darius was deeply grieved over the course of events, it seems that his own faith was strengthened by the good and godly life of Daniel. But the faith of Darius was not the faith of the man of God. I have an idea that even though he hoped for the best he feared the worst. So, against his better judgment and contrary to his own desires, the king had Daniel put into the den of lions. The entire procedure was quite a ceremony, conducted personally by the king and his lords. Daniel was led to the den and pushed in, after which the gate was closed, the lock snapped, and the royal seal put upon the lock which would forbid anyone opening it, "that the purpose might not be changed concerning Daniel" (6:17).

My sense of humor rises at this point. Repeatedly the law of the Medes and Persians is described as the law "which altereth not" (6:8, 12) and which can "not be changed" (6:15, 17). Puny man proposes but the mighty God disposes.

When the body of our Lord was taken down from the cross and buried in the tomb, the chief priests and Pharisees came to Pilate and said, "Command therefore that the sepulchre be made sure. . . . Pilate said unto them, Ye have a watch: go your way, make it as sure as you can. So they went, and made the sepulchre sure, sealing the stone, and setting a watch" (Matthew 27:62-66). They made it as sure as they could, but when they came to the sepulcher our Lord was not there. I like that! The high priest had the apostles locked in a prison cell, but when the guards made their round, the apostles were not in the prison, because "the angel of the Lord by night opened the prison doors, and brought them forth" (Acts 5:17-22). I enjoy reading that! Herod put Peter in prison chained to two soldiers, one on each wrist, and armed soldiers outside the cell to stand guard. But during the night while the three bound men slept, the angel of the Lord came, released the chains from Peter's wrists, and led him free. When the soldiers, to whom Peter was chained, awoke in the morning, Luke says, "there was no small stir among the soldiers, what was become of Peter" (Acts 12:5-10, 18). That amuses me! It delights the believing heart to stand by and wait for God to set aside the foolish laws of man and then do the miraculous.

THE POWER OF GOD (6:18-23)

Then the king went to his palace, and passed the night fasting: neither were instruments of musick brought before him: and his sleep went from him. Then the king arose very early in the morning, and went in haste unto the den of lions. And when he came to the den, he cried

*with a lamentable voice unto Daniel: and the king spake
and said to Daniel, O Daniel, servant of the living God,
is thy God, whom thou servest continually, able to deliver
thee from the lions? Then said Daniel unto the king, O
king, live for ever. My God hath sent His angel, and hath
shut the lions' mouths, that they have not hurt me: forasmuch as before Him innocency was found in me; and also
before thee, O king, have I done no hurt. Then was the
king exceeding glad for him, and commanded that they
should take Daniel up out of the den. So Daniel was taken
up out of the den, and no manner of hurt was found upon
him, because he believed in his God (Daniel 6:18-23).*

King Darius spent a miserable, sleepless night in his
palace, fearfully contemplating the fate of Daniel. He was
genuinely concerned about Daniel as he doubtless condemned himself. His heart was not in agreement with the
treatment Daniel received, yet he had been a party to the
unjust verdict brought against God's servant. He could
neither eat nor sleep over his blunder. No attempt was made
to bring in the customary form of entertainment for a distressed king. I am certain that Daniel in the lions' den had
a more restful night than did the king in his palace.

At daybreak the king himself hastened to the den; he did
not summon a servant to go and get a report for him. As he
approached the den he cried out with a lamentable voice,
"O Daniel, servant of the living God, is thy God, whom
thou servest continually, able to deliver thee from the lions?"
(6:20) Of course God is able! No man ever has a right to
question the ability of the Almighty, for He is the omnipotent Creator and Sustainer of the universe. He was able
to deliver Daniel's friends (3:17), and He could deliver
Daniel, who spent that night not merely with the king of the
beasts, but with their Creator, the King of kings, "the Lion

of the tribe of Judah" (Revelation 5:5). Sometimes in Scripture the lion is used symbolically of Satan and evil (1 Peter 5:8; Revelation 13:2), but it is used also of our Lord Jesus Christ to show forth His great strength and superiority. That night Daniel was blessed and protected by the presence of Him of whom the hymn writer spoke,

> Stayed upon Jehovah
> Hearts are fully blessed,
> Finding as He promised
> Perfect peace and rest.

Of course the preservation of Daniel was a miracle of God. Just how does God perform miracles? He is never limited to one method. Daniel related how God preserved him: "My God hath sent His angel, and hath shut the lions' mouths, that they have not hurt me" (6:22). Yes, I believe in angels. The Scriptures abound in revelation concerning the activities of these spirit beings. I will not insist that either Daniel or the lions saw the angel, but I know the angel was present in the den that night and had the situation in hand. If Nebuchadnezzar did not know about the angel of Jehovah before he cast Daniel's three friends into the fiery furnace, he certainly was informed after their miraculous preservation (3:28). If Darius did not know about angels, Daniel saw to it that he too was informed. The Psalmist said, "For He shall give His angels charge over thee, to keep thee in all thy ways" (Psalm 91:11). "Are they not all ministering spirits, sent forth to minister for them who shall be heirs of salvation?" (Hebrews 1:14) "The angel of the LORD encampeth round about them that fear Him, and delivereth them" (Psalm 34:7). "Bless the LORD, ye His angels, that excel in strength, that do His commandments, hearkening unto the voice of His word" (Psalm 103:20). The fact that

God sent His angel and preserved His servant was demonstration of the power of Daniel's God.

Daniel added another reason why God shut the lions' mouths and protected His child. He said, "Forasmuch as before Him innocency was found in me; and also before thee, O king, have I done no hurt" (6:22). This hardly appears as a rebuke to the king but rather a reminder that the decision to cast Daniel into the den of lions was wrong inasmuch as it impugned Daniel's integrity. The divine deliverance demonstrated the fact that God vindicated Daniel. The seeming disobedience of Daniel in praying to Jehovah was not because of any contempt he had for Darius, but because his first loyalty was to his God.

"So Daniel was taken up out of the den, and no manner of hurt was found upon him, because he believed in his God" (6:23). The fact that Daniel was "taken up" suggests that the "den" was actually a recessed pit. He was in excellent physical condition in spite of the ordeal through which he passed, because he believed in his God. Through faith he was able to brave the lions (Hebrews 11:33). When one reads Hebrews, chapter 11, he is impressed with the fact that the great essential in the lives of the saints is faith. Those heroes of faith knew what it meant to believe God. Would Daniel have been delivered from the lions had he not believed in his God? The inspired New Testament commentary says that those Old Testament saints "through faith . . . stopped the mouths of lions" (Hebrews 11:33). On one occasion our Lord said, "According to your faith be it unto you" (Matthew 9:29). Faith is firm trust in another; it is utter dependence upon the veracity of another. Frequently the Lord Jesus rebuked unbelief with the words, "O ye of little faith" (Matthew 6:30; 8:26; 14:31; 16:8), and upbraided men because of it (Matthew 13:58; 17:20). Daniel knew that the chief requisite for a man of God was faith.

A living faith in the living God will give courage and strength for every emergency of life.

THE PROCLAMATION OF KING DARIUS
(6:24-27)

And the king commanded, and they brought those men which had accused Daniel, and they cast them into the den of lions, them, their children, and their wives; and the lions had the mastery of them, and brake all their bones in pieces or ever they came at the bottom of the den. Then king Darius wrote unto all people, nations, and languages, that dwell in all the earth; Peace be multiplied unto you. I make a decree, That in every dominion of my kingdom men tremble and fear before the God of Daniel: for He is the living God, and stedfast for ever, and His kingdom that which shall not be destroyed, and His dominion shall be even unto the end. He delivereth and rescueth, and He worketh signs and wonders in heaven and in earth, who hath delivered Daniel from the power of the lions (Daniel 6:24-27).

The king's first action was directed at the princes and presidents whose wicked plotting was responsible for the attempt on Daniel's life. They, together with their families, were cast into that same den of lions where those same wild beasts, who were powerless to devour Daniel, devoured those evil men. I feel certain that Daniel did not gloat over the disastrous fate of his foes. Their tragic end was not Daniel's idea but rather an instance of typical Oriental justice. Under the Mosaic law the wives and children would not have been made to suffer the death penalty along with those found guilty of attempted murder (Deuteronomy 24:16). So we must remember that the penalty here was in keeping with pagan laws.

Now follows the proclamation of King Darius. His decree was sent to all the people dwelling "in all the earth" (i.e., the land), meaning, of course, the land and people within his empire. It said that the people should trust Daniel's God. It testified to the fact that He is the living God, His kingdom is an everlasting kingdom, and that He is the God who performs miracles. All of this does not necessarily mean that Darius experienced a genuine conversion to the true God. It merely admits that Daniel's God is a deity capable of performing signs and wonders. However, it appears obvious that a profound impression was made upon Darius by the miracle he had witnessed. How far he entered personally into an experience of the statements contained in his proclamation we shall never know. We do know, however, that when Satan would have extinguished forever the testimony of the true God in Babylon, the light was preserved to shine throughout the earth. The Jewish captives in Babylon were tolerated and permitted to worship Jehovah without persecution. The Psalmist said, "Surely the wrath of man shall praise Thee: the remainder of wrath shalt Thou restrain" (Psalm 76:10).

For some time now I have believed and preached that a man of God in the will of God is immortal until his work on earth is finished. Daniel was such a man, and God preserved him to finish some more work in the divine plan.

THE PROSPERITY OF DANIEL (6:28)

So this Daniel prospered in the reign of Darius, and in the reign of Cyrus the Persian (Daniel 6:28).

This single verse brings our chapter to a close on a high note. Because of his faithfulness Daniel was exalted to a place of honor wherein he was privileged to witness to two kings. This historical portion of the book of Daniel might have concluded with the prophet's death. But instead God permitted him to live and write the vast cyclorama of world events, kingdoms rising and falling, earthly thrones cast down until the Ancient of Days returns to occupy His throne. No greater honor could ever be bestowed upon any man.

There have been servants of God in the world who prayed less, had less faith, and were less persistent in their determination to serve God faithfully than was Daniel, but then they prospered less than did Daniel. This chapter in the life of Daniel should challenge every servant of God never to be afraid of the evils which threaten him, but to believe that God is equal to every emergency. "Thou shalt prosper, if thou takest heed" (1 Chronicles 22:13).

THE PROPHETIC PREVIEW

Just as we have seen a prophetic foreview of things to come in chapters 2, 3, and 4, so there is another prophetic glimpse in chapter 6. The deliverance of Daniel foreshadows the deliverance of another faithful Jewish remnant. Darius foreshadows the man of sin when he sits "in the temple of God, shewing himself that he is God" (2 Thessalonians 2:4). During the tribulation the persecution of the remnant is satanic, but their preservation will be supernatural (Revelation 7:3, 14; 12:13-17). The parallel between the experiences of Daniel and the believing remnant of Israel during the great tribulation is obvious.

G. H. Lang wrote, "All this is prophetic, a revelation of principles perpetually operating. Antichrist will claim for himself divine honors; he alone shall be worshiped. The alternative will be death (Revelation 13:14-15). Again the saints will need endurance to keep the commandments of God and the faith of Jesus (Revelation 14:12). . . . They who endure to the end of those dread days shall be saved physically at the descent of the Son of man (Matthew 24:13-14; Mark 13:13); and at the same time by resurrection shall all who are accounted by the Lord worthy to rule in His kingdom be brought up out of a deeper region than the den of lions."

A. C. Gaebelein wrote, "The deliverance of Daniel once more foreshadows the deliverance of the faithful Jewish remnant. It is strange that expositors and teachers put the Church into this time of the end. The Church, according to the testimony of the New Testament Scriptures, will no longer be on earth when this predicted time of the end comes. We have then seen that these four chapters foreshadow the moral characteristics of the times of the Gentiles, down to the end, when the stone smites the image and it will forever pass away. Self-exaltation, the pride and deification of man, impiety, blasphemy, hatred, persecution, cruelty, man putting himself in the place of God are the leading features."

Commenting on chapter 6, H. A. Ironside said, "It will be necessary now to dwell somewhat particularly upon the typical character of all this. The whole scene points us on to a time when Daniel's people will once more be restored to their land, and there shall rise up among them one who will magnify himself above all that is called God and is worshiped." Dr. Ironside then devoted nine pages in his *Lectures on Daniel* to "The Faithful Remnant."

O. B. Greene said, "There is a deep spiritual lesson in the deliverance of Daniel from the lions' den. Here is a picture of the preservation of Israel through the lion's den of the tribulation period under the reign of Antichrist."

P. R. Newell wrote, "This sixth chapter is significantly prophetic: There will presently appear upon earth a satanically energized man, of whom we will learn important details later in this book of Daniel, who is to demand in fact that which Darius was duped into demanding in principle—worship of himself (2 Thessalonians 2; Revelation 13). Such of God's people who may be there in that evil day may well take courage from Daniel's devotion to his God and from his preservation from otherwise certain terrible death."

In 1893 Edward Dennett wrote, "The deliverance of Daniel is also typical. He prefigures the remnant, God's faithful remnant, who will be found in Jerusalem and in the land during the days of Antichrist's fearful sway. Through the machinations of their enemies they will be cast, as it were, into the lion's den, surrounded on all sides by the various displays of Satan's power, and their destruction will appear to human eyes to be imminent and certain. But God will Himself protect them, and interposing for their release by the appearing of Christ, will bring upon their enemies the very judgment which they had designed for His people."

CHAPTER SEVEN

CHAPTER SEVEN

With this chapter begins the second major division of the book of Daniel. This second half of the book consists of a series of visions, all of them given to Daniel, and all of them interpreted. The vision in chapter 7 was given "In the first year of Belshazzar" (7:1); the vision in chapter 8 was given "In the third year of the reign of king Belshazzar" (8:1); the vision in chapter 9 was given "In the first year of Darius" (9:1); the vision in chapter 10 was given "In the third year of Cyrus king of Persia" (10:1); and the vision in chapters 11 and 12 "in the first year of Darius the Mede" (11:1).

These visions contain remarkable prophecies covering the period of the times of the Gentiles and the great tribulation. Both Israel and the Gentiles pass through this period, and both receive their just retribution from God for their rejection of Jesus Christ. Neither the Church nor the present age of grace are found in Daniel's prophecies, logically or chronologically.

The vision of "four great beasts" (7:3), "which are four kings" (7:17), corresponds to the four metals of the image in chapter 2, thus Daniel's vision parallels Nebuchadnezzar's dream image. We see in these two chapters the principle of parallelism, which is a similarity of construction and meaning in two passages. The four beasts in chapter 7 correspond to the four kingdoms of Babylon, Media-Persia, Greece, and

Rome. The "ten horns," which are "ten kings" (7:7, 24) correspond to the "toes" of the great image (2:41-42) and the "ten horns" in Revelation 13:1 and 17:12. These represent a confederacy of ten nations the details of which we will study later.

Both visions (chapters 2 and 7) are God-given and God-explained, however the stately and impressive image in chapter 2 depicts world rule from the human view, while world dominion as seen in Daniel's vision in the form of wild beasts is the divine view. Man sees the kingdoms of this world as great exhibitions of human prowess; God looks upon them as being bestial in character. The divine viewpoint of the times of the Gentiles shows human government to be brutal and terrible; it is the true picture. The same deterioration of quality as seen in the component metals in the dream image is likewise suggested in the four beasts. In both visions we see the final overthrow of all earthly kingdoms by the second coming of Christ to earth and the interposition of the everlasting kingdom from Heaven, the kingdom that will be universal and in which the rightful sovereignty to Christ will be restored.

THE INTRODUCTION TO THE VISION
(7:1-7)

In the first year of Belshazzar king of Babylon Daniel had a dream and visions of his head upon his bed: then he wrote the dream, and told the sum of the matters. Daniel spake and said, I saw in my vision by night, and, behold, the four winds of the heaven strove upon the great sea.

And four great beasts came up from the sea, diverse one from another. The first was like a lion, and had eagle's wings: I beheld till the wings thereof were plucked, and it was lifted up from the earth, and made stand upon the feet as a man, and a man's heart was given to it. And behold another beast, a second, like to a bear, and it raised up itself on one side, and it had three ribs in the mouth of it between the teeth of it: and they said thus unto it, Arise, devour much flesh. After this I beheld, and lo another, like a leopard, which had upon the back of it four wings of a fowl; the beast had also four heads; and dominion was given to it. After this I saw in the night visions, and behold a fourth beast, dreadful and terrible, and strong exceedingly; and it had great iron teeth; it devoured and brake in pieces, and stamped the residue with the feet of it: and it was diverse from all the beasts that were before it; and it had ten horns (Daniel 7:1-7).

The introductory words of this chapter, namely "In the first year of Belshazzar king of Babylon" (7:1), give the clue as to the time Daniel received the vision in a dream. The first kingdom, namely Babylon, was still in existence when the vision came to Daniel. At a time when the prophet was far advanced in years, he was no doubt devoting much of his time to writing. Belshazzar had left the aging statesman to obscurity, but this afforded Daniel a good opportunity to be used by God as one of the most significant prophetic writers in his time. Daniel received the revelation and wrote every word of it being borne along by the Holy Spirit.

In writing he said that he "told the sum of the matters" (7:1). Leupold suggests this to mean the "essential content" of the dream. "By this term 'sum' the author appears to say that the essential features were culled out of the great variety of details that a long dream presented so as not to present a bewildering array of detail . . . a significant reminder that every word is carefully chosen and to the point; unessential items are passed by."[1] Not less than nine times in this one chapter Daniel said, "I saw" or "I beheld" (verses 2, 4, 6, 7, 9, 11, 13, 21); literally "I was beholding," indicating a continuous action of thoughtfully examining the details in the dream. Here we have a conscientious student being guided by the Spirit of God, therefore we shrink from finding any fault whatever with what the author wrote.

The first detail of the vision is that "the four winds of the heaven strove upon the great sea" (7:2). DeHaan, Gaebelein, Ironside, Lang, Larkin, Newell, and others interpret "the great sea" to mean the Mediterranean Sea. Lang devotes almost three pages in his book seeking to show that the term cannot be used here in a symbolic sense but means literally the Mediterranean Sea. He cites at length numerous passages, among them Numbers 34:6-7; Joshua 1:4; 9:1; 15:11, 12, 47; 23:4; Ezekiel 47:10, 15, 19-20; 48:28.[2] Almost all commentators are in agreement that all four empires reached the Mediterranean coast, if not in their original boundaries, certainly by gradual conquest. At the eastern end of the Mediterranean is the land of Palestine, the geographic center of the earth and the center of God's activities with Israel and the Gentile nations at the second coming of our Lord Jesus Christ.

Symbolically the sea represents Gentile powers that are hostile to God and to Israel. The symbolism seems clear from such passages as Isaiah 8:7-8; 17:12-13; 57:20; Jeremiah 46:7-9; 47:2; Revelation 13:1; 17:1, 15. It is out from the disturbed peoples of the earth that the "four great beasts" (i.e., four nations) arise. The restless nations have known nothing but discord from their very beginning, and

[1] Leupold, *Daniel*, page 282.
[2] Lang, *Daniel*, pages 78-80.

their restlessness has increased continually. This disturbed state of the world gives rise to the conflicts among nations whereby world powers rise up to overthrow one another.

But what is the cause of the commotion in this disturbed society? What is meant by "the four winds of the heaven" (7:2)? If the "four winds" are interpreted as a divine force, then the unrest and unhappy plight of the nations are attributed directly to God. If the "four winds" are intended to symbolize a clash between heavenly agencies and satanic forces, the confusion and conflict among nations are still attributable to God. Further light is thrown upon this passage when we turn to Revelation 7. Here again are "four winds" bent on hurting God's elect during the tribulation. However, a quartet of angels is seen restraining the four winds till the servants of God are sealed in their foreheads. It seems from the context here that divine power is restraining an evil force intending to hurt God's elect. Any disturbance of the sea is caused by some outside force, as a volcanic eruption, an earthquake, or a strong wind. So the nations are in turmoil because of Satan's power. He is called "the prince of the power of the air" (Ephesians 2:2), that "spiritual wickedness in high [heavenly] places" (Ephesians 6:12). In Revelation 7:1 the winds are called "the four winds of *the earth*" because during the tribulation the Church and the Holy Spirit will have departed from the earth, and the man of sin, the devil incarnate, will be in full control. Presently, during the Church Age, the Holy Spirit is restraining the forces of Satan, thereby preventing the Antichrist from appearing to take control of the earth (2 Thessalonians 2:6-10). Of course we know, though world leaders little realize it, that the movements of the nations are in full accord with the providence of God. No matter what takes place among the nations, the child of God rests in the fact that God is behind the scenes directing the scenes He is behind.

The First Beast. "The first was like a lion, and had eagle's wings: I beheld till the wings thereof were plucked, and it was lifted up from the earth, and made stand upon the feet as a man, and a man's heart was given to it" (7:4). This first beast corresponds to the head of gold in the dream image of Nebuchadnezzar in chapter 2, both representing the Babylonian Empire. As gold is the most precious metal, so the lion is recognized as the king among beasts. At first it appeared as a lion with wings, suggesting strength and swiftness displayed by Babylon in conquering other nations surrounding her. But as Daniel studied the scene on the screen, the wings were plucked from the beast, for Babylon's conquests would cease and she would give way to the Persian Empire. No doubt Daniel was acquainted with the figures of winged lions that guarded the gates of the royal palace in Babylon. There was no mistaking the identification of this first beast. There are a number of Scriptures in which these creatures are mentioned as emblems of Babylon. The student should read carefully such passages as Jeremiah 4:7; 48:40; 49:19-22; 50:17, 43-44; Ezekiel 17:3, 12. This is doubtless sufficient evidence to point to a correct interpretation of the first beast.

When Daniel saw the first beast, "It was lifted up from the earth, and made [to] stand upon the feet as a man, and a man's heart was given to it" (7:4). This part of the vision might have reference to Nebuchadnezzar's insanity for a period of seven years, during which time he was debased and lived in the fields eating grass as the oxen. If this is the correct meaning of the latter part of verse 4, then Daniel's vision did not include the dehumanizing of Nebuchadnezzar into a beastlike character, but merely his recovery at the end of seven years, which was the humanizing of the bestial. Since it was made clear to Daniel that the four beasts "are four kings" (7:17), and the first was Nebuchadnezzar and his kingdom of Babylon, it is possible that the reference in the latter part of verse 4 is to the experience of Nebuchadnezzar recorded in chapter 4.

The Second Beast. "And behold another beast, a second, like to a bear, and it raised up itself on one side, and it had three ribs in the mouth of it between the teeth of it: and they said thus unto it, Arise, devour much flesh" (7:5). After Nebuchadnezzar's restoration the Babylonian Empire began to decline. It eventually gave way to the Medo-Persian Empire, in which Persia became the more dominant. The three ribs between the teeth suggest that this new world power had already devoured its prey, conquering Babylon, Egypt, and Lydia.

Just as there is a deterioration of quality in the component metals in the image in chapter 2, so this same difference is indicated between the lion and the bear. The bear is without doubt slower and less regal than the lion, nevertheless the lion eventually was overpowered just as the head of gold surrendered to the breast and arms of silver.

The statement that "it raised up itself on one side" (7:5) has been more literally translated to read, "raised up one dominion," which of course the combined kingdoms of the Medes and the Persians did. Of the Medo-Persian Empire Larkin wrote, "It was ponderous in its movements, and gained its victories by hurling vast masses of troops upon its enemies. Xerxes' expedition against Greece was undertaken with 2,500,000 fighting men. It is easy to be seen that the movements of such enormous bodies of men would 'devour much flesh,' not merely in the shape of food, but by death by exposure, disease, and in battle."[3] The large, lumbering bear is an apt description of a huge, slow-moving but mighty force. The conquests of the Medo-Persian Empire were frightfully destructive.

[3] Clarence Larkin, *The Book of Daniel*, page 121.

The Third Beast. "After this I beheld, and lo another, like a leopard, which had upon the back of it four wings of a fowl; the beast had also four heads; and dominion was given to it" (7:6). Continuing to scrutinize the scene in the vision, Daniel saw a beast, like a leopard, but characterized by four wings and four heads. While the leopard is more slight than the lion and the bear, it is nevertheless powerful and swift and none the less fierce. The lion devours, the bear crushes, the leopard springs upon its prey.

The leopard represents the Grecian Empire, and it is a fit symbol. Greece, under Alexander the Great, overcame its enemies with a swiftness unprecedented in warfare. The speed of his conquests is one of the marvels of the student of history. The four heads denote the dividing of this empire into the four kingdoms of Syria, Egypt, Macedonia, and Asia Minor. Four of Alexander's generals were appointed as heads, and the empire continued as such until it was conquered by the Romans. All students of history will readily recognize these facts.

We should not overlook the significant phrase, "and dominion was given to it" (7:6). The distinctive feature in this statement lies in the fact that the conquests of kings and kingdoms are singled out and supported by the providence of God. "The most High ruleth in the kingdom of men, and giveth it to whomsoever He will, and setteth up over it the basest of men" (4:17). In this connection the following verses from the prophecy of Hosea are highly significant: "I did know thee in the wilderness, in the land of great drought. According to their pasture, so were they filled; they were filled, and their heart was exalted; therefore have they forgotten Me. Therefore I will be unto them as a lion: as a leopard by the way will I observe them: I will meet them as a bear that is bereaved of her whelps, and will rend the caul of their heart, and there will I devour them like a lion: the wild beast shall tear them" (Hosea 13:5-8). World rulers are men of destiny able to go only as far as God allows. Dominion "was given" to these kings.

Nebuchadnezzar in his dream saw this empire as the thighs of brass, while Daniel in his vision beheld the same empire in its true light as God saw it, a leopard, cruel and quick to leap upon its prey.

The Fourth Beast. "After this I saw in the night visions, and behold a fourth beast, dreadful and terrible, and strong exceedingly; and it had great iron teeth: it devoured and brake in pieces, and stamped the residue with the feet of it: and it was diverse from all the beasts that were before it; and it had ten horns" (7:7). Daniel passed quickly over the first three, for it was the fourth that captured his greater interest and which caused him to inquire as to its meaning (7:19).

Before looking at the fourth beast, let us pause to observe closely that the divine view of the times of the Gentiles and the last days presents beasts and not men for symbols of world rulers. God foresaw the beastlike, bloodthirsty passion of great leaders in a rage of aggression and covetousness. The Christian is often charged with being pessimistic about the future plans of man in the earth. But how can he be otherwise in the light of such plain facts in the Bible? The Bible predicts no peace-loving world ruler for the last days. We can expect nothing more than greedy commercialism and political imperialism under the most beastly and barbaric type of warfare. Daniel saw world governments as beasts under the thin veneer of a boasting civilization. It is important that we see this, because most people gullibly swallow the wishful thinking of progressive evolution and social refinement. We thank God for every semblance of success announced by organizations formed to improve human relations; but it is all so temporary. On the horizon today we can see wild beasts and the monstrosities of Daniel's vision just waiting for the opportune moment to pounce upon their prey.

This fourth beast is a nondescript and it became the major concern of Daniel, just as the chief interest in chapter 2 was in the feet and toes of the great image. This fourth beast with *iron* teeth corresponds to the legs and feet of *iron* and clay, while the *"ten horns"* correspond to the implied ten "toes." If our interpretation of this chapter is correct thus far, then the Roman Empire is here depicted in the fourth beast. The final successor to Alexander's dominion was Rome. Daniel saw no exact description of this beast other than that it was dreadful, terrible, and exceedingly strong. The Apostle John saw in his vision of this same beast a composite of the first three: "like unto a leopard, and his feet were as the feet of a bear, and his mouth as the mouth of a lion" (Revelation 13:2). Rome at times has boasted that she did not destroy the cultures of the nations she conquered but rather incorporated them into her own. More shall be said concerning this fourth beast when we examine the interpretation in verses 23-28.

THE INNOVATION OF THE "LITTLE HORN" (7:8)

I considered the horns, and, behold, there came up among them another little horn, before whom there were three of the first horns plucked up by the roots: and, behold, in this horn were eyes like the eyes of man, and a mouth speaking great things (Daniel 7:8).

We now meet with an additional factor, the innovation of the "little horn." An important item to be noticed is that the little horn comes out of the ten horns on the fourth beast.

Not less than four major passages of Scripture treat directly, or else by implication, a prophecy of a future ten-nation confederacy. Two of these are in the book of Daniel (2:31-35, 40-45; 7:7-8, 19-24), and two are in the book of the Revelation (13:1-2; 17:3, 7, 12-18). The implied ten toes and the ten horns are ten kings reigning over a ten-kingdom federation. They are prophetic and should be interpreted as literal prophecy, not in an allegorical or nonliteral sense. The prophecy has not been fulfilled in the past but it is subject to future fulfillment, therefore it is an important feature in determining God's prophetic program as outlined in His Word.

The toes in the image in Daniel 2 are associated with the fourth kingdom, and they do not appear till the time when God establishes His kingdom which shall never be destroyed (Daniel 2:44). This fourth kingdom we have identified as the Roman Empire. The destruction of the fourth kingdom is the prelude to the second coming of Christ to earth to establish His everlasting kingdom. The vision in Nebuchadnezzar's dream image spans the centuries from his day, 600 B.C., to Christ's second coming. Therefore the feet stage of the image, including the toes, is yet future.

The ten horns in the vision in Daniel 7 are likewise associated with the fourth kingdom (7:17, 24), and they too do not appear till the coming of the Son of Man and "His kingdom which shall not be destroyed" (7:14, 27). The amillennial school of thought maintains that the prophecy of the ten kingdoms was fulfilled in the latter phase of the old Roman Empire. I know of no event in history which corresponds to a ten-kingdom confederacy overthrown by another king, and which remains until it is replaced by the kingdom of Heaven. A literal interpretation of this prophecy places it in the future from the standpoint of our present generation.

The ten horns in the vision in Revelation 13:1-2 have an obvious correspondence to the fourth beast with ten horns in Daniel 7. In support of a future ten-nation confederacy, this passage in Revelation adds its weight to both visions previously revealed in Daniel. Here there is no mistaking the fact that the prophecy is still future and not a part of the past history of the Roman Empire.

The ten horns in Revelation 17 are likewise ten kings. The beast here is the same beast appearing in Revelation 13:1, and represents the great political power of the end time just preceding the coming again of Christ to the earth. This passage, along with those in Daniel 2 and 7, and Revelation 13, lead to the conclusion that there will arise a ten-kingdom confederacy within the boundaries of the old Roman Empire. As to exactly which ten nations these might be, we would not choose to speculate. We suggest the possibility of representative countries in Southern Europe, Western Asia, and Northern Africa.

But now let us give attention to the new innovation in the book of Daniel, namely "the little horn" (7:8). At its first appearance, it seems relatively insignificant, appearing on the world scene with no great outward demonstration of the popularity and power which will ultimately be recognized.

First of all, verse 8 says that the little horn has "eyes like the eyes of man." This is as Daniel saw it in the vision. These notable eyes suggest the penetrating insight and discernment of an imposing personality. "And a mouth speaking great things." What he says is spoken against God and is therefore blasphemy; as an orator he will sound plausible and be persuasive.

Here for the first time in Daniel we meet the Antichrist, for this little horn is the man of sin (2 Thessalonians 2:3-4) and the first beast of Revelation 13. He will be satanically inspired (Revelation 13:4, 6). He will make war against the saints, the faithful remnant who will be saved in the great tribulation (Daniel 7:21, 25; Revelation 13:7). The Apostle Paul calls him "the god of this world" (2 Corinthians 4:4) and "the prince of the power of the air" (Ephesians 2:2). That little horn will become big, the last big dictator of this world before the coming again of our Lord Jesus Christ.

Before moving on to the next part of Daniel's vision, I would like to quote from the late W. C. Stevens. He asks the question, "Why beasts for symbols of the empires? We must bow in respect to this expression of the divine estimate of the character of this world's imperial rule. What are the attributes of beasts? To keep their own at any cost within their might; to quarrel over what they do not have but what they want; to fly easily into bloodthirsty rage at any affront, at any aggression, for any coveted object; under passion, to take utmost satisfaction in the blood, the agonies, the loss, the death of the objects of their rage; in a word, to be supreme in rule, in possession, in indulgence, insofar as their power can avail. God foresaw this spirit prevalent in the world empires down to the end."[4]

---

[4] W. C. Stevens, *The Book of Daniel*, page 97.

THE INTERVENTION FROM HEAVEN
(7:9-14)

I beheld till the thrones were cast down, and the Ancient of days did sit, whose garment was white as snow, and the hair of His head like the pure wool: His throne was like the fiery flame, and His wheels as burning fire. A fiery stream issued and came forth from before Him: thousand thousands ministered unto Him, and ten thousand times ten thousand stood before Him: the judgment was set, and the books were opened. I beheld then because of the voice of the great words which the horn spake: I beheld even till the beast was slain, and his body destroyed, and given to the burning flame. As concerning the rest of the beasts, they had their dominion taken away: yet their lives were prolonged for a season and time. I saw in the night visions, and, behold, one like the Son of man came with the clouds of heaven, and came to the Ancient of days, and they brought Him near before Him. And there was given Him dominion, and glory, and a kingdom, that all people, nations, and languages, should serve Him: His dominion is an everlasting dominion, which shall not pass away, and His kingdom that which shall not be destroyed (Daniel 7:9-14).

The scene changed from the terrestrial to the celestial, from the earthly to the heavenly. It must have held a fascination for Daniel, for again he said, "I continued looking." First, thrones appeared. Here the Revised Version is preferred, "I beheld till thrones were placed," that is, placed in position. The Authorized Version implies that the thrones were overthrown, but the commentators all are in agreement that the thrones were being set in an orderly position. The scene corresponds to the one in Revelation 4 and 5. It is one of preparation for judgment. Beastlike men, who have been ruling the earth, are about to be judged and their power taken from them.

The courtroom having been properly arranged, the Judge entered, "and the Ancient of days did sit" (7:9). This name for God, appearing three times in this chapter (7:9, 13, 22), suggests His eternal existence. He has been on the scene for a long time. He is the eternal, self-existent One, the Creator of all things, and He has been viewing the activities of men and demons from His throne in Heaven. Now He is about to wrest the power from the Antichrist and transfer it to the rightful Sovereign, Jesus Christ. The Antichrist cannot prosper forever. There must be an exchange of dominion. The judgment will be a just one. The description of the garment of the Ancient of Days suggests His purity and righteousness and assures all that the Judge will do right (Genesis 18:25).

A further detail not to be overlooked is the mention of fire: "His throne was like the fiery flame, and His wheels as burning fire. A fiery stream issued and came forth from before Him" (7:9-10). The fire represents the divine presence in judgment. "For the LORD thy God is a consuming fire, even a jealous God" (Deuteronomy 4:24, cf., Hebrews 12:29). When the Lord Jesus comes back to judge the earth, it will be "In flaming fire taking vengeance on them that know not God, and that obey not the gospel of our Lord Jesus Christ" (2 Thessalonians 1:8). The angels who execute the judgments of God are called "His ministers a flaming fire" (Psalm 104:4). "The LORD rained upon Sodom and upon Gomorrah brimstone and fire from the LORD out of heaven" (Genesis 19:24). Concerning Nadab and Abihu, Moses wrote, "And there went out fire from the Lord, and devoured them, and they died before the Lord" (Leviticus 10:2). Isaiah prophesied, "For, behold, the Lord will come with fire, and with His chariots like a whirlwind, to render His anger with fury, and His rebuke with flames of fire. For by fire and by His sword will the Lord plead with all flesh: and the slain of the Lord shall be many" (Isaiah 66:15-16). In these and many other passages the fire is clearly a representation of the judgment of the Almighty.

As Daniel continued to study the vision, the scene enlarged and the action increased. While the courtroom was being prepared for the Ancient of Days, "thousand thousands ministered unto Him, and ten thousand times ten thousand stood before Him" (7:10). Here appears an innumerable host who have committed themselves to do God's bidding. Never has so large a number completely dedicated to one purpose ever appeared on the stage of history. Are these men or angels? Leupold says, "The innumerable hosts are without doubt the angels of God." [5] However, I am not certain that he is correct in this. It is possible that we have here two separate groups and that neither group is made up of angels only. If this judgment revealed to Daniel is the judgment of the great tribulation at the return of Christ to establish His millennial kingdom upon the earth, then it should be studied closely with those corresponding passages in Matthew 25:31-46; Revelation 5:11-14; 19:11-21. Those who "ministered unto Him" might include the redeemed of this Church Age who were raptured before the tribulation and who return with Him to the earth. Then the multiplied thousands who "stood before Him" certainly could be those who are to be judged, for it immediately follows that "the judgment was set, and the books were opened." If our viewpoint is correct, Daniel saw in the

[5] Leupold, *Daniel*, page 304.

vision the Judge and His redeemed followers, and those who have rejected Him and who must be judged. With the opening of the books the deeds of the godless were brought to light. God keeps an accurate record of the deeds of men. (See Revelation 20:12-13.) His judgments are just because God Himself is just as well as omniscient.

While the court was being prepared for the judicial session to determine who will enter the kingdom on earth, the little horn raised his voice in blasphemous boasts. The entire scene has a growing fascination for Daniel. Twice in this one verse, he said, "I continued looking." Centuries later the Apostle John saw some of the same that appeared in Daniel's vision (Revelation 13:1-6). Because of his godless and defiant words against the Almighty, "the beast was slain, and his body destroyed, and given to the burning flame" (7:11; see Revelation 19:19-21). Does this burning with fire convey the idea of annihilation, or does it point to eternal punishment? Leupold writes, "The Aramaic original (see margin), correctly rendered, says, the body was given 'to the burning of fire.' This form of the statement does not point so much to annihilation as to perpetual punishment, especially since other Scripture passages indicate with ample fullness the eternal character of the sufferings of the damned." [6]

"As concerning the rest of the beasts, they had their dominion taken away: yet their lives were prolonged for a season and time" (7:12). The other beasts were not dealt with finally as was the little horn. Their dominion was taken from them, but their lives were prolonged for a season, that is, for a definite measured point of time. The Babylonian, Medo-Persian, and Grecian Empires had their power taken from them, but their final judgment awaits the gathering of the nations (Gentiles) as described by the Prophet Joel (Joel 3:1-2) and by our Lord Himself (Matthew 25:31-46).

[6] Leupold, *Daniel,* page 306.

> *I saw in the night visions, and, behold, one like the Son*
> *of man came with the clouds of heaven, and came to the*
> *Ancient of days, and they brought Him near before Him.*
> *And there was given Him dominion, and glory, and a*
> *kingdom, that all people, nations, and languages, should*
> *serve Him: His dominion is an everlasting dominion,*
> *which shall not pass away, and His kingdom that which*
> *shall not be destroyed (7:13-14).*

At this point the prophet of God saw appearing in the vision the last world ruler, the Son of Man, our Lord and Saviour Jesus Christ. This is the climax of the vision presenting the goal of all history. The Son of God comes from Heaven and is invested with authority to take the kingdoms of earth from the Gentiles and to establish His kingdom. His coming as seen by Daniel is the fulfillment of a promise found in the first Messianic psalm where the Ancient of Days says to the Son, "Ask of Me, and I shall give Thee the heathen for Thine inheritance, and the uttermost parts of the earth for Thy possession" (Psalm 2:8). Daniel sees the triumph of Christ and His kingdom over all other kingdoms. He comes in power and great glory as depicted in such passages as Matthew 24 and 25; Mark 14:61-62; Luke 1:32; 2 Thessalonians 2:6-10; Revelation 19 and 20:1-4. The most casual reading of the prophetic Scriptures present clearly the coming kingdom of Christ on the earth, and the most careful scrutiny of these same Scriptures leaves no room whatever to deny His coming and His kingdom. We will not here attempt to present any of the features of this glorious kingdom. The important thing to notice is that He comes with power and authority. Daniel speaks of this event not less than five times in chapter 7 (verses 14, 18, 22, 25, 27).

Daniel sees Him coming "with the clouds of heaven" (7:13). Both in the Old and New Testaments the clouds are seen frequently accompanying Him. They represent the divine presence, thus they follow Him as His mark of identification. The student should examine the following passages: Exodus 13:21; 19:9; 24:16; 34:5; Leviticus 16:2; 1 Kings 8:10; Psalm 18:11-12; 78:14; 97:2-4; Isaiah 19:1; Jeremiah 4:13; Ezekiel 10:4; Nahum 1:3; Matthew 17:5; 24:30; Luke 21:27; 1 Thessalonians 4:17; Revelation 1:7; 14:14.

THE INQUIRY OF DANIEL (7:15-16)

I Daniel was grieved in my spirit in the midst of my body, and the visions of my head troubled me. I came near unto one of them that stood by, and asked him the truth of all this. So he told me, and made me know the interpretation of the things (Daniel 7:15-16).

At this point the action upon the screen ceased and the vision came to an end. He merely reported what he saw, but the revelation affected him deeply. Why was he shaken and disturbed? Being a godly Jew and acquainted with the Scriptures at hand, he would be looking for the coming Messiah with His reign of peace and prosperity. But now he had seen in the vision a long, dark future for the Jewish people, and this naturally grieved him. Here again we see something of Daniel's compassion and concern for his people. The aged prophet knew from Nebuchadnezzar's dream vision that there would be four great world empires to succeed each other before the times of the Gentiles would end. But now as an old man he realized that the end of Gentile world power and the coming of Messiah's kingdom were a long way off.

Before this God had made Daniel an interpreter of the dreams and visions of others; now Daniel was seeking divine help for the meaning of his own vision. Exactly who it was that Daniel approached for information we are not told. Presumably there were heavenly creatures in the vision, probably angels. Possibly there were ministering angels sent by God to Daniel for the express purpose of assisting him. At any rate, Daniel approached one of the angels to inquire after the meaning of the vision. He would not come to any conclusion apart from divine guidance. He must know "the truth of all this."

THE INTERPRETATION OF THE VISION (7:17-18)

These great beasts, which are four, are four kings, which shall arise out of the earth. But the saints of the most High shall take the kingdom, and possess the kingdom for ever, even for ever and ever (Daniel 7:17-18).

The heavenly interpreter informed Daniel that the four beasts are four kings, and it is proper to add that they represent kingdoms. The use of the word "kingdom" in this section supports the fact that these are earthly empires (verses 18, 22, 23, 27). These vicious beasts with a voracious nature depict the character of world leaders during the times of the Gentiles. We saw before in our study that these represent, in order, Babylon under Nebuchadnezzar, Medo-Persia under Darius, Greece under Alexander the Great, and Rome under Caesar, Nero, etc.. This is the general interpretation as stated in verse 17.

There are those who reject this interpretation, that the four beasts represent the four above-mentioned empires of Babylon, Persia, Greece, and Rome, on the ground that the four kingdoms were still in the future. They argue that the words "shall arise" mean that the kingdoms were still future from the time of the vision, but that Babylon had already risen to world power, and was actually near her fall. Such an objection should not disturb us, because everything in the vision is summed up in capsule form. Leupold points out the fact that the imperfect verb *yequmun* translated "shall rise" (A.V.), can be rendered "are destined to arise."[7]

Now for the first time in the book of Daniel we meet with the word "saints." "But the saints of the most High shall take the kingdom, and possess the kingdom for ever, even for ever and ever" (7:18). Who are "the saints of the most High"? The word "saint" appears in both the Old and New Testaments. It is used for Old Testament believers, that is, Israel (Matthew 27:52-53, cf., Exodus 19:6), the tribulation saints, those who will be saved during the tribulation (Revelation 13:7), and of New Testament believers, those who are saved in the Church Age (1 Corinthians 1:2; Ephesians 1:1; Philippians 1:1; etc.). Daniel used the word not less than seven times (7:18, 21, 22, 25, 27; 8:24), always with reference to his own people Israel. The Church saints are not in view in the book of Daniel since they will have been caught up to Heaven before the "little horn" makes war with the Jewish saints, that believing remnant of the last days. Israel is an earthly people associated with the land of Palestine, therefore it is Israel who is to possess the earthly kingdom. Israel will obtain it because it is bestowed by Him whose right it is to give it. They have not sought world dominion as have Gentile world rulers, but it becomes theirs by divine bestowment. See Revelation 20:4.

[7] Leupold, *Daniel*, page 317.

THE INTERROGATION AFTER
THE FOURTH BEAST (7:19-22)

*Then I would know the truth of the fourth beast, which
was diverse from all the others, exceeding dreadful, whose
teeth were of iron, and his nails of brass; which devoured,
brake in pieces, and stamped the residue with his feet;
And of the ten horns that were in his head, and of the
other which came up, and before whom three fell; even of
that horn that had eyes, and a mouth that spake very great
things, whose look was more stout than his fellows. I beheld, and the same horn made war with the saints, and
prevailed against them; Until the Ancient of days came,
and judgment was given to the saints of the most High;
and the time came that the saints possessed the kingdom
(Daniel 7:19-22).*

Daniel had no difficulty understanding the meaning of
the first three beasts, however this unnamed fourth beast he
did not fully comprehend. So he turned again to God for
further light, stating in detail what he wanted to know. He
asked about the "ten horns . . . and of the other which came
up, and before whom three fell" (7:20). The description of
the fourth beast in the interrogation here differs little from
that given in verses 7 and 8. There is one noticeable difference, however, namely the horn that appeared later is not
called here "a little horn," but appears "more stout" (or
sturdier) than his fellows. We point out this fact lest the
reader of Scripture pass lightly over what might appear to
be an unnecessary repetition. All such passages should

invite a closer examination. It seems that the "little horn" is projecting himself into a place of prominence and power above his contemporaries.

We come now to the final mention of the words, "I beheld," or, "I kept looking." There was a continuous action in the vision which engaged the uninterrupted attention of Daniel. That "same horn," about which he was asking, showed his hatred for the saints, declared war on them, and prevailed against them. This war against the saints is new in the vision, and no doubt Daniel made this a major point of inquiry. What Daniel saw here is a brief period in the last part of the tribulation. Commenting on that same time and event, the Apostle John wrote, "And it was given unto him [the little horn] to make war with the saints, and to overcome them: and power was given him over all kindreds, and tongues, and nations" (Revelation 13:7). As to the time element associated with this persecution, the reader should look up Revelation 11:3; 12:6; 13:5. Antichrist fulfills the prediction in all of these passages.

But the little horn's reign of terror does not last long, only "until the Ancient of days came." Only the personal return of Christ to the earth can bring to pass the deliverance of God's saints. The little horn was winning the victory until the King of kings put in His appearance, stopped the attack upon His saints, rendering the divine verdict in their favor. So with the appearance of God's Son from Heaven, the saints of the Most High were avenged of their persecutor and given their portion in Messiah's kingdom. Here is a clear prophecy describing a blessed experience awaiting the saved remnant of earthly Israel.

THE INTERPRETATION CONCLUDED
(7:23-28)

> *Thus he said, The fourth beast shall be the fourth king-*
> *dom upon earth, which shall be diverse from all kingdoms,*
> *and shall devour the whole earth, and shall tread it down,*
> *and break it in pieces. And the ten horns out of this king-*
> *dom are ten kings that shall arise: and another shall rise*
> *after them; and he shall be diverse from the first, and he*
> *shall subdue three kings. And he shall speak great words*
> *against the most High, and shall wear out the saints of*
> *the most High, and think to change times and laws: and*
> *they shall be given into his hand until a time and times*
> *and the dividing of time. But the judgment shall sit, and*
> *they shall take away his dominion, to consume and to*
> *destroy it unto the end. And the kingdom and dominion,*
> *and the greatness of the kingdom under the whole heaven,*
> *shall be given to the people of the saints of the most High,*
> *whose kingdom is an everlasting kingdom, and all domin-*
> *ions shall serve and obey Him. Hitherto is the end of the*
> *matter. As for me Daniel, my cogitations much troubled*
> *me, and my countenance changed in me: but I kept the*
> *matter in my heart (Daniel 7:23-28).*

Here again (verse 23) it is stated that the fourth beast
shall be the fourth kingdom upon earth and the mightiest
of all the kingdoms preceding it, for it "shall devour the
whole earth, and shall tread it down, and break it in pieces"
(7:23). At the turn of the twentieth century this prediction
of a world ruler seemed to many to be fantastically unbelievable. However, modern communication systems, jet

travel, and destructive weapons of warfare have erased all doubts as to its possible fulfillment. Our modern world has shrunk.

This last world power will be different in that ten kings will arise from it. Again we make the point that the ten horns, which arise from the last world empire, are ten kings, and that they correspond to the toes of the image of Daniel 2. They reign simultaneously until they are subdued by the little horn. These ten kings are over ten kingdoms, a federation of ten nations which constitute the formation of the fourth empire in its last days. This is the revived Roman Empire, for at no time in history did the Roman Empire ever exist in this form. We see no ground whatever for placing an historical interpretation on these ten kings and the little horn, because this fourth kingdom is immediately succeeded by the kingdom of the Son of Man (7:26-27). No event in the past answers in the smallest degree to this prediction in Daniel's prophecy.

Since the ten arise "out of" this fourth kingdom, there seems to be an indication that the fourth did not completely pass out of existence, but rather continued in some form until the ten-horn federation combines. Keep in mind the fact that the fourth beast is alive when the ten horns and the little horn appear, which leads to the conclusion that the Roman Empire, though it collapsed as a world power, has been smoldering through the centuries. Out of political Rome has emerged ecclesiastical Rome, but a political federation of states will rise again. The little horn, who is an eleventh king, will rise to power by subduing three of the ten kings, thereby gaining for himself the balance of power.

Verse 25 teaches that the little horn, who has now become a great horn, and who is the Antichrist, is a blasphemer who elevates himself above God and speaks out against Him (Revelation 13:5-6). Also his attitude toward the tribulation saints is that of hatred and persecution (Revelation 13:13-17). His continual purpose and design is to harass and harm them. The very fact of their existence and prosperity shall arouse his anger against them. Another feature of his short reign will be his intention "to change times and laws." These times and laws, I take it, have reference to the Jewish feasts inasmuch as his persecution is aimed at the Jewish people. However, the period of his reign is short:

"Time"—	1 year
"Times"—	2 years
"Dividing of time"—	$\frac{1}{2}$ year
	$3\frac{1}{2}$ years

These three-and-one-half years correspond to Daniel 12:7, the forty-two months in Revelation 11:2 and 13:5, and the twelve hundred and sixty days in Revelation 11:3 and 12:6. It is the last half of the seventieth week in Daniel 9:24-27. Our Lord spoke of this period in the Olivet Discourse in Matthew 24:15.

"But the judgment shall sit, and they shall take away his dominion, to consume and to destroy it unto the end" (7:26). The thrones are arranged, the Judge takes His seat (7:9), and the court is about to go into session. The beast must be put down and his dominion must be overthrown forever. The prophecy of David will then be fulfilled, "Let God arise, let His enemies be scattered: let them also that hate Him flee before Him. As smoke is driven away, so drive them away: as wax melteth before the fire, so let the wicked perish at the presence of God" (Psalm 68:1-2). Thus the career of the Antichrist will come to an end.

Following the dethronement of the little horn, the kingdom from above will be set up on the earth (7:27). The King of kings will be enthroned upon His holy hill of Zion. His kingdom will embrace the whole inhabited earth, for its greatness is said to extend "under the whole heaven." Thus, consequent upon the judgment upon, and the removal of, the last of the four world empires, the kingdom of the Son of Man shall be established. The earth will then be cleared of every oppressor, and the prayer, "Thy kingdom come" will be fully answered.

"Hitherto is the end of the matter" (7:28). This was the end of the vision, and nothing more was divulged to Daniel at that time. However, he concluded, "I kept the matter in my heart." He knew that this was a revelation from God and therefore should not be put aside or treated lightly.

Deep soul exercise should follow every revelation we receive from God. May our Lord grant to each of us an earnest desire to hide His Word in our hearts, as did Mary also (Luke 2:19). Peter wrote that one of the purposes of studying prophecy is "that ye take heed . . . in your hearts" (2 Peter 1:19).

CHAPTER EIGHT

The Ministry of Prophetic Revelation
(8:1-2)
The Miracle of Prophetic Fulfillment
(8:3-12)
The Messengers of Prophetic Illumination
(8:13-18)
The Method of Prophetic Interpretation
(8:19-24)
The Man of Prophetic Consummation
(8:25-27)

CHAPTER EIGHT

It might help the student to be reminded again that the events recorded in the book of Daniel are not set down in chronological order, which means, of course, that the chapters have not been arranged chronologically. The chronological order of the chapters would be 1, 2, 3, 4, 7, 8, 5, 9, 6, 10, 11, 12.

Another observation to be made here is that the book of Daniel was written originally in two different languages: the Chaldean (Aramaic) and the Hebrew. According to these two languages the book can be outlined as follows: 1:1—2:3 (Hebrew); 2:4—7:28 (Aramaic); 8:1—12:13 (Hebrew).

There are reasons for this difference. The first section (1:1—2:3) relates the fall of Jerusalem at the hands of Babylon and the deportation of the Jewish people; it is in Hebrew. The second section (2:4—7:28) records those details and events which have to do chiefly with the Gentile rule, tracing out the course of the times of the Gentiles. The change to Aramaic, being the popular language of that day, would enable the Chaldeans to read and understand the message. The third section, which is the portion before us now, beginning with chapter 8, is occupied largely with the Jewish people and their place in God's prophetic plan. Thus there is a return to the Hebrew language.

From here on we shall see that God's purpose was to show to Daniel that which would befall the Jews in the latter times. It is true that Daniel discussed the times of the Gentiles in chapter 8, but the prophecy treated them from the standpoint of their relationship to Israel. Persecution of a severe nature was to come upon Israel at the hands of Gentiles, and God was here predicting that persecution. One of the purposes of this second half of the book is to prepare Israel for that time of suffering. Since the tribulation was to be of an extreme sort, God would not expose the nation to it totally unprepared.

THE MINISTRY OF PROPHETIC REVELATION (8:1-2)

In the third year of the reign of king Belshazzar a vision appeared unto me, even unto me Daniel, after that which appeared unto me at the first. And I saw in a vision; and it came to pass, when I saw, that I was at Shushan in the palace, which is in the province of Elam; and I saw in a vision, and I was by the river of Ulai (Daniel 8:1-2).

Two years had elapsed between Daniel's vision of chapter 7 and the one recorded here, the former coming to him "In the first year of Belshazzar king of Babylon" (7:1), and the latter "In the third year of the reign of king Belshazzar" (8:1). The prophet had two years to meditate on the vision of the four beasts before God imparted this further knowledge to him. We know that the vision came to Daniel in a dream because he said it was *"after that which appeared unto me at the first."* It was a divinely directed prophetic dream because it bore witness to the clear foreknowledge and predetermined purposes of God. No one but God could foretell the coming centuries and their happenings, therefore the book of Daniel is a divine prophecy, and that in spite of theological skeptics and infidels who refuse to believe in the supernatural and the miraculous in prophecy.

If the student will fix in his mind, or keep before him, the chronological order of events in the book of Daniel, he will not fail to see the ministry of prophetic revelation. Actually the revelation in chapter 8 was given to Daniel before the fall of Babylon as recorded in chapter 5. Daniel could interpret the handwriting on the wall in chapter 5 because already he had received the prophecy in chapter 8. When Daniel interpreted Nebuchadnezzar's dream in chapter 2, he knew that Babylon would be overpowered by a second kingdom, and in turn the second would give way to a third kingdom; but he did not know at that time exactly which nations they would be. In chapter 8 he was told precisely who the two succeeding kingdoms would be (8:20-21).

Another prophetic detail comes before us in verse 2. The exact geographic location in the vision is said to be "at Shushan in the palace, which is in the province of Elam . . . by the river of Ulai" (8:2). Since Persia was to figure in the overthrow of Babylon, the geographical setting of the vision was significant inasmuch as Shushan was the capital of Persia where Nehemiah and Esther lived (Nehemiah 1:1; Esther 1:2-5; 2:3-5). In his dream vision in the chapter before us Daniel was transported into the next empire to succeed Babylon.

Was Daniel transported to Persia in body or in spirit? The fact that this is a vision leads us to accept the view that the prophet was there in spirit only, as when Ezekiel was transported to Jerusalem (Ezekiel 8:3), and John was carried into the wilderness (Revelation 17:3).

The Spirit of prophetic revelation here bears clear witness

to the omniscience of God. McGee comments, "The events foretold in this vision were fulfilled within 200 years. Such fulfillment is so remarkable that the liberal critic insists upon a later dating of Daniel. He maintains that Daniel was written *after* these events had transpired, and so is merely an historical record. It is an attempt to get rid of the miraculous which is embarrassing to his system of interpretation."[1]

THE MIRACLE OF PROPHETIC FULFILLMENT (8:3-12)

Then I lifted up mine eyes, and saw, and, behold, there stood before the river a ram which had two horns: and the two horns were high; but one was higher than the other, and the higher came up last. I saw the ram pushing westward, and northward, and southward; so that no beasts might stand before him, neither was there any that could deliver out of his hand; but he did according to his will, and became great. And as I was considering, behold, an he goat came from the west on the face of the whole earth, and touched not the ground: and the goat had a notable horn between his eyes. And he came to the ram that had two horns, which I had seen standing before the river, and ran unto him in the fury of his power. And I saw him come close unto the ram, and he was moved with choler against him, and smote the ram, and brake his two horns: and there was no power in the ram to stand before him, but he cast him down to the ground, and stamped upon him: and there was none that could deliver the ram out of his hand. Therefore the he goat waxed very great: and when he was strong, the great horn was broken; and for

---

[1] J. Vernon McGee, *Delving Through Daniel,* page 65.

> *it came up four notable ones toward the four winds of*
> *heaven. And out of one of them came forth a little horn,*
> *which waxed exceeding great, toward the south, and to-*
> *ward the east, and toward the pleasant land. And it waxed*
> *great, even to the host of heaven; and it cast down some*
> *of the host and of the stars to the ground, and stamped*
> *upon them. Yea, he magnified himself even to the prince*
> *of the host, and by him the daily sacrifice was taken away,*
> *and the place of his sanctuary was cast down. And an host*
> *was given him against the daily sacrifice by reason of*
> *transgression, and it cast down the truth to the ground:*
> *and it practised, and prospered (Daniel 8:3-12).*

One of the strongest evidences for the divine inspiration
and inerrancy of the Scriptures is the fact of fulfilled prophecy. God alone can predict in advance what is going to occur
hundreds of years hence. This is one of the miracles of
inspiration. An example of this is before us.

In the vision Daniel saw, there appeared a ram with two
horns. The ram represented Persia (8:20). The two horns
offer no problem. They are the two component parts of the
kingdom, Media and Persia. Of the two, "the higher came
up last" (8:3). Media enjoyed supremacy before Persia, but of
the two, Persia became the greater power. Cyrus the Persian
was mightier than Darius the Mede. Cyrus had pushed his
way "westward, and northward," and later his son extended
the kingdom "southward" to Egypt. For 200 years Persia
expanded her empire with irresistible force, for "he did
according to his will, and became great" (8:4). The three
points of the compass in verse 4 agree to the "three ribs"
in 7:5.

The breast and arms of silver (2:32), the bear (7:5), and
the ram (8:3) all represent the Medo-Persian Empire. But
why a ram in this later vision? The ram was the national
emblem of Persia, a ram being stamped on Persian coins as

well as on the headdress of Persian emperors. The sturdy strength of the ram enables it to thrust an enemy from its path. But even such a mighty empire as Persia must give way to one stronger.

There is prophetic harmony in the various visions of Daniel, and the rise of Persia was a miracle of prophetic fulfillment. The student should take note of the consistent agreement which exists between Daniel's visions. Little wonder the modern skeptics avow their disbelief in miracles and prophecy. But let us not miss the wonder of it all. The miracle of prediction and fulfillment should strengthen the faith of the child of God and challenge the thinking of every honest doubter.

As Daniel looked on with deep interest, giving close attention to all that God was showing to him in the vision, the action increased. With the appearance of the ram the points of the compass loomed large in the vision. Now there appeared suddenly from the west, the land of the sunset, an "he goat." His speed of travel was so fast that he literally skimmed along without touching the ground. The striking feature of the goat was "a notable horn between his eyes" (8:5). Its appearance was as sudden and startling as was that of the ram. In hot anger, and showing great strength, the goat moved directly toward the ram, butted the ram, breaking the ram's horn and trampling it to total submission. The goat emerged the victor, but although he conquered the ram, "the great horn was broken; and for it came up four notable ones toward the four winds of heaven" (8:6-8).

Here again Daniel was not left in doubt as to the meaning of the he goat. "The rough goat is the king of Grecia: and the great horn that is between his eyes is the first king" (8: 21). The goat represented Greece, the next kingdom to follow that of the Medes and Persians. The conflict between these two kingdoms was a fight to the finish, the ram rule coming to an end and with its downfall, the rise to greatness of the goat rule. The humiliating defeat of Xerxes at the battle of Salamis marked the beginning of the end of Persian rule. "The great horn . . . the first king" was Alexander the Great. The speed with which he conquered the known civilized world of his day is one of the best-known facts associated with the warfare of history. Alexander's amazing ability to strike suddenly and conquer speedily is typified in the four wings of the leopard in chapter 7, verse 6. His speedy overthrow of Persia was as complete and thorough as was imaginable.

What followed was indeed a strange sight. When the goat had waxed very great and strong, reaching the zenith of its power, the protruding prominent horn was broken off, and four horns appeared in its place. Alexander, "the great horn . . . the first king," died unexpectedly and prematurely at the age of thirty-three. Following his death "four notable" horns, four generals in Alexander's army, divided his empire into four parts. Cassander took over the European area, ruling over Macedonia and Greece. Lysimachus took over a large part of Asia Minor, ruling over Thrace and Bithynia. Seleucus took over the eastern portion of the empire, ruling over Syria and Babylonia. Ptolemy took over Egypt and portions of North Africa. These "four notable" horns correspond to the four heads of the leopard to whom dominion was given (7:6).

Once more we view the miracle of prophetic fulfillment, for the predictions came to pass more than two hundred years after Daniel had written his prophecy. Only God could have revealed to Daniel that the coming centuries would produce those nations and the predicted events associated with them. In Daniel's time Greece was a group of small and insignificant states. No one but God could have fore-known and predetermined their union under one great king, the rapid conquests of that king, his abrupt and sudden death as seen in the horn being "broken," and the rise of four other rulers, none of which would measure to the stature of Alexander.

Then in the vision, God showed to Daniel "a little horn" (8:9). It was seen coming out of one of the four horns. First, there had been "the great horn." This had been broken off and replaced with the four horns. Now out of one of the four there appeared this little horn. This was a strange sight indeed, a horn issuing forth from a horn. At first, the sight could not have been too impressive, for it was merely a little horn. And who among men could have predicted what its future might be? But as Daniel watched it closely, the "little horn . . . waxed exceeding great." It is difficult for us to visualize, and therefore equally difficult to explain, how the little horn grew, or developed, toward the south, the east, and the pleasant land. But most of the commentators are in agreement that there is a consistency and a continuity running throughout the vision. The great horn and the four horns were rulers over empires, and so it follows that the little horn is likewise a man who rises to great power. Moreover it is only reasonable to assume that there might be a close relationship as to time. Just as Greece succeeded Persia, and Alexander's four generals succeeded him, so the little horn followed after the divided Grecian Empire.

The question before us now is, who is the little horn? We know that he rises out of one of the four divisions of Alexander's empire. But which one? In 175 B.C. there arose from the Seleucidan dynasty in Syria a man whom history tells us was Antiochus Epiphanes, son of Antiochus the Great. He continued as king from 175 B.C. until 164 B.C., ruling from Antioch. This man was an avowed foe of Jehovah and His people. He forbade the Jews to practice circumcision, ordered sacred Jewish writings to be destroyed, mocked the

Levitical offerings and sacrifices by actually offering a sow upon the altar and scattering the broth in the holy sanctuary (8:11-12). He was known as "Epiphanes the Madman," who at one time slew one hundred thousand Jews. Some of his diabolical actions and wicked atrocities are recorded in the first book of the Maccabees. Many years before he was born, Daniel saw in the vision this man and his wicked work. Centuries before it all happened it had been predicted in detail.

There have been some good and able teachers of God's Word who believed that the little horn in 8:9 is to be identified with the little horn in 7:8, and that both therefore are one and the same, namely, the Antichrist. However, there is one detail which leads us to make a difference between these two little horns. The little horn in chapter 7 arises out of the fourth kingdom; the little horn in chapter 8 comes out of the third kingdom. Verses 10-12 in chapter 8 are admittedly difficult to interpret, however in their primary association I feel that they have to do with Antiochus Epiphanes and are therefore historical from our point of view. If his unholy and profane acts, which he perpetrated against God and the Temple, are hard to conceive and comprehend, then we dare believe that he was a demon-possessed man.

Having identified the little horn (8:9-12) with Antiochus Epiphanes, in its primary interpretation, let me add that I see in this portion of Daniel's vision the possibility of a double prophecy. It could be that we have here a prophecy with both a near and a far fulfillment, the first or partial fulfillment in Antiochus and the final or perfect fulfillment in Antichrist. The wicked Antiochus is at least a type, or a remarkable foreshadowing of Antichrist. Luther commented, "This chapter in Daniel refers to both Antiochus and Antichrist." Jerome said that the Jews of his time looked upon this prophecy as yet to have a further fulfillment in another king yet to rise and do after the fashion of Antiochus. When our Lord mentioned "the abomination of desolation, spoken of by Daniel the prophet" (Matthew 24: 15), He was referring to an event yet future and not looking back upon something in the past. Some statements in the interpretation of Daniel's vision which indicate a later and larger fulfillment of the prophecy are: "For at the time of the end shall be the vision" (8:17); "The last end of the indignation" (8:19).

From these statements it seems that there is a fulfillment of this prophetic vision which has to do with the end time and the man of sin. Both Antiochus and Antichrist exercise a strange superhuman power which is, of course, by the permissive will of God. Why would God permit such a thing to come to pass? The answer lies in the words, "by reason of transgression" (8:12), that is, because of the national transgression of Israel. The remnant returned to the land, but they did not turn back to God, a fact not to be denied as to Israel's past and also as to her present status in the land today.

The past hatred of Antiochus and the future hatred of Antichrist is directed against the Jews. The little horn "waxed great, even to the host of heaven; and it cast down some of the host and of the stars to the ground, and stamped upon them" (8:10). God's chosen people, who are His stars, are literally cast down and trampled upon. (Read Genesis 15:5; 22:17; Daniel 12:3.) This has occurred in the past under the persecutions of Pharaoh, Haman, Antiochus, Hitler, and many others, and it will be so in the future under Antichrist. (Read 2 Thessalonians 2:3-12 and Revelation 13 and 17.)

THE MESSENGERS OF PROPHETIC ILLUMINATION (8:13-18)

Then I heard one saint speaking, and another saint said unto that certain saint which spake, How long shall be the vision concerning the daily sacrifice, and the transgression of desolation, to give both the sanctuary and the host to be trodden under foot? And he said unto me, Unto two thousand and three hundred days; then shall the sanctuary be cleansed. And it came to pass, when I, even I Daniel, had seen the vision, and sought for the meaning, then, behold, there stood before me as the appearance of a man. And I heard a man's voice between the banks of Ulai, which called, and said, Gabriel, make this man to understand the vision. So he came near where I stood: and when he came, I was afraid, and fell upon my face: but he said unto me, Understand, O son of man: for at the time of the end shall be the vision. Now as he was speaking with me, I was in a deep sleep on my face toward the ground: but he touched me, and set me upright (Daniel 8:13-18).

After Daniel's vision of the ram, the goat, the four horns, and the little horn, he heard two saints discussing the time element in the vision. He was not left to guess what the meaning of the vision might be. The "saint" or "holy one" here is undoubtedly an angel, one of God's created intelligences other than man. Here, as elsewhere, they are God's messengers of prophetic illumination. The messenger that illumined Daniel was not a man, but Daniel merely said, "there stood before me as the appearance of a man" (8:15). This angel was identified as Gabriel (8:16), the same divinely-sent messenger who was to appear again to Daniel (9:21), and centuries later to Zacharias and Mary (Luke 1:19, 26). Peter, writing still later by divine inspiration, reminded us that angels were messengers of prophecy, "which things the angels desire to look into" (1 Peter 1:11-12). It was just such an angel that God used to signify to the Apostle John the message of the Revelation (Revelation 1:1). Among the angelic hosts, Gabriel and Michael only are called by the special title "archangel" (Jude 9; Revelation 12:7), meaning "chief messenger," suggesting that there is not general knowledge of things to come among all of the angels.

The first detail disclosed by these messengers of prophetic illumination had to do with the matter of time. The first angel asked, "How long shall be the vision?" (8:13) That is to say, How long will this desecration of the sanctuary and persecution of God's people at the hands of the little horn last? The answer came back from the second angel, "Unto two thousand and three hundred days; then shall the sanctuary be cleansed" (8:14). Whatever else the angels discussed up to this point was not important to Daniel because it was not necessary to the prophet's understanding of the vision. But the matter of the duration of the little horn's atrocities against God and His people was relevant.

Both Pember and Leupold point out the fact that the literal Hebrew expression for "days" is "evenings—mornings," so that the most feasible and simplest interpretation would be a period of twenty-four hours. This means that there were to be 2,300 repetitions of the evening and morning sacrifices to be polluted at the hands of the little horn. In his unpublished notes on Daniel, Dr. Wilbur M. Smith said, "This period of 2,300 days is the length of time during which the sanctuary was desecrated by the army of Antiochus Epiphanes, 171 B.C. to December 25, 165 B.C." The priest, Judas Maccabeus, drove out the Syrian army in 165 B.C., at which time the Temple was cleansed and rededicated after its pollution. This cleansing was thereafter celebrated at the feast of lights, and it was probably this feast mentioned by John in John 10:22.

In verses 15 and 16 Daniel continued to look and to inquire for further information concerning the meaning of the vision. In response to his seeking, there suddenly appeared a figure like that of a man, and the figure, an angel, spoke in a human voice. The voice called upon Gabriel, God's interpreting angel, to give to Daniel clear understanding of the vision (8:16).

With the appearance of the figure and the voice, Daniel became fearful, though he did not lose consciousness (8:17). The fact that Daniel was overcome and fell face downward should not surprise any of us. The Scriptures relate that men were overcome with dread and awe when in contact with a heavenly being. We meet with this again in chapter 10 (verses 9, 15, 17). Moses had such an awe-inspiring experience at the burning bush (Exodus 3). Isaiah saw his own sinfulness when in the presence of the seraphim (Isaiah 6:5). Ezekiel fell upon his face when he saw an appearance with the likeness of Jehovah's glory (Ezekiel 1:28). When the angel of Jehovah appeared to Manoah and his wife, Manoah said, "We shall surely die, because we have seen God" (Judges 13:22). It was with good reason that men feared death when in contact with a heavenly being from outer space because Jehovah had said, "There shall no man see Me, and live" (Exodus 33:20). How sinful the human heart must be, that at the mere presence of a sinless being man should be so completely awe-stricken!

Then Gabriel, the messenger of prophetic illumination, having come near to where Daniel stood, commenced to speak. At the sound of this voice from another world, Daniel lapsed into a swoon and fell face downward to the ground, whereupon Gabriel touched the old prophet of God and helped him to his feet (8:17-18). The mere touch of the angel restored Daniel from his helpless state, im-

244 The Prophecies of Daniel

parting the necessary strength to receive intelligently and with understanding the interpretation of the vision.

THE METHOD OF PROPHETIC INTERPRETATION (8:19-24)

And he said, Behold, I will make thee know what shall be in the last end of the indignation: for at the time appointed the end shall be. The ram which thou sawest having two horns are the kings of Media and Persia. And the rough goat is the king of Grecia: and the great horn that is between his eyes is the first king. Now that being broken, whereas four stood up for it, four kingdoms shall stand up out of the nation, but not in his power. And in the latter time of their kingdom, when the transgressors are come to the full, a king of fierce countenance, and understanding dark sentences, shall stand up. And his power shall be mighty, but not by his own power: and he shall destroy wonderfully, and shall prosper, and practise, and shall destroy the mighty and the holy people (Daniel 8:19-24).

A method of prophetic interpretation, one which we have already spoken of in our study of this chapter, deserves further attention here. A prophecy may have a first and fragmentary fulfillment centuries before its full and final fulfillment. I see in Daniel 8 two end-time periods. Both of these periods witness the wrath of God being extended to His chosen people. The first of these periods of wrath commenced with the Babylonian captivity and concluded with the atrocities of Antiochus, after which there was deliverance. The second of these periods is yet future. It will commence with the beginning of the seventieth week (Daniel 9:24-27) and conclude with the atrocities of Antichrist, after which there will be deliverance. This method of prophetic interpretation must be employed if we are to understand clearly some of the great prophetic passages in the Bible. Look closely at the following: "For unto us a child is born, unto us a son is given: and the government shall be upon His shoulder: and His name shall be called Wonderful, Counsellor, The mighty God, The everlasting Father, The Prince of Peace. Of the increase of His government and peace there shall be no end, upon the throne of David, and upon His kingdom, to order it, and to establish it with judgment and with justice from henceforth even for ever. The zeal of the LORD of hosts will perform this" (Isaiah 9:6-7). In this one passage there is a compound prophecy with a double fulfillment and centuries divide the two. The partial fulfillment occurred when the child (Christ) was born, but the world awaits the final fulfillment when the government of this world will be upon His shoulders and He will rule His kingdom from the throne of David. Here is a dual prophecy in which the two comings of Christ are predicted.

"And the angel said unto her, Fear not, Mary: for thou hast found favour with God. And, behold, thou shalt conceive in thy womb, and bring forth a son, and shalt call His name JESUS. He shall be great, and shall be called the Son of the Highest: and the Lord God shall give unto Him the throne of His father David: And He shall reign over the house of Jacob for ever; and of His kingdom there shall be no end" (Luke 1:30-33). Here again we have a compound prophecy with a double fulfillment and centuries dividing the two. The same messenger of prophetic illumination who appeared to Daniel appeared to Mary. He is Gabriel, God's chief angelic interpreter. In one sweeping statement Christ's two comings are predicted. Here are both the cradle and the crown. This dual prophecy has been only partially fulfilled in our Lord's birth. The world still awaits His second coming when He shall receive the throne of David and reign over the house of Jacob forever.

It is this method of prophetic interpretation that must be employed if Daniel 8 is to be understood and confusion avoided. In the section before us (verses 19-24), I see both the near and far fulfillment, Antiochus and the tribulation which has been fulfilled in the past, and Antichrist and the great tribulation which is still ahead for God's chosen people Israel.

Verses 19-22 cover that first and fragmentary fulfillment. Here we have the ram with two horns representing Media and Persia (8:20), the rough goat with the great horn representing Greece and Alexander (8:21), and the divided kingdom of Greece ruled by Alexander's four generals after his death (8:22). Following the reign of these four kings, "a king of fierce countenance" (8:23), whom we believe to be Antiochus Epiphanes, arose. He was a man "understanding dark sentences," that is, a crafty politician and a master of intrigue, skilled in double dealing. His strength grew until he became mighty, "but not by his own power," that is, his craft and cunning were imparted to him by another, presumably Satan. He was a monster who crushed all who stood in his way, including some of the holy people (8:24).

THE MAN OF
PROPHETIC CONSUMMATION (8:25-27)

And through his policy also he shall cause craft to prosper in his hand; and he shall magnify himself in his heart, and by peace shall destroy many: he shall also stand up against the Prince of princes; but he shall be broken without hand. And the vision of the evening and the morning which was told is true: wherefore shut thou up the vision; for it shall be for many days. And I Daniel fainted, and was sick certain days; afterward I rose up, and did the king's business; and I was astonished at the vision, but none understood it (Daniel 8:25-27).

It is most difficult to pinpoint exactly where the division appears in the chapter between the first fulfillment of the prophecy in Antiochus and its final fulfillment in Antichrist. Frankly, I see a blending of these two personalities both in the vision and the interpretation. But there does seem to be a clear application of this prophecy to a time yet future when there is apostasy in the whole earth, that "latter time" at the end of the age of which Paul wrote, "Now the Spirit speaketh expressly, that in the latter times some shall depart from the faith, giving heed to seducing spirits, and doctrines of devils" (1 Timothy 4:1). Antiochus is the type in some measure of the Antichrist who is to appear "in the last end of the indignation" (8:19). Let us say that the historical fulfillment is prophetic of a later fulfillment.

From the descriptive statements in this chapter concerning the little horn one can hardly miss the similarity between Antiochus and Antichrist. The vision has to do with two men who will be energized by Satan. Each is mighty, "but not in his power" (8:22). "The dragon gave him his power, and his seat, and great authority" (Revelation 13:2). Of Judas it is written that "Satan entered into him" (John 13:27). "Whose coming is after the working of Satan with all power and signs and lying wonders" (2 Thessalonians 2:9). Antiochus invaded the holy place, usurping the place of God (8:11-12). Antichrist "opposeth and exalteth himself above all that is called God, or that is worshipped; so that he as God sitteth in the temple of God, shewing himself that he is God" (2 Thessalonians 2:4). Antiochus made war against the "holy people" (8:24). Of Antichrist it is written, "And it was given unto him to make war with the saints, and to overcome them: and power was given him over all kindreds, and tongues, and nations" (Revelation 13:7). Our Lord described this in Matthew 24:15-22. Of Antiochus it was predicted, "He shall magnify himself in his heart" (8:25), meaning that in his own opinion he shall be great. John wrote prophetically of the Antichrist, "And there was given unto him a mouth speaking great things and blasphemies" (Revelation 13:5). Antiochus is but a forerunner in miniature of the coming Antichrist.

Possibly the strongest evidence in the chapter in support of a fulfillment yet future is in verse 25, where we read that "he shall also stand up against the Prince of princes; but he shall be broken without hand" (8:25). The Prince of princes can be none other than our Lord Jesus Christ. He only is more than a match for the Antichrist. The Seed of the woman shall bruise the serpent's head (Genesis 3:15). Christ is the Man of prophetic consummation. The world awaits His return to the earth, and when He comes the Antichrist "shall be broken without hand" (8:25), that is, without the aid of a human hand. The stone "cut out without [human] hands" (2:34) shall crush the serpent without human aid. "Whom the Lord shall consume with the spirit of His mouth, and shall destroy with the brightness of His coming" (2 Thessalonians 2:8). "These shall make war with the Lamb, and the Lamb shall overcome them: for He is Lord of lords, and King of kings" (Revelation 17:14). "And out of His mouth goeth a sharp sword, that with it He should smite the nations: and He shall rule them with a rod of iron: and He treadeth the winepress of the fierceness and wrath of Almighty God" (Revelation 19:15).

When the arrogant Lucifer sought to dethrone God and deify himself, he was smitten by God and duly humbled (Isaiah 14:12-14). Ever since the hour of that first fall he has not ceased his attack against God and the people of God. His vicious assaults have continued for centuries against everything that is right and holy. He has shared his powers with wicked men whose minds he controlled. But the coming of the Son of Man, the man of prophetic consummation, will bring to an end the beastlike rule of Antichrist in the last days. This sinister foe of the people of God shall have his power broken finally and forever, and in that day our Lord Jesus Christ will have the pre-eminence in "all things" (Colossians 1:18). The believer's hope is in the justice and judgment of God who will one day, and possibly soon, give to His beloved Son His rightful place in the earth. The "prince of this world" (John 12:31; 14:30; 16:11) will be no match for the Prince of princes.

Supernatural, divine judgment will at last overtake Satan, the beast, and the false prophet. Of the latter two it is written, "These both were cast alive into a lake of fire burning with brimstone" (Revelation 19:20). These enemies of righteousness will be "broken," utterly shattered into submission and helplessness.

Our chapter concludes with the angel's parting words to Daniel: "And the vision of the evening and the morning which was told is true: wherefore shut thou up the vision; for it shall be for many days" (8:26). The disclosure concerning the future had come to an end, and now Daniel was told that everything he saw in the vision was truth and therefore it was not to be questioned. Daniel was told to "shut up the vision," that is, to preserve it, for it had to do with a time far into the future. Leupold says, "As far as the more immediate future was concerned, Daniel might have transmitted the truth to faithful men by word of mouth; and it might have lived on by sound tradition until the times for which it was intended. But in that case it would have been completely lost for that 'time *far* in the future.' So Daniel was to take such precautions about the preservation and manifolding of the manuscript as might be necessary so that the document could be preserved for a long time to come. Nothing about it was intended to be kept secret."

Yes, "the vision . . . is true." It proved to be true in the first and partial fulfillment when Antiochus cut off the evening and morning sacrifices. Now we await the final and perfect fulfillment in the coming of the Prince of princes, the man of prophetic consummation, our Lord and Saviour Jesus Christ.

"And I Daniel fainted, and was sick certain days; afterward I rose up, and did the king's business; and I was astonished at the vision, but none understood it" (8:27). The strain on the aging prophet was more than he could bear, so that exhaustion and temporary sickness overcame him. Such manifestations of divine power and prophetic revelation are too great for any man to receive without being affected in some way. With Daniel it was but a recurrence of an earlier weakness. If we could imagine ourselves being visited by an angel from Heaven, then given a glimpse into the future known only to God, and see empires crumbling and our own people suffering, we must agree that such an experience would appall us. So it should! Yet the positive factor in our chapter is most encouraging, namely the Antichrist's tyranny will be broken at the time of our Lord's coming again to the earth.

CHAPTER NINE

THE PRAYER (9:1-23)

The Promptings of the Prayer
The Pursuit of the Prayer
The Penitence in the Prayer
The Particulars in the Prayer
The Petition in the Prayer
The Power in the Prayer

THE PROPHECY (9:24-27)

The Meaning of the Prophecy
The Mathematics in the Prophecy
The Message in the Prophecy
The Man of Sin in the Prophecy
The Messiah in the Prophecy

CHAPTER NINE

If one were asked to make a list of the greatest chapters in the Bible on the subjects of prayer and prophecy, Daniel 9 would have to be included in the list. Here we have what I believe to be the greatest chapter in the entire Bible. I know of no portion of Scripture that surpasses it in grandeur and content in its relation to the two aforementioned subjects. These amazing twenty-seven verses are among the most searching and satisfying ever to come to my own heart.

Other men have expressed their highest praise of this chapter in Daniel. Sir Edward Denny called it "the backbone of prophecy." H. A. Ironside called it "the greatest of all time-prophecies." Concerning the verses in this chapter H. C. Leupold wrote, "They unroll a panorama of history that is without parallel even in the sacred Scriptures." Philip R. Newell calls it "the greatest chapter in the book (Daniel), and one of the greatest of the entire Bible." Any man of unprejudiced mind who will examine this chapter carefully in the light of other Scriptures and history, will readily admit to its divine inspiration and amazing accuracy.

We will examine this chapter under two headings: *the prayer* and *the prophecy*.

THE PRAYER (9:1-23)

In the first year of Darius the son of Ahasuerus, of the seed of the Medes, which was made king over the realm of the Chaldeans; In the first year of his reign I Daniel understood by books the number of the years, whereof the word of the LORD *came to Jeremiah the prophet, that he would accomplish seventy years in the desolations of Jerusalem. And I set my face unto the Lord God, to seek by prayer and supplications, with fasting, and sackcloth and ashes: And I prayed unto the* LORD *my God, and made my confession, and said, O Lord, the great and dreadful God, keeping the covenant and mercy to them that love Him and to them that keep His commandments; We have sinned, and have committed iniquity, and have done wickedly, and have rebelled, even by departing from Thy precepts and from Thy judgments: Neither have we hearkened unto Thy servants the prophets, which spake in Thy name to our kings, our princes, and our fathers, and to all the people of the land. O Lord, righteousness belongeth unto Thee but unto us confusion of faces, as at this day; to the men of Judah, and to the inhabitants of Jerusalem, and unto all Israel, that are near, and that are far off, through all the countries whither Thou hast driven them, because of their trespass that they have trespassed against Thee. O Lord, to us belongeth confusion of face, to our kings, to our princes, and to our fathers, because we have sinned against Thee. To the Lord our God belong mercies and forgivenesses, though we have rebelled against Him; Neither have we obeyed the voice of the* LORD *our God, to walk in His laws, which He set before us by His servants the prophets. Yea, all Israel have trans-gressed Thy law, even by departing, that they might not obey Thy voice; therefore the curse is poured upon us, and the oath that is written in the law of Moses the servant of God, because we have sinned against Him. And He hath confirmed His words, which He spake against us, and against our judges that judged us, by bringing upon us a great evil: for under the whole heaven hath not been done as hath been done upon Jerusalem. As it is written in the law of Moses, all this evil is come upon us: yet made we not our prayer before the* LORD *our God, that we might turn from our iniquities, and understand Thy truth. Therefore hath the* LORD *watched upon the evil, and brought it upon us: for the* LORD *our God is righteous in all His works which He doeth: for we obeyed not His voice. And now, O Lord our God, that hast brought Thy people forth out of the land of Egypt with a mighty hand, and hast gotten Thee renown, as at this day; we have sinned, we have done wickedly. O Lord, according to all Thy righteousness, I beseech Thee, let Thine anger and Thy fury be turned away from Thy city Jerusalem, Thy holy mountain: because for our sins, and for the iniqui-ties of our fathers, Jerusalem and Thy people are become a reproach to all that are about us. Now therefore, O our God, hear the prayer of Thy servant, and his supplica-tions, and cause Thy face to shine upon Thy sanctuary that is desolate, for the Lord's sake. O my God, incline Thine ear, and hear; open Thine eyes, and behold our desolations, and the city which is called by Thy name: for we do not present our supplications before Thee for our righteousnesses, but for Thy great mercies. O Lord, hear; O Lord, forgive; O Lord, hearken and do; defer not, for Thine own sake, O my God: for Thy city and Thy people are called by Thy name. And whiles I was speaking, and praying, and confessing my sin and the sin of my people Israel, and presenting my supplication before the* LORD *my God for the holy mountain of my God; Yea, whiles I was speaking in prayer, even the man Gabriel, whom I had seen in the vision at the beginning, being caused to fly swiftly, touched me about the time of the evening oblation. And he informed me, and talked with me, and said, O Daniel, I am now come forth to give thee skill and understanding. At the beginning of thy supplications the commandment came forth, and I am come to shew thee; for thou art greatly beloved: therefore understand the matter, and consider the vision (Daniel 9:1-23).*

The order of the two divisions in this chapter is important. Before this significant prophecy was made known to Daniel, he was found on his knees before the Word of God and in prayer. There are three significant ninth chapters in the Old Testament, all of them containing a prayer of a similar nature: Ezra 9, Nehemiah 9, and Daniel 9. In each instance a servant of God was on his knees before the Word of God, earnestly interceding for the people of God. The Old Testament prophets did not sit in a passive state waiting for a revelation from God through a dream, a vision, or a voice. They were "holy men of God" (2 Peter 1:21) who spent much time in prayer, searching for the message and meaning of prophecy (1 Peter 1:10-12). When the deep things of God baffled them they followed the only true course, that of asking God (James 1:5) and trusting the Holy Spirit to show them (1 Corinthians 2:9-11). Prayer and an understanding of God's Word are linked together.

The Promptings of the Prayer (9:1-2). Verse one tells us the time of the prayer: "In the first year of Darius the son of Ahasuerus." Darius was not the conqueror who became king in his own right, but rather he "was made king over the realm of the Chaldeans" by Cyrus. The exact boundaries of the entire kingdom are not known, however we do know that when Cyrus the Persian conquered Babylon, he placed his uncle Darius on the throne at Babylon to rule that part of the new Medo-Persian kingdom. The fact that no monuments have been found which indicate a ruler in Media or Persia by the name of Darius need not disturb us. The absence of a record does not stand up as an argument against the book of Daniel. Those destructive critics of the Word of God will one day learn their lesson, but for some of them it will be too late. The fact that this Darius was "*made* king" agrees with the statement made earlier that "Darius the Mede *received* the kingdom" (5:31 R.V.).

The events in chapter 9 follow chronologically those in chapter 5, so that 9:1 follows 5:31. The time of Daniel's prayer and prophecy was the year 538 B.C. or 537 B.C. It was a critical time and an hour of much confusion. That fateful night of Belshazzar's death and Babylon's fall could hardly have been forgotten. A new form of government had the people in an unsettled state. Quite possibly Daniel himself was somewhat perplexed.

At that time of upheaval and uncertainty Daniel occupied himself with the Scriptures. The text says he was reading the "books," especially the book of the Prophet Jeremiah. Exactly how many books in the Old Testament were written at that time, and how many of those Daniel had in his possession, we do not know. We do know, however, that he had the book of Jeremiah; he doubtless had read such passages as Jeremiah 24:5-10; 25:11-12; 29:10, and possibly the prayer of Solomon as recorded in 1 Kings 8:47-52. Daniel's secret lay in his regular and right use of the Scriptures. This is the best possible prompting to prayer. Bible reading and prayer stand or fall together. If your prayer life is lacking, take up the Word of God and give yourself to quiet and reflective reading. Daniel was reading his Bible and it was that which prompted him to pray.

There is a particular detail that fastened upon Daniel as he read, namely that "He [God] would accomplish seventy years in the desolations of Jerusalem" (9:2). God had given to Jeremiah detailed information concerning the desolation and captivity of His people Israel. "And this whole land shall be a desolation, and an astonishment; and these nations shall serve the king of Babylon seventy years. And it shall come to pass, when seventy years are accomplished, that I will punish the king of Babylon, and that nation, saith the LORD, for their iniquity, and the land of the Chaldeans, and will make it perpetual desolations" (Jeremiah 25:11-12). As Daniel was reading he caught a fresh glimpse of the fact that the "seventy years" were almost expired. The old prophet, now approaching ninety years of age, must have rejoiced in heart as he realized that his people stood on the threshold of a new day. The study of the prophetic Scriptures had given to this careful student insight into an impending event.

Now Daniel doubtless knew this passage well, having read it many times before; therefore he knew exactly what was coming to pass. His heart and conscience were greatly exercised as the result of his study of prophecy. Too often our interest in the prophetic Scriptures is of a curious and speculative nature, or else we conclude that God will carry out His sovereign purpose no matter what we do, and so we do not concern ourselves about those matters. But when Daniel realized that a great prophecy affecting his people was about to be fulfilled, he commenced to pray. The prospect of the restoration of his people and the downfall of their adversary drew him into the presence of God. When a man of God believes the promises of God his faith becomes active, not passive. Faith always tends to draw the believing one to God.

The Pursuit of Prayer (9:3). "And I set my face unto the Lord God, to seek by prayer and supplications, with fasting, and sackcloth, and ashes" (Daniel 9:3). Daniel might have hurried to his people whom the prophecy concerned, for indeed he had good news to tell them. How we students of prophecy delight to preach our prophetic findings and rush into print with our "amazing new discoveries"! But not so Daniel! This seasoned saint of God set his face to seek the Lord, meaning that with deep devotion and intense desire he consciously turned to God. He did not glibly recite a prayer made up of mere idle words and pious phrases. He earnestly pursued God. True prayer, which has for its foundation the Word of God, will drive the man of God to the holy of holies.

Praying the Bible way is "praying in the Holy Ghost" (Jude 20); it is to "pray with the understanding" (1 Corinthians 14:15), "Praying always with all prayer and supplication in the Spirit" (Ephesians 6:18); it is to "Pray without ceasing" (1 Thessalonians 5:17); "and not to faint" (Luke 18:1). When we pray the Bible way we do not "ask amiss" (James 4:3). The Biblical pursuit of prayer is necessary to a proper understanding of prophecy. The right pursuit of prayer will seek God's will at any cost. Can we say with Daniel, "I set my face unto the Lord God"?

The Penitence in the Prayer (9:3). Daniel's prayer was accompanied by "fasting, and sackcloth, and ashes" (Daniel 9:3). Leupold says, "Fasting and sackcloth and ashes are employed as auxiliary means to aid devotion. Fasting helps to keep the mind unencumbered and also reminds him who practices it that he has not deserved even food from God. To remove clothing and to substitute a coarse wrap strongly reminds the supplicant that not even the comforts of good clothing are his right and due reward. Ashes were put upon the head as a token of grief since Daniel sincerely grieved over his and his people's sins."[1] These were outward marks of internal contrition and penitence. As the dignified prime minister, Daniel was accustomed to going about in his official robe, but here he laid aside the garment of his earthly office and came to God in prayer as a penitent.

It is only when true penitence exists in the heart, as is so markedly exemplified by Daniel, that there can be power in prayer. Three steps, or links, are seen in the accomplishment of God's purposes for His people and the holy city Jerusalem. First, the *prophecy* of Jeremiah; secondly, the *prayer* of Daniel; thirdly, the *proclamation* of Cyrus. All three played an important role, and not the least of them was the prayer of Daniel. W. C. Stevens wrote, "Penitent supplication was to be a necessary spiritual condition of restoration from Babylonian exile."[2]

The Particulars in the Prayer (9:4-15). The prayer is marked first by confession. Daniel said, "And I prayed unto the LORD my God, and made my confession, and said . . . We have sinned, and have committed iniquity, and have done wickedly, and have rebelled, even by departing from Thy precepts and from Thy judgments" (Daniel 9:4-5). Daniel knew that confession of sin is a first requisite to a successful prayer life and the subsequent blessing of God. Now if there was one man in Babylon who, from his own behavior and condition of his own heart, might not have needed to confess sins, that man was Daniel. From his youth, when Jerusalem fell and he was led captive to Babylon, he refused to defile himself.

[1] Leupold, *Daniel*, page 380.
[2] Stevens, *Daniel*, page 133.

But what brought Daniel to this place of confession? I suggest two things. First, he recognized that Israel's spiritual unpreparedness was preventing the Lord from doing for His people all that He had promised. There is an unaltered and unalterable principle in the Word of God which says, "If I regard iniquity in my heart, the Lord will not hear me" (Psalm 66:18). "The LORD is far from the wicked: but He heareth the prayer of the righteous" (Proverbs 15:29). "He that turneth away his ear from hearing the law, even his prayer shall be abomination" (Proverbs 28:9). A true and genuine confession will not hide anything; rather it is straightforward, without excuse, offering no palliation of guilt. When we are aware of our being caught in sin, having lost the blessing of God, there is only one course to follow: "If we confess our sins, He is faithful and just to forgive us our sins, and to cleanse us from all unrighteousness" (1 John 1:9). If we Christians were to have the same attitude toward the sins of our nation as did Daniel in dealing with the sins of his nation, we would be on our knees confessing our personal and national sins. The blessing of the Lord would follow. We are caught up in the sins of our day and age but until we come before God in true penitence and confession there can be no national blessing. The sins of Israel brought Daniel to the place of confession.

A second thing that brought Daniel to the place of confession was his heart attitude toward God, his reflections on the nature and attributes of God. His descriptive language is unsurpassed. "O Lord, the great and dreadful [awe-inspiring] God, keeping the covenant and mercy to them that love Him, and to them that keep His commandments" (Daniel 9:4), "O Lord, righteousness belongeth unto Thee" (9:7). "To the Lord our God belong mercies and forgivenesses" (9:9). "The LORD our God is righteous in all His works which He doeth" (9:14). This is the language of a soul occupied with God: who and what God is. Prayer is the occupation of the soul with its needs; worship is the occupation of the soul with God, and yet the two are inseparably linked together. This explains, in part at least, why this purest of men is confessing sin. As Daniel meditated upon the glories and perfection of Jehovah, his own heart became blacker against the pure, spotless, white background of a holy God. No man can have a true concept of himself until he draws near to God. Isaiah testified, "I saw also the Lord. . . . Then said I, Woe is me! for I am undone; because I am a man of unclean lips, and I dwell in the midst of a people of unclean lips: for mine eyes have seen the King, the LORD of hosts" (Isaiah 6:1, 5). When we see God for what He is, and our own hearts for what they are, we are uncomplaining because we know then that whatever God's dealings with us might be, they are just. Here is a prayer which might well be read frequently by us all if we want God's blessing in a sinful and sorrowful world. O, how we need to examine our thoughts and search our hearts as regards the cause and contents of our prayers!

The Petition in the Prayer (9:16-19). After penitence, confession, and worship, faith becomes emboldened to petition its desires of the Lord. Daniel's first and greatest concern was that God's anger and fury be turned away from the holy city of Jerusalem, the location of the Temple and the center of God's rule and government. He petitioned God for His "sanctuary" (9:17). Mark the selflessness in the prayer: every request is "for the Lord's sake" (9:17, 19). There is nothing asked for "me and my wife and our son and his wife." All must be for God's glory. Daniel did not ask one single thing for himself; rather his whole heart went out in supplication for the honor of God's name in the earth. It was this spirit that gripped Paul when he wrote, "Now I be-seech you, brethren, for the Lord Jesus Christ's sake, and for the love of the Spirit, that ye strive together with me in your prayers to God for me" (Romans 15:30). The apostle urged the saints to join him in prayer "for the Lord Jesus Christ's sake."

Does the reader detect something new and strange in this kind of praying? If so, let him reflect upon who God is. Let him turn from his own selfish wants and ponder the needs of others. Only as we have an intimate and experiential knowledge of Him, whose help we seek, will our prayers be effective. Read carefully and slowly verses 16-19, and note the expressions "*Thy* righteousness . . . *Thy* city Jeru-salem, *Thy* holy mountain . . . *Thy* people . . . *Thy* face . . . *Thy* sanctuary . . . *Thy* name." Such praying will set in mo-tion the power of God.

The Power in the Prayer (9:20-23). Actually the prayer was not completed. It must have been a delightful experience for Daniel to have his prayer interrupted by a sudden answer from Heaven. The elderly saint of God was given a foretaste of millennial blessing when, according to God's own Word, "Before they call, I will answer; and while they are yet speaking, I will hear" (Isaiah 65:24). Daniel said, "Yea, whiles I was speaking in prayer, even the man Gabriel, whom I had seen in the vision at the beginning, being caused to fly swiftly, touched me about the time of the evening obla-tion" (Daniel 9:21). Notice at what point the prayer was in-terrupted: "O Lord, hear; O Lord, forgive; O Lord, hearken and do; defer not, for Thine own sake, O my God: for Thy city and Thy people are called by Thy name" (9:19). Mark the words, "defer not." Actually Daniel was pleading in humility and contrition, "O Lord, hear and act at once; please do not delay." Observe the urgency in his appeal for immediate action on God's part, and praise God for the on-the-spot response. Heaven is not far from the child of God who prays as did Daniel. Think of it: the very second we pray according to the divine pattern, our petition has reached God! With equal rapidity God can come to us. We read that the angel Gabriel came "swiftly" (9:21).

There is something to be said concerning the time Gabriel was sent to Daniel. It was "about the time of the evening oblation" (9:21). The time of the evening *sacrifice* was the hour for prayer and the worship of Jehovah. Ezra wrote, "And at the evening sacrifice I arose up from my heaviness; and having rent my garment and my mantle, I fell upon my knees, and spread out my hands unto the LORD my God" (Ezra 9:5). Now we know that there were no Jewish sacrifices being offered in Babylon. Moreover, almost seventy years before the time of Daniel's prayer, the Temple at Jerusalem had been destroyed. But though there was no temple nor altar, Daniel had never forgotten the hour of the evening sacrifice. The holy city and Temple were desolate, but Daniel's heart never ceased to be an altar at the dedicated hour of sacrifice. Away in exile in pagan Babylon, a holy man of God met with God at a stated hour. The time of the evening sacrifice was between three and four o'clock in the afternoon, referred to in Scripture as the "ninth hour" (Acts 3:1; 10:3, 30). It was at the hour when Old Testament sacrifices were offered, that ninth hour, that God's Lamb died at Calvary (Matthew 27:46; Mark 15:34). Those smoking sacrifices in Old Testament times pointed to the offering of our Lord Jesus Christ.

At the hour when sacrifices would have been offered at Jerusalem, Daniel was on his knees before God presenting himself a living sacrifice (see Romans 12:1). The time element in Daniel 9:21, namely the time of the evening sacrifice, suggests that there is only one way by which a sinful

man can come to God. That way is through Jesus Christ in
His death on the cross. Our Lord said, "I am the way, the
truth, and the life: no man cometh unto the Father, but by
Me" (John 14:6). The only way a man can reach God is to
"enter into the holiest by the blood of Jesus" (Hebrews
10:19-22). When Daniel sought God on divinely provided
grounds God answered at once. The distance between
Heaven and earth is no longer than it takes a penitent and
honest heart to call upon God through faith in Jesus Christ.

May Daniel's experience and blessing become ours. But
in order to obtain it we, like Daniel, must give ourselves to
the Word of God and prayer. God does not give special and
sudden visions of illumination to fanatical minds apart from
what He has written in His Word. Daniel lived a holy life,
and he was regular and consistent in studying the Scriptures.
"The effectual fervent prayer of a righteous man availeth
much" (James 5:16).

THE PROPHECY (9:24-27)

*Seventy weeks are determined upon thy people and
upon thy holy city, to finish the transgression, and to make
an end of sins, and to make reconciliation for iniquity, and
to bring in everlasting righteousness, and to seal up the
vision and prophecy, and to anoint the most Holy. Know
therefore and understand, that from the going forth of the
commandment to restore and to build Jerusalem unto the
Messiah the Prince shall be seven weeks, and threescore
and two weeks: the street shall be built again, and the
wall, even in troublous times. And after threescore and
two weeks shall Messiah be cut off, but not for Himself:*

and the people of the prince that shall come shall destroy the city and the sanctuary; and the end thereof shall be with a flood, and unto the end of the war desolations are determined. And he shall confirm the covenant with many for one week: and in the midst of the week he shall cause the sacrifice and the oblation to cease, and for the over-spreading of abominations he shall make it desolate, even until the consummation, and that determined shall be poured upon the desolate (Daniel 9:24-27).

Here all teachers and commentators are compelled to exercise thought and prayer in their attempt to expound these three verses. As early as 400 A.D., Jerome discovered so many different interpretations offered by many teachers that he wrote, "Because it is unsafe to pass judgment upon the opinions of the great teachers of the Church, and to set one above another, I shall simply repeat the view of each and leave it to the reader's judgment as to whose explanation ought to be followed." At the start of the fifth century Jerome was already acquainted with nine interpretations. Because of the multiplicity of interpretations, some pastors and teachers have despaired completely of pursuing a study of this passage and arriving at any certain conclusion. Certainly this passage, like all Scripture, has but one primary interpretation.

We enter now upon the remarkable prophecy of the "seventy weeks." As Daniel was on his knees with the Word of God open before him, he was praying that the Lord would bless the Word to his heart. In answer to his prayer, God gave to him the revelation of truth we are about to study. Let us keep in mind, then, that the prophecy of the "seventy weeks" is an answer to prayer. While he was praying, confessing his sin and the sins of his people, and presenting his supplication before the Lord, the angel Gabriel flew swiftly to this saint on his knees (9:20-21).

"And he informed me, and talked with me, and said, O Daniel, I am now come forth to give thee skill and understanding . . . . Therefore understand the matter, and consider the vision" (9:22-23). In consequence of the prayer, special skill and understanding were to be given to Daniel to interpret this important message from God. Among the reasons why God immediately sent an answer to Daniel's prayer is that Daniel was a man "greatly beloved," which means "most desired" or "very precious." It is a remarkable thing to see one of this earth who is so greatly beloved in Heaven that angels are assigned to respond immediately to his prayers. This does not suggest in the least any favoritism on God's part, but rather that Daniel exercised himself to holy living and was thereby living where God answers prayer. He who waits upon the Lord is certain to have Heaven's closest attention.

The prophecy is next disclosed: "Seventy weeks are determined upon thy people and upon thy holy city, to finish the transgression, and to make an end of sins, and to make reconciliation for iniquity, and to bring in everlasting righteousness, and to seal up the vision and prophecy, and to anoint the most Holy" (9:24). On the background of the seventy years' captivity, which was then expiring, God projected a new *chronology* of events relating to the Jewish nation.

The Meaning of the Prophecy. The first matter of importance is that we understand the meaning of the term "weeks." There is no disagreement among students of the Hebrew language as to the meaning of the word "weeks" in the passage we are now studying. It is the word *heptad*, meaning a unit of measure. A *heptad* is used to designate a collection of seven things, just as we would use the word "dozen" to designate a collection of twelve things. However, the word "dozen" does not stand alone. If I enter a food store and ask the clerk for a dozen, he would reply, "a dozen of what?" Do I want a dozen eggs, a dozen doughnuts, or a dozen something else?

Gabriel said to Daniel, "Seventy heptads [or sevens] are determined" (9:24). Here then are seventy sevens, but seventy sevens of what? It is clear in the context that the prophecy is dealing with time. But time is made up of units of varied duration. Are these seventy sevens of seconds, minutes, hours, days, weeks, months, or years? I am led to the conclusion that the seventy sevens in Daniel 9:24-27 have to do with years. While I would not insist that there is any connection between the "seventy years" in verse 2 and the "seventy weeks" in verse 24, I would direct the reader's attention to the fact that what Daniel was reading in the book of Jeremiah, and what he was writing, had to do with "years." As one reads other passages of Scripture it appears that the Jews recognized a week of seven years as well as a week of seven days.

Among the Hebrews there were not less than three classifications of "weeks." First, there was the week of days, which was reckoned from one sabbath to another. The following verses illustrate the sabbath week: "Remember the sabbath day, to keep it holy. Six days shalt thou labour, and do all thy work: But the seventh day is the sabbath of the LORD thy God: in it thou shalt not do any work, thou, nor thy son, nor thy daughter, thy manservant, nor thy maidservant, nor thy cattle, nor thy stranger that is within thy gates: For in six days the LORD made heaven and earth, the sea, and all that in them is, and rested the seventh day:

wherefore the LORD blessed the sabbath day, and hallowed it" (Exodus 20:8-11).

Secondly, there was the week of years, which was reckoned from one sabbatical year to another, and which consisted of seven years. The following verses illustrate the sabbatical week of years: "Six years thou shalt sow thy field, and six years thou shalt prune thy vineyard, and gather in the fruit thereof; But in the seventh year shall be a sabbath of rest unto the land, a sabbath for the LORD: thou shalt neither sow thy field, nor prune thy vineyard. That which groweth of its own accord of thy harvest thou shalt not reap, neither gather the grapes of thy vine undressed: for it is a year of rest unto the land. And the sabbath of the land shall be meat for you; for thee, and for thy servant, and for thy maid, and for thy hired servant, and for thy stranger that sojourneth with thee, And for thy cattle, and for the beast that are in thy land, shall all the increase thereof be meat" (Leviticus 25:3-7).

Thirdly, there was the week of seven times seven years, or forty-nine years, which was reckoned from one jubilee to another. The following verses illustrate the jubilee week: "And thou shalt number seven sabbaths of years unto thee, seven times seven years; and the space of the seven sabbaths of years shall be unto thee forty and nine years. Then shalt thou cause the trumpet of the jubile to sound on the tenth day of the seventh month, in the day of atonement shall ye make the trumpet sound throughout all your land. And ye shall hallow the fiftieth year, and proclaim liberty throughout all the land unto all the inhabitants thereof: it shall be a jubile unto you; and ye shall return every man unto his possession, and ye shall return every man unto his family. A jubile shall that fiftieth year be unto you: ye shall not sow, neither reap that which groweth of itself in it, nor gather the grapes in it of thy vine undressed. For it is the jubile; it shall be holy unto you: ye shall eat the increase thereof out of the field. In the year of this jubile ye shall return every man unto his possession" (Leviticus 25:8-13).

The phrase, "seven sabbaths of years shall be unto thee forty and nine years," was understood by Israel to mean weeks of years. The period of seven years was looked upon as one week.

There is another passage, to which we draw the reader's attention, which shows that this word "week," which is the word "seven," may mean seven years. The student should turn in his Bible to the interesting narrative in Genesis 29:15-28. Here the time period that Jacob agreed to work for Laban, so that he might have Rachel for his wife, is referred to interchangeably by the two expressions, "seven years" and "one week." Verses 27 and 28 show this clearly: "Fulfill her week, and we will give thee this also for the service which thou shalt serve with me yet seven other years. And Jacob did so, and fulfilled her week: and he gave him Rachel his daughter to wife also." Here there can be no question that the terms "week" and "seven years" are used synonymously. (See also Leviticus 23:15-16.)

Returning now to Daniel 9, the conclusion is that the prophecy of the "seventy weeks" refers to seventy sevens of years, or 490 years. Daniel had been reading in Jeremiah of the seventy years' captivity in Babylon. Then it is as though God said, "Yes, Daniel, you have discovered rightly that the seventy years captivity recorded by Jeremiah are coming to their end. But now I want to show you another *seventy*, a time period within which I shall accomplish all My plans for My people and My holy city."

The number *seven* has always represented completion, or perfection, so that our prophecy is dealing with a period of time in which God will bring to perfection a work of greatest moment which has to do with Israel and the land of Palestine.

The Mathematics in the Prophecy. There follows next in this great prophecy three divisions of the "seventy weeks."

> *Know therefore and understand, that from the going forth of the commandment to restore and to build Jerusalem unto the Messiah the Prince shall be seven weeks, and threescore and two weeks: the street shall be built again, and the wall, even in troublous times. And after threescore and two weeks shall Messiah be cut off, but not for Himself: and the people of the prince that shall come shall destroy the city and the sanctuary; and the end thereof shall be with a flood, and unto the end of the war desolations are determined (Daniel 9:25-26).*

The first thing Daniel was to know and understand was that the "seventy weeks" were to be divided into three parts:

1. Seven sevens (7 × 7) or 49 years.

The first period of 49 years, which was the starting point of the prophecy, would commence with "the commandment to restore and to build Jerusalem." Now there were not less than three decrees involving the restoration of worship at Jerusalem, the reconstruction of the Temple, and the rebuilding of the city of Jerusalem which included the city wall.

The first decree was issued by Cyrus in 538 B.C. and is recorded by Ezra (Ezra 1:1-4; 5:13-17). See also Isaiah 44:28; 45:1-4; 2 Chronicles 36:22-23. This decree was limited to the rebuilding of the Lord's house, the completion of which is recorded in Ezra 6. Since the decree of Cyrus did

272 The Prophecies of Daniel

not include the rebuilding of the city and the wall, but merely the Temple of Zerubbabel, we dismiss it as the "commandment" spoken of in Daniel 9:25. This decree does not satisfy the requirements which God gave to Daniel for the commencement of the 490 years.

The second decree was made by Darius in 517 B.C. and is recorded in Ezra 6:1-12. However, here Darius merely reaffirmed the proclamation of Cyrus with reference to the building of the Temple. Again no mention is made of restoring and building the city and the wall.

The third decree, issued by Artaxerxes in 445 B.C., fits more exactly those specifications given by God in Daniel 9:25. It is recorded in Nehemiah 2 and it seems from the details in the record that this is the correct starting point of our great prophecy. Artaxerxes gave Nehemiah permission to build "the wall of the city" (Nehemiah 2:8, 13-15), and God's servant said to the people, "Come, and let us build up the wall of Jerusalem" (2:17). "So the wall was finished" (6:15). From the time of the decree of Artaxerxes to the close of the Old Testament canon, which concluded with the prophecy of Malachi, covers "seven weeks," or seven sevens of years, which total 49 years.

2. Sixty-two sevens (62 × 7) or 434 years.

The first cycle of 49 years, while mentioned separately from the 434 years, is yet joined to it, the two cycles combined totaling 483 years.

> *And after threescore and two weeks shall Messiah be cut off (9:26).*

That is, 483 years after the decree of Artaxerxes, another significant prophecy would be fulfilled, namely Messiah should be cut off. We will discuss more fully later the person of Messiah, however, in order that we might understand the mathematics in the prophecy, we will at this point identify Messiah as our Lord Jesus Christ.

Now we must be careful to weigh the matter of Bible chronology wisely, avoiding dogmatism except where specific time is given in certain passages. However, two books by the late Sir Robert Anderson, *Daniel in the Critic's Den* and *The Coming Prince,* have impressed me greatly. Sir Robert has traced the time from the day that Artaxerxes gave permission to Nehemiah to rebuild Jerusalem until the first "Palm Sunday," when our Lord publicly presented Himself to Israel as their King, to be exactly 483 years (seven sevens of years or 49 years, plus sixty-two sevens of years or 434 years). However, in Sir Robert's calculations these years were Jewish years of 360 days, made up of twelve months of thirty days each.

The time period in verse 26 presents one of the most amazing prophecies in the Bible. Here is stated the exact time of Christ's rejection, a prediction given more than four centuries before He was born. Had the Jews of Christ's day believed Daniel's prophecy, they would have known that Jesus of Nazareth was their promised Messiah and King. What a stinging rebuke to man's unbelief!

3. The seventieth seven or 7 years.

This brings us to the seventieth week described in verse 27. It is the "one week" remaining of the 70 weeks, or 490 years.

> *And he shall confirm the covenant with many for one week: and in the midst of the week he shall cause the the sacrifice and the oblation to cease, and for the overspreading of abominations he shall make it desolate, even*

*until the consummation, and that determined shall be
poured upon the desolate (9:27).*

We have seen that there was no lapse of time between the
seven weeks (49 years) and the sixty-two weeks (434 years),
so that the first 483 years of the prophecy ran their course
successively, without interruption.

Now the question that confronts us is, did the seventieth
week (7 years) run its course successively, without interruption, meaning of course that it is now past and its prophecy
has already been fulfilled? The answer is a clear and em-
phatic, No! The sixty-nine weeks are separated from the
last week by an interval of time. Verse 26 refers to the death
of Christ and the destruction of Jerusalem in 70 A.D., while
verse 27 passes on to a time yet future. The seventieth week
of seven years awaits its fulfillment at some future date. The
full "seventy weeks" might have run their course without
interruption had the Jews received Christ as their Messiah
and the rightful Heir to David's throne. But they rejected
Him and crucified Him, and as a consequence they are
scattered over all the earth with no recognized relationship
with God. We cannot lose sight of the fact that the entire
prophecy has to do with Daniel's people (the Jews) and the
"holy city" (Jerusalem).

Of course Gabriel did not reveal to Daniel that the seventieth week did not follow immediately upon the expiration
of the sixty-ninth week. Between the second and third parts
of the cycle, embracing the full 490 years, there is an indefinite period of time. It is the present Church Age which
had its commencement at Pentecost and will conclude at
the appearing of Christ in the air to gather His Church to
Himself (John 14:2-3; 1 Thessalonians 4:16-17). Our Lord
said to the Jews, "Therefore say I unto you, The kingdom
of God shall be taken from you, and given to a nation bring-

ing forth the fruits thereof" (Matthew 21:43). Presently God is not dealing with Jews merely, but with all mankind, Jews and Gentiles, so that all who accept His Son Jesus Christ are born spiritually into His kingdom (John 3:3). After Pentecost the apostles recognized the gap between the sixty-ninth and seventieth weeks. At Antioch Paul gathered the church together, and "they rehearsed all that God had done with them, and how He had opened the door of faith unto the Gentiles" (Acts 14:27). James reminded the brethren how God appeared to the Gentiles to take out from among them a people for His name; then, quoting Amos the prophet, he added, "*After this* I will return, and will build again the tabernacle of David, which is fallen down" (Acts 15:13-17, cf., Amos 9:11). This present age is that to which Paul referred as "the dispensation of the grace of God. . . . Which in other ages was not made known unto the sons of men" (Ephesians 3:2,5).

There is then a "gap" or "parenthesis" between the sixty-ninth and seventieth weeks, an undetermined period of time not included in the writings of the Old Testament prophets. It appears from our study of the Scriptures that God reckons time with the Jews only when He is dealing with them nationally. This fact is illustrated early in Israel's history and it is recorded by Moses in Exodus 12:2, where we read, "This month shall be unto you the beginning of months." God had cut out those years that were spent in Egyptian bondage. In the history of the Jewish state, Daniel 9:26 marks another gap which commenced with their rejection of Jesus Christ.

Should anyone regard the idea of a gap between the sixty-ninth and seventieth weeks as forced, let him consider that such instances are common in the prophetic Scriptures. For example, David wrote, "The face of the LORD is against them that do evil, to cut off the remembrance of them from the earth" (Psalm 34:16). Did you ever take note of the prophetic gap in this verse? You see it clearly when you read Peter's quotation of it. Peter wrote, "The face of the Lord is against them that do evil" (1 Peter 3:12). But the Holy Spirit prevented Peter from adding the last part of Psalm 34:16, namely "to cut off the remembrance of them from the earth," for the reason that this act of God is one of future judgment.

A similar illustration of a gap in prophecy is found in our Lord's message from Isaiah 61:1-2, when He taught in the temple at Nazareth. Isaiah said, "The Spirit of the Lord GOD is upon men . . . To proclaim the acceptable year of the LORD, and the day of vengeance of our God." However, when our Lord read from this very passage, He said, "The Spirit of the Lord is upon Me . . . To preach the acceptable year of the Lord" (Luke 4:18, 19). Then Luke adds, "He closed the book" (verse 20). Why did He conclude His reading in the middle of a sentence, thereby omitting the words, "and the day of vengeance of our God"? Because "the day of vengeance" or judgment would not come until after "the acceptable year," that is, until the age of grace had run its course." So between the words "LORD" and "and" in Isaiah 61:2, there is a gap of an undetermined period of time. Other illustrations of prophetic gaps are clearly identified in Isaiah 9:6 and Luke 1:31-33.

Our conclusion is that the seventieth week is not to be viewed as chronologically consecutive with the other sixty-nine, but it is separated from them by an indefinite period of time. We are presently living in that time period.

The Message in the Prophecy. What message was there in the prophecy for Daniel and his people? We have already taken note of the fact that Daniel learned about the rebuilding of Jerusalem and the city wall. But in verse 24 six things were mentioned which should occur during the marked-out period of 490 years. These six special announcements should be looked at carefully, one at a time:

1. "To finish the transgression." This was the first and most important item on the list. Keep in mind the fact that this was a national "transgression" since the prophecy has to do with Daniel's "people." Observe also that the definite article appeared in the text: "*the* transgression." The central theme in Daniel's prayer was the transgression of his people, a transgression which was to culminate in "*the* transgression." The word "transgression" combines the idea of rejection and apostasy, so that *the* transgression would be Israel's final rejection of Messiah. The final putting away or "finishing" this transgression is still future for the Jews.

While it is true that the atonement of Christ is sufficient for the whole world, Israel continues to reject Him and thereby remains even now in disfavor with God. But when Christ comes to earth again, at the end of the seventieth week, and the Jews are in their own land, they will recognize and receive Him as their Messiah and shall experience the forgiveness and cleansing which He alone can provide. In that day the people will say, "Surely He hath borne our griefs, and carried our sorrows: yet we did esteem Him stricken, smitten of God, and afflicted. But He was wounded for our transgressions, He was bruised for our iniquities: the chastisement of our peace was upon Him; and with His stripes we are healed. All we like sheep have gone astray; we have turned every one to his own way; and the Lord hath laid on Him the iniquity of us all" (Isaiah 53:4-6). God said, "And it shall come to pass in that day, that I will seek to destroy all the nations that come against Jerusalem. And I will pour upon the house of David, and upon the inhabitants of Jerusalem, the spirit of grace and of supplications: and they shall look upon Me whom they have pierced, and they shall mourn for Him, as one mourneth for his only son, and shall be in bitterness for Him, as one that is in bitterness for his firstborn. . . . In that day there shall be a fountain opened to the house of David and to the inhabitants of Jerusalem for sin and for uncleanness" (Zechariah 12:9-10; 13:1). "And the Redeemer shall come to Zion, and unto them that turn from transgression in Jacob, saith the LORD" (Isaiah 59:20). Paul, when quoting Isaiah 59:20, said, "And so all Israel shall be saved" (Romans 11:26). The perfect consummation of Messiah's redeeming work will be realized when He comes again at the end of the seventy weeks. At that time the whole course of Israel's transgression will have come to an end.

2. "To make an end of sins." To "make an end" is literally to "seal up" or "restrain." At the coming again of Jesus Christ to establish His rule in the earth, "The Lord God shall give unto Him the throne of His father David: And He shall reign over the house of Jacob for ever; and of His kingdom there shall be no end" (Luke 1:32-33). During His reign He will "seal up sin," that is, restrain sin as a criminal is restrained when locked in a prison cell and the doors are sealed, or as God seals up the stars so that they do not shine (Job 9:7), or as He shuts up heaven that it cannot rain (Deuteronomy 11:17). When God puts a new Spirit within His people, He will "shut up" or "seal up" her sins so that they will not break forth again (Ezekiel 36:26-27). "Neither shall they defile themselves any more with their idols, nor with their detestable things, nor with any of their transgressions: but I will save them out of all their dwelling-places, wherein they have sinned, and will cleanse them: so shall they be My people, and I will be their God" (Ezekiel 37:23). "By this therefore shall the iniquity of Jacob be purged; and this is all the fruit to take away his sin" (Isaiah 27:9). "For this is My covenant unto them, when I shall take

away their sins" (Romans 11:27). During Christ's reign on earth, which follows immediately after the seventieth week, the devil himself is "shut up" or sealed in the bottomless pit (Revelation 20:1-3). In that day sin will have run its course in Israel and will be locked up, never to do its evil work again. Thank God for that coming day when sin shall not break forth again.

3. "To make reconciliation for iniquity." Here the word "reconciliation" means "atonement" or "covering." It implies an effective covering for sin whereby the sinner is reconciled to God. Daniel confessed, "We have sinned, and have committed iniquity" (9:5), and God responded by telling Daniel that there is a day yet future when Israel's sins will be pardoned and forgiven. The sins of all men, Jews and Gentiles, have been atoned for in Christ's death at Calvary. But though our Lord's death is *sufficient* for all, it is *efficient* only where men will receive Him. Israel is still living in rejection of her Messiah, hence her atonement awaits the acknowledgment of Him as the only Redeemer. When Israel accepts the propitiatory sacrifice of Jesus Christ, her iniquities will be pardoned and forgiven, and this is exactly what will come to pass when the "seventy weeks" have expired. Let us bear in mind the fact that this has a special meaning for Israel as a nation. However, the application is not to the Jews as a nation in this dispensation. If a Jew wants to be saved today he must turn to Jesus Christ, for in Him only there is salvation (Acts 4:12). In the Body of Christ no distinction is made between Jew and Gentile (Galatians 3:26-28; Colossians 3:10-11).

4. "To bring in everlasting righteousness." Summing up as far as we have examined the first three of the six things mentioned, the time for "transgression . . . sins . . . and iniquity" has run its allotted course so that these must now be checked. This will be done by the introduction of a new

age when Christ shall usher in the righteousness of the ages. At that time Israel will be in a state of right relation to God, and then shall there be righteousness in the earth. Jeremiah wrote of that day and its new covenant, "Behold, the days come, saith the LORD, that I will make a new covenant with the house of Israel, and with the house of Judah: Not according to the covenant that I made with their fathers in the day that I took them by the hand to bring them out of the land of Egypt; which My covenant they brake, although I was an husband unto them, saith the LORD: But this shall be the covenant that I will make with the house of Israel; After those days, saith the LORD, I will put My law in their inward parts, and write it in their hearts; and will be their God, and they shall be My people. And they shall teach no more every man his neighbor, and every man his brother, saying, Know the LORD: for they shall all know Me, from the least of them unto the greatest of them, saith the LORD: for I will forgive their iniquity, and I will remember their sin no more" (Jeremiah 31:31-34).

Christ's millennial reign on earth will be a kingdom of righteousness. That righteousness will not merely be available to Israel, but she will possess it through Him. "Righteousness shall go before Him; and shall set us in the way of His steps" (Psalm 85:13). "He shall judge the world with righteousness, and the people with His truth" (Psalm 96:13). "Righteousness and judgment are the habitation of His throne" (Psalm 97:2). God said to Israel, "I will restore thy judges as at the first, and thy counsellors as at the beginning: afterward thou shalt be called, The city of righteousness, the faithful city" (Isaiah 1:26). "Righteousness shall be the girdle of His loins" (Isaiah 11:5). "The work of righteousness shall be peace; and the effect of righteousness quietness and assurance for ever" (Isaiah 32:17). "In His days Judah shall be saved, and Israel shall dwell safely: and this is His name whereby He shall be called, THE LORD OUR RIGHTEOUSNESS" (Jeremiah 23:6).

5. "To seal up the vision and prophecy." After the seventieth week, when Israel worships the Messiah and has been forgiven and cleansed from her sin and has entered into her glory, all prophetic predictions and announcements will be fulfilled so that faith will give place to sight. All of God's promises to Israel will be a blessed reality. All prophecies shall be done with (1 Corinthians 13:8) because the purpose of the visions and prophecies will be fully and finally realized. In the second of these six things we saw that sin was to be sealed up, and now vision and prophecy are to be sealed up. God is going to make good all that He has spoken by the mouth of all His holy prophets (Acts 3:18, 21). When Israel's transgressions have ceased, and her communion with God is unbroken, there will be no further need of vision and prophecy. Prophecy was not introduced into the world by God until after sin entered. The first overt prophecy is related to sin and redemption (Genesis 3:15). God's prophets have been a despised and rejected company, but one day the divine authority and authenticity of the prophet's message will be vindicated.

6. "To anoint the most Holy." There is not perfect agreement among conservative students as to the exact meaning of the term "The most Holy." Some have rendered it, "the holy of holies," while others believe it should be translated "most Holy One," the first referring to a place and the latter to a person. Larkin is quite sure that "the 'most holy' is a place, not a person. The reference is doubtless to the most holy place of the new millennial Temple as described in Ezekiel 41:1—42:20, whose erection is still future." [3] Lang agrees to this when he says, "In the place of the Tabernacle

---

[3] Larkin, *Daniel,* page 179.

and former temples . . . a new holy of holies shall be anointed. . . . The holy of holies of this prophecy, the innermost shrine of the grand Temple described by Ezekiel, will be no mere continuation of former sanctuaries."[4] The American Standard Version renders "most Holy" as "a most holy place." We know from other passages in the Bible that there is to be one, and possibly two temples built in Jerusalem (Amos 9:11; Acts 15:16) in which there will be an altar and a "holy place." The anointing of the "holy place" will be by the divine presence, so that both a place and the person could be included here.

In these six things that are mentioned in verse 24, Israel has God's message in the prophecy, the sum of all the blessings the nation is yet to receive. Here we are given to see the results of God's dealings with Israel at the end of the 490 years. All of God's promises will then be fulfilled.

The Man of Sin in the Prophecy. "And he shall confirm the covenant with many for one week: and in the midst of the week he shall cause the sacrifice and the oblation to cease, and for the overspreading of abominations he shall make it desolate, even until the consummation, and that determined shall be poured upon the desolate" (9:27).

Here is another remarkable prophecy. "The prince that shall come" (9:26), Antichrist, that man of sin appears at the commencement of the seventieth week. Here is the dreadful beast of Revelation 13:1 who will occupy a place of leadership in the United States of Europe. He is the "little horn" who will be accepted as prince of the Jewish state in the place of Messiah-Prince whom they rejected. The Jews will be in their land with the Beast promising them political and religious protection. This is the "covenant" he makes with Israel "for one week" (seven years). He will permit them to rebuild the Temple for the purpose of offer-

[4] Lang, *Daniel,* page 132.

ing sacrifices and oblations to God. They will look upon him as their man of destiny.

But when all appears to be going well, the man of sin will issue a decree that all Jewish worship must cease. This he will do "in the midst of the week," that is, three and one-half years after the commencement of the seventieth week. The middle of the week commences that period we call "the great tribulation" (Matthew 24:21, 29; Revelation 7:14), "the time of Jacob's trouble" (Jeremiah 30:7), characterized by an unprecedented wave of anti-Semitism. Isaiah describes this covenant with the Antichrist as "your covenant with death . . . and with hell" (Isaiah 28:18). Our Lord spoke of this very time when He said, "When ye therefore shall see the abomination of desolation, spoken of by Daniel the prophet, stand in the holy place, (whoso readeth, let him understand:) Then let them which be in Judaea flee into the mountains: Let him which is on the housetop not come down to take any thing out of his house: Neither let him which is in the field return back to take his clothes. And woe unto them that are with child, and to them that give suck in those days! But pray ye that your flight be not in the winter, neither on the sabbath day: For then shall be great tribulation, such as was not since the beginning of the world to this time, no, nor ever shall be" (Matthew 24: 15-21).

Zechariah described the same period when he wrote, "Behold, the day of the LORD cometh, and thy spoil shall be divided in the midst of thee. For I will gather all nations against Jerusalem to battle; and the city shall be taken, and the houses rifled, and the women ravished; and half of the city shall go forth into captivity, and the residue of the people shall not be cut off from the city" (Zechariah 14:1-2). This destruction will immediately precede the coming again of Jesus Christ to the earth, for Zechariah continues, "Then shall the LORD go forth, and fight against those nations, as when He fought in the day of battle. And His feet shall stand in that day upon the mount of Olives, which is before Jerusalem on the east, and the mount of Olives shall cleave in the midst thereof toward the east and toward the west, and there shall be a very great valley; and half of the mountain shall remove toward the north, and half of it toward the south" (14:3-4). The Apostle John was given to see that same awful period when he wrote, "And there was given me a reed like unto a rod: and the angel stood, saying, Rise, and measure the temple of God, and the altar, and them that worship therein. But the court which is without the temple leave out, and measure it not; for it is given unto the Gentiles: and the holy city shall they tread under foot forty and two months" (Revelation 11:1-2). Note the time element of "forty and two months" (verse 2) and "a thousand two hundred and threescore days" (verse 3). Using 360 days to the year, which was the Jewish way of calculating the year, John corroborated the exact time given to Daniel in the interpretation of his vision. John's forty-two months (3½ years and 1,260 days) is the same as the last half of the seventieth week in Daniel 9:27. Jesus, Daniel, Zechariah, and John were all foretelling the destruction of Jerusalem, and since John wrote after the destruction of that city in 70 A.D., the prophecy is unfulfilled as of now.

Speaking of the great tribulation our Lord said, "And when ye shall see Jerusalem compassed with armies, then know that the desolation thereof is nigh. . . . for there shall be great distress in the land, and wrath upon this people. And they shall fall by the edge of the sword, and shall be led away captive into all nations: and Jerusalem shall be trodden down of the Gentiles, until the times of the Gentiles be fulfilled" (Luke 21:20, 23-24). The times of the Gentiles will not be fulfilled until the end of the seventieth week.

Israel's present possession of Jerusalem, the result of her capturing that city in June 1967 in the brief Israeli-Arab war, is temporary. After the Church has been taken out of the world, Antichrist will appear on the scene (2 Thessalonians 2:7-8) and will make a "covenant" (pact or agreement) with Israel. She will agree to the Antichrist's offer in hope of receiving protection against the nations she knows will converge upon her. Isaiah calls it a covenant with death and Hades (28:18) because Antichrist will be raised from the underworld of the dead (Revelation 13:3; 17:8) by Satan himself, who has the power of death (Hebrews 2:14; Revelation 13:15). So clever will be the Antichrist's deception that Israel will accept him as her messiah and mistake the great tribulation for the millennium.

The Messiah in the Prophecy. Our Lord Jesus Christ is mentioned in the prophecy in Daniel 9:25-26. He is called "Messiah the Prince." However the mention of Him here does not go prophetically beyond His death. It is His crucifixion that is referred to when Gabriel said, "And after threescore and two weeks shall Messiah be cut off." Israel rejected her Prince and Messiah, and now for 2,000 years she has been trodden down of the Gentiles. But the end is not yet. Israel's future is not in any help she receives from Gentile nations; it is not in the false promises of the Antichrist, but in the coming again of her true Messiah, the Lord Jesus Christ.

We should keep in mind the fact that Matthew 24 is the key to the interpretation of Daniel 9:26-27. The disciples asked our Lord, "What shall be the sign of Thy coming, and of the end [consummation] of the world [age]?" (Matthew 24:3) The age referred to is, of course, that age marked by the end of the great tribulation as is stated in the context (verses 21, 29), the end of the seventieth week. Included in those indications of the approaching end of the age, whose end will be climaxed by Christ's coming again to the earth, He said, "When ye therefore shall see the abomination of desolation, spoken of by Daniel the prophet, stand in the holy place, (whoso readeth, let him understand)" (Matthew 24:15). This then is a clear sign to the Jews of the tribulation that their Messiah will return. When the seventieth week begins, God will once again take up His dealings with the nation of Israel, fulfilling the prophecy of Daniel 9:27 through the appearing of the Antichrist. When the seventieth week has ended, Christ will return, Israel will recognize and receive Him, and then the nation will enter the millennial rest.

Clarence Larkin wrote, "From this we see that Daniel's seventieth week (Daniel 9:24-27), Jesus' Olivet Discourse (Matthew 24), and John's seals, trumpets, and vials (Revelation 6:1 to 18:24) cover the same period, and are Jewish and have no reference to the Christian Church. Daniel draws the outline in his seventieth week, Jesus roughs in the picture in His Olivet Discourse, and John fills in the details in the book of Revelation."[5]

But Daniel's seventieth week is not the end of all things. God said through His prophet, "Behold, the days come, saith the LORD, that I will make a new covenant with the house of Israel, and with the house of Judah: Not according to the covenant that I made with their fathers in the day that I took them by the hand to bring them out of the land of Egypt; which My covenant they brake, although I was an husband unto them, saith the LORD: But this shall be the covenant that I will make with the house of Israel; After those days, saith the LORD, I will put My law in their inward parts, and write it in their hearts; and will be their God, and they shall be My people. And they shall teach no more every man his neighbour, and every man his brother, say-

[5] Larkin, *Daniel,* page 197.

ing, Know the LORD: for they shall all know Me, from the least of them unto the greatest of them, saith the LORD: for I will forgive their iniquity, and I will remember their sin no more" (Jeremiah 31:31-34). God's "new covenant" will follow the Antichrist's false covenant, and it will be expressly for Israel. (See Hebrews 8:8-13.)

The end of the seventieth week is marked by a great victory of Christ over Antichrist. The Seed of the woman will then crush the head of the serpent. The Antichrist will lead the kings of the earth to make war against God's Son, but the King of kings and Lord of lords shall triumph (Revelation 19:11-21). The grand terminus of the seventy weeks will be the day when a redeemed, regenerated, and cleansed Israel will possess the land which God gave unconditionally to their father Abraham. In that day Israel's Messiah will be worshiped by all Jews, and then peace, prosperity, and purity shall prevail in the holy city.

No one can state with certainty at what moment our Lord shall appear in the air from Heaven: "the dead in Christ shall rise first: Then we which are alive and remain shall be caught up together with them in the clouds, to meet the Lord in the air" (1 Thessalonians 4:16-17), but it could be nearer than any of us think. Beloved brethren in Christ, let us look for and love His appearing from day to day.

If these lines are being read by one who has never been saved, turn to Christ at once before this fleeting day of grace has run its course.

CHAPTER TEN

CHAPTER TEN

The three remaining chapters of the book of Daniel (10—12) combine to make one unit of thought. They belong together, therefore these three chapters should be read through several times at one sitting. We have discovered that each of the first nine chapters contains one major subject, so that the chapter divisions are quite excellent. Chapter 10 marks a departure from that pattern.

This part of the book of Daniel is no doubt the least read and studied. Most commentators who have written on this book have given less space to these last three chapters than to any three which preceded them. Therefore our approach to this final section of Daniel's prophecy demands humility and our human best, guided by the Holy Spirit. There is hardly anything in the Bible quite like these three chapters.

The subject matter unfolds in some detail the end of "the times of the Gentiles," those events which will occur during the seventieth week and on to the return of Christ to the earth in glory. A key phrase essential to a proper understanding of the entire vision is in verse 14: "Now I am come to make thee understand what shall befall thy people in the latter days: for yet the vision is for many days," that is, the end of these days. So in this last vision and final message to Daniel there is given to him the last revelation of things to come. The introduction to this revelation is in chapter 10.

THE CONCERN OF DANIEL (10:1-3)

*In the third year of Cyrus king of Persia a thing was re-
vealed unto Daniel, whose name was called Belteshazzar:
and the thing was true, but the time appointed was long:
and he understood the thing, and had understanding of
the vision. In those days I Daniel was mourning three full
weeks. I ate no pleasant bread, neither came flesh nor
wine in my mouth, neither did I anoint myself at all, till
three whole weeks were fulfilled (Daniel 10:1-3).*

A specific date introduces our chapter, "In the third year
of Cyrus king of Persia." Then there follows another time
period involving an exact day and month of the year (10:4).
It must have thrilled the hearts of God's prophets to keep
written records of the divine movements, especially when
those movements were a fulfillment of a promise or a
prophecy. There are numerous incidents of these revelations
involving time, such as the birth of Isaac (Genesis 17:21,
cf., 21:2); the bondage of Israel (Genesis 15:13, cf., Exodus
12:40); the birth of John the Baptist (Luke 1:11-22, cf.,
1:57-64); and Israel's seventy years in captivity (Jeremiah
25:8-12, cf., Daniel 9:2). Whenever God gave a revelation
to His prophets, they knew the importance of the divine
message. So it was in the third year of Cyrus' reign that
Daniel received the vision. By that time Daniel had reached
the ripe years of ninety plus.

In verse 1 the vision is referred to as "a thing." The text
says "a *thing* was revealed . . . the *thing* was true . . . he understood the *thing*." By the word "thing" is meant the *word*
or the entire *revelation* in the vision. There were a number of

things in the vision, that is, a number of connected events which would make up the whole "thing." Even though the final fulfillment of the vision was in the distant future, it was made clear to Daniel, for he "had understanding of the vision."

At the time of the vision Daniel was greatly troubled, so much so that he mourned and fasted three weeks. From Ezra 1:1-4 we learn that it was two years at least since Cyrus had issued his decree permitting Daniel's people to return to Palestine. The concern of Daniel might have been caused from a lack of interest on the part of his people to return to the land. From the twelve tribes then in captivity, only 49,697 desired to return to Jerusalem (Ezra 2:64-65; Nehemiah 7:66). The seventy years of captivity had expired; at the time of this last vision it was about seventy-two years since the first deportation, and now only a meager number had wanted to return. Daniel mourned for the lack of concern in the hearts of the Jews.

His burden was increased by the fact that those who did return were being hindered by enemies who occupied Jerusalem during the absence of his people. Zerubbabel, who led the first deportation back after the seventy years, was able to lay the foundation of the Temple, and this caused the people to rejoice (Ezra 3). But at that time Rehum and Shimshai, the Jews' adversaries, hindered the work. This double burden weighed heavily on the aging prophet's heart causing him soul travail which led him to pray and fast. He refrained from eating "pleasant bread," meaning the more attractive foods and delicacies. His heart was so burdened that he gave no thought to life's luxuries. Such self-denial and the denial of self our Lord laid down as requisites for true discipleship (Luke 14:26-27, 33). Do we give ourselves to prayer and self-denial when the work of God slows down and Satan attacks our brethren who serve

God? Do we grieve over the suffering and adversities of the workmen and work of God? Daniel did! And well might all believers mourn over the interested few and the victories of the enemy! Once upon a time God said, "To this man will I look, even to him that is poor and of a contrite spirit, and trembleth at My word" (Isaiah 66:2).

Because of the sadness in his heart Daniel refused to anoint himself. He said, "Neither did I anoint myself at all" (10:3). The anointing of the body was usually practiced on days of fasting and joy (Amos 6:6-7). It was an ancient custom to put unguents on the body. Today both men and women apply costly perfumes, bath lotions, deodorants, and the like. Daniel had no desire to exalt his external appearance while his internal state was one of sorrow and mourning. From 2 Samuel 14:2 one may assume that during periods of sorrow and mourning the anointing of the body was omitted. There is a time to mourn, and blessed are they that mourn at the proper time (Matthew 5:4). Both at the beginning and end of Daniel's history we find him abstaining from certain foods and habits (1:8-12), such abstinence as would contribute to spiritual growth and knowledge.

THE COMING OF THAT "CERTAIN MAN"
(10:4-9)

And in the four and twentieth day of the first month, as I was by the side of the great river, which is Hiddekel; Then I lifted up mine eyes, and looked, and behold a certain man clothed in linen, whose loins were girded with fine gold of Uphaz: His body also was like the beryl, and his face as the appearance of lightning, and his eyes as lamps of fire, and his arms and his feet like in colour to polished brass, and the voice of his words like the voice of a multitude. And I Daniel alone saw the vision: for the men that were with me saw not the vision; but a great quaking fell upon them, so that they fled to hide themselves. Therefore I was left alone, and saw this great vision, and there remained no strength in me: for my comeliness was turned in me into corruption, and I retained no strength. Yet heard I the voice of his words: and when I heard the voice of his words, then was I in a deep sleep on my face, and my face toward the ground (Daniel 10:4-9).

The time and geographical location of this last great vision are first identified. It came to Daniel "in the four and twentieth day of the first month" (10:4). The twenty-fourth day of the first month would include the Passover and feast of unleavened bread. The Passover was held on the fourteenth day of the month Abib (Exodus 23:15), later called Nisan (Nehemiah 2:1), and the feast of unleavened bread on the fifteenth to the twenty-first days of that same month. The nearness of these festival days, which commemorated Israel's deliverance, might have been further reason why Daniel fasted and mourned.

Daniel then tells where he saw the vision: "I was by the side of the great river, which is Hiddekel" (10:4). This is not the Euphrates River in Babylon, but the Tigris just outside Babylon. It is mentioned in Genesis 2:14.

On this significant occasion the vision appeared to Daniel without any preliminary indication. He said, "I lifted up mine eyes, and looked, and behold a certain man" (10:5). Who is this "certain man"? I must warn you now that little help will be derived from the commentators apart from the interestingly presented divergent views. The titles in the bibliography listed in this book are about equally divided, one-half holding to the view that the "certain man" is our Lord Jesus Christ, and the other half telling why he could not have been Christ but rather a created angel. On the side of those who believe him to be Christ there are Gaebelein, Kelly, Larkin, McGee, P. R. Newell, Petrie. Holding to the view that he is a created angel one will note Dennett, Ironside, King, Lang, Leupold, Stevens, Tathem.

In 1948 I wrote a brief exposition of the book of Daniel in which I said, "This glorious person set forth in verses 5-9 is none other than our Lord Jesus Christ." Then in 1958, when I was a pastor in Detroit, I wrote another exposition of Daniel in which I said, "Some attempts have been made to identify him as *the* angel of the LORD, the eternal Word, thus a theophany or preincarnate appearance of Jesus Christ. It is true that the description of him here does call to mind the vision John saw of the ascended Christ in Revelation 1:13-16. But Daniel 10:13 pretty much settles it for me that we have here a created angel. He was not the Lord of all angels, but merely one of the Lord's angels." Now I have let you in on a secret: In 1948 I was very sure; in 1958 I had reversed my former conclusion; now in 1968 I am not certain that I know just who this certain man is.

Those who hold to the view that the man in Daniel's vision was a created angel do so mainly on the ground that he needed the help of Michael when he was withstood by the prince of the kingdom of Persia (10:13). They deem it unthinkable that our Lord should require help in conflict. In further support of the view that the man is not Christ is the argument that the whole narrative is a continuous interview with one being, a messenger sent from God, who admits that he was not able alone to overcome the opposition of the wicked angel, the prince of Persia. One writer says,

"My mighty Jesus is not dependent upon even the arch-angel."

In favor of this "certain man" being Christ, reference is made to the striking similarity of the man in Daniel's vision to the vision of Christ as seen by John in Revelation 1:12-16. The two descriptions do seem to be of the same person. Moreover the effect of the visions upon Daniel and John are much the same. A number of commentators believe that Daniel did not see Christ in a preincarnate form, but that he saw the postincarnate Christ as Moses and Elijah saw Him on the Mount of Transfiguration. Mention is made also of the close comparison of Daniel 10:7 with Acts 9:7. Daniel alone was permitted to see the vision, but the men in his presence saw nothing. Saul of Tarsus alone could distinguish the words of Christ, but the men who journeyed with him to Damascus could not perceive with their physical senses.

The question has been asked, "If this personage is a spirit being, then why is he called 'a certain man'?" The word "angel" means literally "messenger," or, as in our present chapter, a celestial being who is a messenger of God. But does an angel ever appear in bodily form, that is, as a man? The writer to the Hebrews said, "Be not forgetful to entertain strangers: for thereby some have entertained angels unawares" (Hebrews 13:2). I believe we have an illustration of angels appearing as men in Genesis 18, when the Lord visited Abraham in the company of two angels. We think also of Manoah's wife in Judges 13, of whom it is recorded, "And the angel of the LORD appeared unto the woman. . . . Then the woman came and told her husband, saying, A man of God came unto me, and his countenance was like the countenance of an angel of God" (verses 3, 6).

Angels are created beings (Ephesians 1:21; Colossians

1:16), and inasmuch as they are spirit beings (Hebrews 1:14) they are without bodies in their original state, that is, bodies of flesh and bones. After our Lord arose from the dead He appeared to His disciples, "But they were terrified and affrighted, and supposed that they had seen a spirit. And He said unto them, Why are ye troubled? and why do thoughts arise in your hearts? Behold My hands and My feet, that it is I Myself: handle Me, and see; for a spirit hath not flesh and bones, as ye see Me have" (Luke 24:37-39). Though angels do not have terrestrial (or earthly) bodies, they do have celestial (or heavenly) bodies. Man receives his terrestrial or natural body from the earth, but angels are not given such a body at the time of their creation; thus man is said to be made "lower than the angels" (Hebrews 2:7). "There are . . . celestial bodies, and bodies terrestrial. . . . There is a natural body, and there is a spiritual body" (1 Corinthians 15:40, 44). The sect of the Sadducees, who were the infidels of Christ's day, did not believe in angels nor in the resurrection. Our Lord told them that angels have bodies adapted to their environment (Luke 20:27-36; Acts 23:8).

It has been a source of encouragement to many of God's children to experience the ministry of those heavenly attendants. Angels are endowed by God with great power and might (Psalm 103:20; 2 Peter 2:11), and it seems that this strength is expanded in the interest of the people of God. An angel came to Gideon (Judges 6:11); to Ornan (1 Chronicles 21:15-20); to Hezekiah (2 Chronicles 32:21); to Zacharias (Luke 1:11); to Mary (Luke 1:26-28); to Peter (Acts 12:7, 11); to Paul (Acts 27:23).

Angels were present at the creation of the world (Job 38:4-10), which fact tells us that they predate the creation as recorded in Genesis 1:1. They are associated with the great events pertaining to our Lord, such as His birth (Luke 2:8-14); temptation (Matthew 4:1-11); transfiguration (Matthew 17:1-8); resurrection (Luke 22:39-46); and His ascension (Acts 1:10-11). The prophetic Scriptures are clear in stating that angels will attend Him when He comes to earth the second time (Matthew 13:39; 24:31).

In our Lord's message about little children He indicated that they have their angels, or rather, that angels are assigned to these little ones (Matthew 18:10).

Such is the work of the holy, unfallen angels of God. They may appear unseen, or indwelling some godly man or woman in order to accomplish the purpose of God.

Well, there you have it, and I leave the choice with each to decide for himself. Both views cannot be correct. Personally, I find it hard to conceive how divine omnipotence can know weakness, or how the almighty Creator can be withstood by one of His finite creatures. However, if McGee is correct in his view, namely that Daniel did not see the preincarnate Christ, but rather a preview of the postincarnate Christ as He appeared on the Mount of Transfiguration, then I can see the possibility of the weakness in Christ's humanity. Who is this "certain man"? "Now we see through a glass, darkly; but then face to face: now I know in part; but then shall I know even as also I am known" (1 Corinthians 13:12).

When those who were present with Daniel fled from the vision, the prophet of God was left alone, but his strength had gone from him. The divine revelation was almost too much for the man of God to bear. His companions were unable to receive the least of the revelation. Only the man whose perceptions are sharpened by concern and contrition receives fresh revelations from God. As was mentioned before, an analogous case is that of Saul of Tarsus and his companions on the road to Damascus. It is possible for one to be close to the presence and power of God, but through lack of spiritual perception, miss the message. The man with a humble and contrite heart is "a man greatly beloved" (10:11, 19), meaning a man of "desires" or "delights," one in whom God delights (Deuteronomy 10:15; Isaiah 62:4). "God resisteth the proud, and giveth grace to the humble" (1 Peter 5:5). The fasting and mourning, coupled with the impact of the vision from another world, left Daniel exhausted, possibly in a state of unconsciousness. The record says, "Therefore I was left alone, and saw this great vision, and there remained no strength in me: for my comeliness was turned in me into corruption, and I retained no strength" (10:8).

THE COMMUNICATION OF THE ANGEL
(10:10-12)

> *And, behold, an hand touched me, which set me upon my knees and upon the palms of my hands. And he said unto me, O Daniel, a man greatly beloved, understand the words that I speak unto thee, and stand upright: for unto thee am I now sent. And when he had spoken this word unto me, I stood trembling. Then said he unto me, Fear not, Daniel: for from the first day that thou didst set thine heart to understand, and to chasten thyself before thy God, thy words were heard, and I am come for thy words (Daniel 10:10-12).*

As the aged Daniel lay in a state of exhaustion, God sent a ministering angel to impart strength to him. Here we see one of the many instances where angels perform as ministering spirits to God's heirs of salvation (Hebrews 1:13-14). How much of the angel's presence was detected by Daniel we are not told, but we do know he was aware of the hand touching him. This touch of God through His angel was to arouse Daniel to enable him to stand. The truth that is to be conveyed is that the angel was preparing Daniel so that he would be fully capable of receiving the interpretation of the vision. This seems clear from the angel's words, "O Daniel, a man greatly beloved, understand the words that I speak unto thee." At this word the old prophet stood up, but still weak and trembling.

We should bear in mind the fact that God sent His ministering angel to a man of prayer and faith. The angel testified to this when he said, "Fear not, Daniel: for from the first day that thou didst set thine heart to understand, and to chasten thyself before thy God, thy words were heard, and I am come for thy words" (10:12). Daniel had spent three weeks travailing in prayer and fasting for his people Israel; then there followed the stunning and shocking vision, so that his weakness was very great. Thus it was a holy and dedicated man who was made aware of the fact that he was "dearly beloved" by God, a man in whom God delighted greatly. It is not to the selfish and unfaithful that this heavenly ministry comes. We recall how in times of human weakness our Saviour Himself was strengthened by angels (Matthew 4:11; Luke 22:43).

The angel's first assuring and encouraging words to Daniel were, "Fear not" (10:12). There is no basis for fear in the heart of the trusting child of God. Why so? The answer was given to Daniel. "From the first day that thou didst set thine heart to understand, and to chasten thyself before thy God, thy words were heard, and I am come for thy words" (10:12). The angel was saying that when Daniel began to pray, three weeks before, God at once dispatched His heavenly messenger to go to the prophet's aid. Here is a precious lesson related to the believer's prayer life: "thy words were heard." True, Daniel did not get immediate response to his prayer, but then the answer that is *delayed* must not be interpreted as having been *denied.* The answer was forthcoming even though Daniel did not know it for three full weeks. At the very beginning of his intercession God went into action in behalf of His child and servant. Not only was the prayer heard at once in Heaven but it was likewise answered at once in Heaven. It is healthy for the child of God, who is in the will of God, to know that his prayers are always heard and answered, even though the answer be a *direct* one, a *delayed* one, or a *denial.*

Beloved Christian, as we walk in communion with our blessed Lord, we may rest in the assurance that when we take our place before the throne of grace in prayer, we have immediate access to God. Moreover, we should be encouraged in our prayer life just to know that God hears us. "And this is the confidence that we have in Him, that, if we ask any thing according to His will, He heareth us: And if we know that He hear us, whatsoever we ask, we know that we have the petitions that we desired of Him" (1 John 5:14-15). Here the Apostle John is enlarging somewhat upon the truth in the angel's statement to Daniel; namely that the believer who desires the will of God, and who has confidence in the wisdom and power of God, knows he will receive what he asks. The word "confidence" in John's statement means "boldness." What a wonderful thing it is for a child of God to be able to "come *boldly* unto the throne of grace, that we may obtain mercy, and find grace to help in time of need" (Hebrews 4:16). When God's will becomes our will, we are enabled to express our minds *boldly* (with freedom of speech) in His presence, and that without fear of embarrassment, for we know that He hears us. We may not get the answer to our petitions immediately, but we know that He hears us, and that "the time of the promise" is God's time and not ours (Acts 7:17). Dr. Roy L. Laurin has said: "As a matter of *fact* the answer may be long in coming, but as a matter of *faith* it is ours at the time of our asking." Daniel prayed for three full weeks, and though he had received no answer from God, he was given the assurance that his prayer had been heard.

THE CONFLICT IN THE SPIRIT WORLD
(10:13, 20)

> *But the prince of the kingdom of Persia withstood me one and twenty days: but, lo, Michael, one of the chief princes, came to help me; and I remained there with the kings of Persia (Daniel 10:13).*
>
> *Then said he, Knowest thou wherefore I come unto thee? and now will I return to fight with the prince of Persia: and when I am gone forth, lo, the prince of Grecia shall come (Daniel 10:20).*

These two verses of Scripture contain an amazing disclosure, giving to us a rare glimpse into the unseen world of spirit forces. Here is revealed a conflict that is totally disregarded by most people in our civilized world. Actually it is the struggle behind all struggles that are recorded on the pages of history.

When Daniel commenced to pray about the distressed state of his people Israel, God at once dispatched one of His holy angels to minister to His aged and weakened prophet. Enroute from Heaven to earth "the prince of the kingdom of Persia" stood against the angel of the Lord, engaging him in a struggle for twenty-one days, thereby preventing him from reaching Daniel during those three weeks.

Now who is this "prince of the kingdom of Persia"? There are varied and conflicting answers given that are hardly worthy of mention here. This "prince" is not Cyrus, the king of Persia. As a matter of fact he is not a man at all; he is an angel, an evil angel. In the New Testament evil angels are called demons. No mere man could withstand an angel. If one angel was able to slay 185,000 men in the Assyrian army, surely no individual man would be a match for one of God's holy ones (2 Kings 19:35, Isaiah 37:36). We are certain that Cyrus, the king of Persia, was not somewhere in outer space confronting an angel of God enroute from Heaven to earth.

As to the reality of spirit beings called demons, the scriptural testimony is clear. There are skeptics who dismiss as a remnant of medieval superstition the Biblical teaching about a personal devil and demons, but we know demons and demonic activity in the affairs of men exist, because the Word of God says so. Both the Old and New Testaments are replete with the activities of this host, and, after all, divine revelation is the most important witness. For Old Testament evidence the student should examine Leviticus 17:7, Deuteronomy 32:17; 2 Chronicles 11:15; Psalm 106:36-37; Isaiah 13:21; 34:14. In these passages it seems certain that the reference is to demonic conceptions.

In the New Testament various descriptive words and phrases are employed synonymously to identify evil spirits. They are called "spirits" (Matthew 12:45); "unclean spirits" (Matthew 12:43; Mark 1:23-27); "unclean devil" (or demon) (Luke 4:33); "seducing spirits" (1 Timothy 4:1); "spirits of devils" (or demons) (Revelation 16:14). (See also 1 Corinthians 10:20-21.) They are intelligent spirit-beings, evil and vicious, with power to hurt man physically, mentally, and morally.

These evil spirits do enter and control the bodies of human beings. They can paralyze one's voice, thereby rendering him dumb (Matthew 9:32-33); smite with blindness (Matthew 12:22); impart superhuman strength (Mark 5:1-4); torment the body and mind as to induce a suicidal mania (Mark 9:17-29); cause a disease and control it in one's body over a long period of time (Luke 13:11-17). To these we can add testimonies from the inspired writings of Peter (1 Peter 5:8; 2 Peter 2:4), James (James 2:19), and John (John 7:20; 8:44; 10:20-21; Revelation 2:13; 9:20; 12:7-9; 16:14; 20:2). These passages will suffice to prove the existence of evil spirits and the functions they exercise.

But before returning to our text in Daniel, we should give some thought and expression to the term "principalities," a word which appears no less than eight times in the New Testament (Romans 8:38; Ephesians 1:21; 3:10; 6:12; Colossians 1:16; 2:10, 15; Titus 3:1). The commentaries on these Epistles say little about this term. The word "principalities" may be better translated "governments." In some smaller countries the ruler is called the "prince," and the area over which he rules, or exercises authority, is his principality. On three occasions our Lord referred to Satan as "the prince of this world" (John 12:31; 14:30; 16:11), and twice the devil is called "the prince of devils" (or demons) (Matthew 9:34; 12:24). The plurality of the principalities suggests there are many of them, and it is probable that a demon, or prince, is set over each principality. These evil forces are called "the rulers of the darkness of this world" (Ephesians 6:12), and it is this army of evil princes against whom Christ and His own are in conflict.

In Daniel 10 "the prince of the kingdom of Persia" (verse 13) and "the prince of Grecia" (verse 20) are evil spirits who entered into rulers of world governments so as to influence those governments to oppose the people of God and the Word and work of God. What we have here is an actual case of demonism in world government. The vision that Daniel saw, when interpreted, was actually a prophecy of events commencing with his own time and his own people and culminating in the return of Jesus Christ to the earth, all of which included the final overthrow of Satan and his wicked world system. Therefore when Daniel prayed for the spiritual victory of his people, there should be no surprise among us that Satan would interfere with the response from God. It was a conflict of spirits in the spirit-world. An evil angel was at war with a good angel, and since an evil angel cannot do good works, it is conclusive that evil was intended. Such a conflict between a good and a bad angel over the body of Moses is recorded in Jude 9.

But all the human agencies on earth linked with those superhuman agencies in the skies cannot through their combined strength and strategy thwart the purposes of God. The angel said to Daniel, "Lo, Michael, one of the chief princes, came to help me" (10:13). The name Michael means "who is like God." He is called "Michael the archangel" (Jude 9), who will seemingly accompany our Lord when He comes in the air to gather His Church to Himself (1 Thessalonians 4:16).

It appears from Revelation 12, Daniel 10, and Jude 9 that Michael is associated with the warfare carried on between good and bad angels. The important prophetic passage in Revelation, still awaiting fulfillment, points to this fact. John wrote, "And there was war in heaven: Michael and his angels fought against the dragon; and the dragon fought and his angels, And prevailed not; neither was their place found any more in heaven. And the great dragon was cast out, that old serpent, called the Devil, and Satan, which deceiveth the whole world: he was cast out into the earth, and his angels were cast out with him. And I heard a loud voice saying in heaven, Now is come salvation, and strength, and the kingdom of our God, and the power of his Christ: for the accuser of our brethren is cast down, which accused them before our God day and night. And they overcame him by the blood of the Lamb, and by the word of their testimony; and they loved not their lives unto the death" (Revelation 12:7-11). This warfare is not among disorganized forces, but with demons under the well-trained leadership of Satan and the unfallen angels under the leadership of Michael. It will be the final conflict between these two separate hosts when Michael and his angels cast out the devil and his angels (Luke 10:18, cf., Revelation 12:9). In that day Satan will strike his final blow against God's chosen people Israel, but he will be no match for Michael.

After Michael casts him out of Heaven, he will muster his forces for his final all-out attack against Israel and her land. Again he will control the minds of world rulers, bringing them together for the last conflict on earth at Armageddon. John writes, "And I saw three unclean spirits like frogs come out of the mouth of the dragon, and out of the mouth of the beast, and out of the mouth of the false prophet. For they are the spirits of devils, working miracles, which go forth unto the kings of the earth and of the whole world, to gather them to the battle of that great day of God Almighty" (Revelation 16:13-14). This Scripture shows clearly the intimate relationship of demon-spirits with world leaders of nations and governments. But when all the governmental powers of the earth have combined their strength, and that energized by all the combined strength of the demon-spirits, they are utterly overthrown at the coming of our Lord Jesus Christ.

Satan, acting through "the prince of the kingdom of Persia," would have prevented the angel from giving to Daniel the interpretation of the vision, but Michael withstood him. Nothing could separate Daniel from the love of God. Paul wrote, "I am persuaded, that neither death, nor life, nor *angels,* nor *principalities,* nor *powers* . . . shall be able to separate us from the love of God, which is in Christ Jesus our Lord" (Romans 8:38-39). Surely those three terms, "angels, principalities, powers," are related to those evil spirit beings we are discussing, else why would they want to separate us from the love of God? We are in the same kind of conflict that engaged Daniel, "For we wrestle not against flesh and blood, but against principalities, against powers, against the rulers of the darkness of this world, against spiritual wickedness in high places" (Ephesians 6:12). Yes, the devil has his world rulers of darkness, one for Russia, one for China, one for Japan, one for Germany, one for Italy, one for the United States of America, etc., etc. But his time is running out. The future for the Church and Israel is bright with prospect. Isaiah wrote, "And it shall come to pass in that day, that the LORD shall punish the host of the high ones that are on high, and the kings of the earth upon the earth" (Isaiah 24:21). Both the high ones on high (angels) and the kings on the earth, in league with one another, will be brought to nought.

Let us look now at Daniel 10:20. "Then said he, Knowest thou wherefore I come unto thee? and now will I return to fight with the prince of Persia: and when I am gone forth, lo, the prince of Grecia shall come" (10:20). Was the angel telling Daniel that after the conflict with the prince of Persia he was going to engage in combat with another demon, namely "the prince of Grecia"? That is exactly right! At the time the angel spoke this word to Daniel, the Medo-Persian Empire had about two hundred years yet to run before the rise of Greece. Satan was at that time ready with a trained angel awaiting the rise of those few wandering Grecian tribes into a vast and influential empire. But the omniscient and omnipotent God was prepared for the attack upon His people two centuries hence.

I would like to continue this interesting discussion; however, we must hasten on. But before doing so, I must pass on to my reader a helpful paragraph from H. C. Leupold on the ministry of God's angels: "A helpful thought is suggested here: the good angels of God cooperate harmoniously with one another in the performance of their work in the kingdom of God. One helps the other where help is needed. That is one example of how God's will is done in Heaven, according to the third petition. The perfect unity of the Church is in evidence at least in the kingdom of glory. And the fact that certain of these angels of God are great and mighty does not cause any rivalry or opposition among them." [1] An excellent lesson is here for our personal application.

THE CAUSE OF THE ANGEL'S COMING (10:14-21)

Now I am come to make thee understand what shall befall thy people in the latter days: for yet the vision is for many days (10:14).

Here is stated the specific purpose of the angel's coming to Daniel, namely, to impart to him that necessary understanding of that which appeared in the vision. This state-

[1] Leupold, *Daniel*, page 459.

ment from the angel is most significant because it presents the key to the right interpretation of the rest of the book of Daniel. It tells us that the prophecy will have its final fulfillment at the end of the seventieth week and Christ's second advent to earth, and that it reaches to the concluding calamities to befall Israel. If we fail to bear this in mind we are likely to place a wrong interpretation on the meaning of the prophecy. It is this broad scope of the vision that arrested the attention of Daniel. Though there are some preliminary events in the vision, the emphasis is upon the Jewish people in the time of the end.

This news concerning more calamities yet to come for Israel had its effect upon Daniel. He simply stared toward the ground and was speechless (10:15). He was overcome with awe and weakness, awe because of the presence of God's angel, and weakness because of the bad news concerning his people. From the human point of view it was almost too much for the old prophet to bear. But the prophecy in the vision was true, therefore the angel could not withhold this revelation of truth even though it affected Daniel deeply, leaving him with a strange weakness.

Then for the fourth time Daniel experienced the touch of God. There had been the touch of *understanding* (8:18), the touch of *unction* (9:21), the touch of *undergirding* (10:10), and now the touch of *utterance*.

> *And, behold, one like the similitude of the sons of men touched my lips: then I opened my mouth, and spake, and said unto him that stood before me, O my lord, by the vision my sorrows are turned upon me, and I have retained no strength (10:16).*

David prayed, "O Lord, open Thou my lips; and my mouth shall shew forth Thy praise" (Psalm 51:15). Without the touch of God upon our lips we would not speak those things which glorify Him. When God said to Jeremiah, "I ordained thee a prophet unto the nations," Jeremiah replied, "Ah, Lord GOD! behold, I cannot speak." The prophet continued, "Then the LORD put forth His hand, and *touched* my mouth. And the LORD said unto me, Behold, I have put My words in thy mouth" (Jeremiah 1:5-9). Isaiah had a similar experience when God was looking for a man who would speak for Him. The prophet said, "I am a man of unclean lips." Then he added, "Then flew one of the seraphims unto me, having a live coal in his hand, which he had taken with the tongs from off the altar: And he laid it upon my mouth, and said, Lo, this hath *touched* thy lips" (Isaiah 6:5-7). After the divine touch Isaiah went forth to speak for God. A strange weakness overcomes many believers when given the opportunity to speak for Jesus Christ. But to men of prayer and faith, as was Daniel, the touch of utterance comes from God. Daniel said, "Then I opened my mouth, and spake." The touching of our lips is for the purpose of enabling us to speak God's message for Him as well as speaking directly to God.

The cause of the angel's coming is further revealed in the next two verses.

> *Then there came again and touched me one like the appearance of a man, and he strengthened me, And said, O man greatly beloved, fear not: peace be unto thee, be strong, yea, be strong. And when he had spoken unto me, I was strengthened, and said, Let my lord speak; for thou hast strengthened me (10:18-19).*

This is the fifth and final touch of God upon Daniel. It is the touch of *undertaking.* The one who touched Daniel was an angel, but he was in appearance like a man. When Daniel was touched it felt to him like the physical touch of a man. The purpose of this touch was to undertake for Daniel through the impartation of physical strength. Daniel said that immediately before this touch "there remained no strength in me" (10:17). But in his weakness God sent a holy angel to undertake for his faithful servant. When Job was broken in body and spirit he testified of God, "He would put *strength* in me" (Job 23:6). The Psalmist added his testimony saying, "The LORD is the *strength* of my life" (Psalm 27:1); and again, "The LORD is my *strength*. . . . and He is the saving *strength* of His anointed" (Psalm 28:7, 8). "The LORD will give *strength* unto His people" (Psalm 29:11). "God is our refuge and *strength*" (Psalm 46:1; 81:1). "God is the *strength* of my heart" (Psalm 73:26). Men of prayer and faith are those who experience the divine touch which undertakes for them in the time of human weakness. Such men were Moses, who could say, "The LORD is my *strength*" (Exodus 15:2); David (2 Samuel 22:33); Isaiah (Isaiah 12:2); Jeremiah (Jeremiah 16:19); Habbakuk (Habbakuk 3:19); and Paul (2 Corinthians 12:9-10). One of the great and familiar promises in God's Word, which has encouraged many saints down through the centuries, was penned by Isaiah: "Fear thou not; for I am with thee: be not dismayed; for I am thy God: I will *strengthen* thee; yea, I will help thee; yea, I will uphold thee with the right hand of My righteousness" (Isaiah 41:10). Ezra bore witness to such a touch from the Almighty when he said, "I was *strengthened* as the hand of the LORD my God was upon me" (Ezra 7:28).

Many churches today are marked by a well-organized, heavily staffed, and adequately financed impotency. This manifest weakness lies in the fact that too many church leaders have cut themselves off from the source of power; they are out of touch with God. The need of the hour is a fresh touch from Heaven, and I believe this touch can come to every believer in Christ who wants it and will seek it. When it comes it will not be the touch of an angel but the touch of the indwelling Holy Spirit. When we confess our sins and cease to grieve and quench Him, a new and strange power will possess us, providing a divine enduement and an enabling unmatched by human cleverness. Our Lord said, "Ye shall receive power, after that the Holy Ghost is come upon you" (Acts 1:8). In two of Paul's prison prayers he requested of God that this touch would be given to the churches, and then he wrote to the believers at Ephesus: "For this cause I bow my knees unto the Father of our Lord Jesus Christ, Of whom the whole family in heaven and earth is named, That He would grant you, according to the riches of His glory, to be *strengthened* with might by His Spirit in the inner man" (Ephesians 3:14-16). (See also Colossians 1:11.) May God touch your life and mine as He touched Daniel and others.

In addition to the physical touch, there came to Daniel the encouraging word, *"Fear not:* peace be unto thee" (10:19). Here we see at once how God comes to His own to allay their fears and speak peace. The Word of God contains many such instances.

When Abram feared his *foes*, God said, *"Fear not*, Abram: I am thy shield" (Genesis 15:1). To Abram came the assuring word of God's *protection*. The child of God need not fear men or demons because God is his shield to protect him against such fears. When Moses feared Og, the king of Bashan, the Lord assured Moses, *"Fear* him *not:* for I have delivered him into thy hand" (Numbers 21:34). Fear not!

When Hagar feared *famine*, God sent the message to her, saying, *"Fear not.* . . . And God opened her eyes, and she saw a well of water" (Genesis 21:15-21). To Hagar came the assuring word of God's *provision*. A similar "fear not" was spoken to Isaac, Abraham's son. Isaac had large herds and flocks needing an ample supply of water. The old homestead had been adequately supplied by the wells that his father Abraham had dug. But the Philistines had filled in the wells, threatening a water shortage and ultimate famine. Then God appeared to him and said, "*Fear not*, for I am with thee, and will bless thee" (Genesis 26:24). No child of God living in the will of God need ever fear a shortage of his material needs. David testified, "I have been young, and now am old; yet have I not seen the righteous forsaken, nor his seed begging bread" (Psalm 37:25). Paul testified from a prison cell, "But my God shall supply all your need according to His riches in glory by Christ Jesus" (Philippians 4:19). Fear not!

When Jacob fainted because of *faithlessness*, God spoke to him one night and said, "*Fear not* to go down into Egypt; for I will there make of thee a great nation: I will go down with thee into Egypt; and I will also surely bring thee up again" (Genesis 46:3-4). To the faithless, fainting Jacob came the assuring word of God's *promise*. Why did he need this word of promise? It appears quite clear. When his sons returned from Egypt and told him Joseph was alive, the record says, "And Jacob's heart fainted, for he believed them not" (Genesis 45:25-26). Unbelief has been the cause of much heart trouble. If your heart is failing because of unbelief, turn to the promises of God, "for He is faithful that promised" (Hebrews 10:23). "For all the promises of God in Him are yea, and in Him Amen, unto the glory of God by us" (2 Corinthians 1:20). His promises are called "great and precious" (2 Peter 1:4). Believe them! Appropriate them by faith! The Old Testament heroes "through faith . . . obtained promises" (Hebrews 11:33). The next time you set out to read through your Bible, note the oft-repeated phrase, "as He promised," and your heart will reach out by faith. (See Exodus 12:25; Numbers 14:40; Deuteronomy 1:11; 6:3; 9:28; 10:9; 12:20; 19:8; 26:18; Joshua 22:4; 23:5, 10, 15; 1 Kings 2:24; 5:12; 8:20, 56; 2 Chronicles 6:20.) Fear not!

When Moses faced the natural *forces* of the Red Sea, God said, "*Fear* ye *not*, stand still, and see the salvation of the LORD which He will shew to you to day" (Exodus 14:13). To Moses had come the assuring word of God's *providence*, and the national leader passed the word on to his people. The fear of natural forces such as floods, hurricanes, earthquakes, tornadoes, lightning, and the like have played havoc with men's nerves. This fear is a common one, even among Christians, but we sometimes fail to reckon on the providence of God, His foresight and care over His own. He is not only the Creator of all things, but "by Him all things consist" (Colossians 1:17); that is, because of Him all things harmonize or hold together. The forces of nature might at times seem to be out of control, but actually God is "upholding all things by the word of His power" (Hebrews 1:3). The real test of our faith in God's providence is a fearless heart when the forces of nature appear to be against us. Fear not!

When Joshua feared *failure* at Ai, "The LORD said unto Joshua, *Fear not*, neither be thou dismayed: take all the people of war with thee, and arise, go up to Ai: see, I have given into thy hand the king of Ai, and his people, and his city, and his land: And thou shalt do to Ai and her king as thou didst unto Jericho and her king: only the spoil thereof, and the cattle thereof, shall ye take for a prey unto yourselves: lay thee an ambush for the city behind it" (Joshua 8:1-2). To Joshua came the assuring word of *prospect*. The sin of Achan resulted in a tragic defeat of Israel's army at Ai. Joshua, the commander-in-chief, was stricken with fear. At that moment the prospect for the nation's future was not bright. Then Jehovah spoke His encouraging "Fear not" to his distraught child. The sin had been confessed and judged, and God assured Joshua that the past could be forgotten and that one who had failed in the past could go on and succeed. Failure need not spell finished. Do not permit a past failure to haunt you and spoil your future. David sinned, but when he confessed and forsook his sin God gave him another chance. Jonathan's encouraging word to the failing, fleeing David was, "*Fear not:* for the hand of Saul my father shall not find thee" (1 Samuel 23:17). The cause of David's failure did not blot out the bright prospect for the future. Never allow failure to strike fear to your heart, but say with the Apostle Paul, "This one thing I do, forgetting those things which are behind, and reaching forth unto those things which are before, I press toward the mark for the prize of the high calling of God in Christ Jesus" (Philippians 3:13-14). Fear not!

When Israel feared the *future* God spoke through the Prophet Isaiah assuring them of His *presence*: "But now thus saith the LORD that created thee, O Jacob, and He that formed thee, O Israel, *Fear not:* for I have redeemed thee, I have called thee by thy name; thou art Mine. When thou passest through the waters, I will be with thee; and through the rivers, they shall not overflow thee: when thou walkest through the fire, thou shalt not be burned; neither shall the flame kindle upon thee" (Isaiah 43:1-2). No doubt there are many believers in Christ in our own day who have not learned to leave their future in God's hands. There is the fear of loneliness, of losing salvation, of bodily harm, and on and on. Many Christians have worried themselves to sickness of mind and body through fear of the future. How foolish! God says to His own, "I have created thee and I have redeemed thee. Thou art Mine." Think of it! We are His possession by both His creative and redemptive right. These two verses from Isaiah's pen are freighted with encouragement:

> God's power—"The LORD . . . created thee."
> God's purchase—"I have redeemed thee."

God's possession—"Thou art Mine."
God's presence—"I will be with thee."
God's protection—"The rivers . . . shall not overflow
thee . . . thou shalt not be burned."

The Lord Jesus said, "Lo, I am with you alway, even unto
the end of the world. Amen" (Matthew 28:20). Fear not!

God's "Fear not" spoken to Daniel gave strength to heart
and mind immediately. Daniel testified, "And when he had
spoken unto me, I was strengthened" (10:19).

Daniel was now ready to receive the message and interpretation of the vision. This is the subject of first importance
to be discussed in the concluding two chapters, dealing with
matters of which God alone has the truth. So the angel said
to Daniel, "But I will shew thee that which is noted in the
scripture of truth: and there is none that holdeth with me
in these things, but Michael your prince" (10:21). Chapter
10 has shown how Daniel was being prepared to receive the
revelation which follows in chapter 11. God only has accurate records of the future, and He reveals that future to those
who love Him and are thus prepared to receive it. The
Apostle Paul stresses this fact in 1 Corinthians 2:9-11. So
Daniel was about to receive that prophetic revelation which
was recorded in the Scripture of truth. It is healthy for us to
bear in mind that God shows His truth, not to the natural
(or unregenerate) man (1 Corinthians 2:14), but to the
spiritually minded (1 Corinthians 2:15-16). The child of
God who is in fear and unrest is not ready to understand the
prophetic Word. The heart that does not enjoy the peace of
God will not enjoy nor desire the Word of God.

CHAPTER ELEVEN

CHAPTER ELEVEN

As was noted earlier, chapters 10, 11, and 12 combine to present one prophetic vision from the time of Darius the Mede to the second coming of Christ to the earth at the end of the seventieth week. Moreover, that which is written here is "the scripture of truth" (10:21), suggesting that it is true prophecy inspired by God. Our Lord Jesus Christ placed His seal of approval upon the contents of the book of Daniel in His statements in Matthew 24:15 and Mark 13:14.

Before we proceed with the study of chapter 11, I would remind the reader that the contents of this book were not intended for classroom use nor for the scholar who desires to pursue a critical examination of the text. Such an attempt here would not be in keeping with the rest of the book. For those who desire a more laborious examination of the historical data, I refer you to the selected bibliography listed at the end of this book. Also much helpful information will be found in the historical and prophetic commentary of 561 pages by Samuel Sparkes, published in 1858.

Here in Daniel 11 we have a clear demonstration of two facts: the first is that prophecy sheds light on the future by foretelling it, and the second is that history is a verification of prophecy. As a matter of fact, history is so accurately foretold here that the critics claim a much later date for the writing of Daniel than that held by evangelical scholars.

Daniel lived till about 534 B.C., which was after the third year of Cyrus' reign. To say that the book of Daniel was not written until the second century, one must discredit it as a fraud. We believe the book belongs to the time of that Daniel of whom Ezekiel wrote (Ezekiel 14:14, 20), and therefore is a revelation of the miracle of prophecy. Why should it be thought a thing incredible that God should foretell the course of history? Even though there are some historical difficulties that are not clear, we part company with those who date the book of Daniel between 167 B.C. and 160 B.C.

Though Daniel never claimed to be a prophet, and nowhere in the Old Testament is he called a prophet, part of the book that bears his name is prophecy. This "scripture of truth" (10:21), is a part of the "all scripture" inspired by the Holy Spirit (2 Timothy 3:16), and written by the holy man Daniel as he was carried along by the Holy Spirit (2 Peter 1:21). Here is one of the most amazing prophecies in all the Bible.

The division between chapter 10 and 11 is unfortunate. Verse 1 of chapter 11 should be included in chapter 10; therefore we will commence our study of the chapter at verse 2. However, dividing the chapter now under consideration is not so simple a task. From our point of view some of the chapter is now history. It was all prophecy when Daniel saw the vision, for he saw the details in advance of their actual happening. That portion of the vision which is now history stands as a verification of prophecy. Daniel understood these things before they came to pass; we see them in the light of historical verification. Possibly the most difficult portion of the interpretation is to determine where the gap appears in the chapter, that is, where the fulfilled prophecy ends and the unfulfilled begins.

FROM AHASUERUS TO ANTIOCHUS
(11:2-20)

And now will I shew thee the truth. Behold, there shall stand up yet three kings in Persia; and the fourth shall be far richer than they all: and by his strength through his riches he shall stir up all against the realm of Grecia. And a mighty king shall stand up, that shall rule with great dominion, and do according to his will. And when he shall stand up, his kingdom shall be broken, and shall be divided toward the four winds of heaven; and not to his posterity, nor according to his dominion which he ruled: for his kingdom shall be plucked up, even for others beside those. And the king of the south shall be strong, and one of his princes; and he shall be strong above him, and have dominion; his dominion shall be a great dominion. And in the end of years they shall join themselves together; for the king's daughter of the south shall come to the king of the north to make an agreement: but she shall not retain the power of the arm; neither shall he stand, nor his arm: but she shall be given up, and they that brought her, and he that begat her, and he that strengthened her in these times. But out of a branch of her roots shall one stand up in his estate, which shall come with an army, and shall enter into the fortress of the king of the north, and shall deal against them, and shall prevail: And shall also carry captives into Egypt their gods, with their princes, and with their precious vessels of silver and of gold; and he shall continue more years than the king of the north. So the king of the south shall come into his kingdom, and shall return into his own land. But his sons shall be stirred up, and shall assemble a multitude of great forces: and one shall certainly come, and overflow, and pass through: then shall he return, and be stirred up, even to his fortress. And the king of the south shall be moved with choler, and shall come forth and fight with him, even with the king of the north: and he shall set forth a great multitude; but the multitude shall be given into his hand. And when he hath taken away the multitude, his heart shall be lifted up; and he shall cast down many ten thousands: but he shall not be strengthened by it. For the king of the north shall return, and shall set forth a multitude greater than the former, and shall certainly come after certain years with a great army and with much riches. And in those times there shall be many stand up against the king of the south: also the robbers of thy people shall exalt themselves to establish the vision; but they shall fall. So the king of the north shall come, and cast up a mount, and take the most fenced cities: and the arms of the south shall not withstand, neither his chosen people, neither shall there be any strength to withstand. But he that cometh against him shall do according to his own will, and none shall stand before him: and he shall stand in the glorious land, which by his hand shall be consumed. He shall also set his face to enter with the strength of his whole kingdom, and upright ones with him; thus shall he do: and he shall give him the daughter of women, corrupting her: but she shall not stand on his side, neither be for him. After this shall he turn his face unto the isles, and shall take many: but a prince for his own behalf shall cause the reproach offered by him to cease; without his own reproach he shall cause it to turn upon him. Then he shall turn his face toward the fort of his own land: but he shall stumble and fall, and not be found. Then shall stand up in his estate a raiser of taxes in the glory of the kingdom: but within few days he shall be destroyed, neither in anger, nor in battle (Daniel 11:2-20).

Daniel was told that there would be three kings of Persia, followed by a fourth who would be richer than them all. These three kings were Ahasuerus (Ezra 4:6; Esther 1:1), Artaxerxes, and Darius Hystaspis (all of whom are referred to in Ezra 4:6-24). The fourth king of great wealth is undoubtedly Xerxes, who invaded Greece in 480 B.C., accumulating riches through conquest. The secular historical records tell us that this fourth king, Xerxes, spent four years gathering together and training more than two million men from every part of his empire. Now there were more than four kings in the Medo-Persian Empire, but these, along with details of military expeditions, were omitted from Daniel's vision. Verse 2 described the breast and arms of silver which formed a part of the image in chapter 2. When revealed to Daniel this was a prophecy of the future, but now we are looking back to it as history. The vast army of Xerxes passed over the Hellespont in seven days and nights on bridges of boats which were laid for that purpose. The Greeks withstood him in that bloody slaughter at the straits of Thermopylae, but he went on to conquer. Thus did Xerxes "stir up all against the realm of Grecia" (11:2).

In verse 3 the "mighty king" is Alexander the Great. He avenged his own defeat by invading and destroying the Persian Empire in 332 B.C. His kingdom was represented in the belly and thighs of brass (2:32) and the rough goat (8:5-8, 21-22). As was mentioned before (8:8, 22), his kingdom was divided into four parts, but none of his successors were able to rule with his strength and authority. While Alexander was still rising, he was cut off.

Keep in mind the fact that Daniel was not attempting here to write the entire history of Persia and Greece, but merely those details which were shown him in the vision. This accounts for more than one hundred years of history between verses 2 and 3.

Every student of history knows that Daniel 11:1-4 was literally fulfilled. It is not likely that any of the rulers whose names were mentioned had any idea whatever that through them the prophecies of God were being fulfilled. But they were, nevertheless, so that we have here either a remarkable fulfillment of a divinely revealed prophecy or else a horrible literary fraud. We know the latter is unthinkable, because we have here the inerrancy of "the scripture of truth." Such are the ways of God. On this interpretation of verses 1-4 all evangelical scholars are agreed.

It is at verse 5 that we meet with a difference of interpretation on the part of evangelicals. Most of the commentators are in agreement with the view that verses 5-35 constitute a detailed prophecy of the conflicts between Syria and Egypt following the dividing of the Grecian Empire and the rise of Antiochus Epiphanes of Syria. Then, beginning at verse 36, the prophecy passes into the distant future, beyond the present Church Age, to the time of the end and the last wicked ruler, the Antichrist. This is the interpretation we will follow in our present study.

However, there have been men of God, equally capable in their interpretation of the Scriptures, who omit entirely the separate period from verse 5 to verse 36 as referring to the wars of the Ptolemies to the rise of Antiochus Epiphanes. They teach that at verse 5 the prophecy passes from the Grecian Empire directly to the end times and the Antichrist. G. H. Lang has written well on this view; however, he has left this writer unconvinced that he is correct.

Verses 5-20 record the wars between Syria and Egypt. They are referred to in terms of geographical relationship to Palestine, the Holy Land being the point of geographical definition (see Deuteronomy 32:8-9). "The king of the south" (11:5) means Egypt, being south of Palestine. "The king of the north" (11:6), then, is Syria, being north of Palestine. From here on to verse 20 everything has to do with the king of the south and the king of the north. What we see here is an accurate account of the continuing conflicts between the Egyptian Ptolemies of the south and the Syrian Seleucidae of the north. The details of this period, covering about 130 years, were not given to Daniel, however the records are available in history books.[1] Dr. Ironside suggested, as his reason why only two of the four kingdoms are involved here, the fact that the angel told Daniel he would show him what would befall his people, the Jews, and that only the kings of the north and south are directly related to Israel and the land of Palestine.

> *And in the end of years they shall join themselves together; for the king's daughter of the south shall come to [literally, be married to] the king of the north to make an agreement (11:6).*

The alliance between the two rulers was effected through the marriage of the Egyptian princess, Berenice, daughter of Ptolemy II in the south, to Antiochus Theos (the divine) in the north. This marriage could be consummated only after Antiochus had divorced his wife Laodice. It was a political marriage for the purpose of establishing an alliance between the two rulers.

> *But she shall not retain the power of the arm; neither shall he stand, nor his arm: but she shall be given up, and*

[1] Wilbur M. Smith, *Egypt in Biblical Prophecy*, pages 157-188.

they that brought her, and he that begat her, and he that
strengthened her in these times (11:6).

Here is given the prophecy that the marriage of Berenice
and Antiochus, as well as the alliance between the kings of
the north and south, would end in calamity. Berenice did
not retain the power of the king's wife. When her father
died not long after the marriage, Antiochus Theos aban-
doned her and brought back his first wife, Laodice. Though
she did return to him, she never forgave him for putting her
away in order that he might be free to marry the Egyptian
Berenice. In her heart lay a secret determination to gain
her revenge. At the earliest opportunity she had both her
husband Antiochus and Berenice murdered. There was thus
fulfilled the prophecy, "she [Berenice] shall not retain the
power of the arm; neither shall he stand, nor his arm"
(11:6). With the throne vacant, Laodice had her son
Seleucus Callinicus crowned in his father's stead.

But all was not to remain peaceful. When word reached
Egypt that Berenice had been slain, her brother Ptolemy
Euergetes set out to avenge his sister's death. He led an
army north to Syria, seized the port of Antioch, sacked the
temples, and carried back to Egypt large quantities of gold,
silver, and Syrian idols. All of this was the fulfillment of
that which Daniel saw in the prophetic vision.

> *Out of a branch of her roots shall one stand up in his*
> *estate, which shall come with an army, and shall enter*
> *into the fortress of the king of the north, and shall deal*
> *against them, and shall prevail: And shall also carry cap-*
> *tives into Egypt their gods, with their princes, and with*
> *their precious vessels of silver and of gold; and he shall*
> *continue more years than the king of the north (11:7-8).*

Here Egypt is identified as the king of the south. Jerome
reported that Ptolemy Euergetes brought back with him

40,000 talents of silver, 4,000 talents of gold, and 2,000 costly idol statues.

This victory for the south did not mean the cessation of conflict between Syria and Egypt. Verse 9, according to Leupold, should read, "But one shall come against the realm of the king of the south but shall return to his own land." Commenting on this verse Leupold says, "To have the king of the south carry on this expedition is a meaningless translation (A.V.). Therefore the third person singular should be construed as involving an indefinite subject—'one shall come.' This one is the Syrian king Seleucus Callinicus who reigned 247-226 B.C., and of whom it is known that he did conduct an expedition against Egypt, though without success. The Syrian had to 'return to his own land.'" [2] Dr. A. C. Gaebelein, in 1911 published his book on Daniel, in which he set forth a literal translation of verse 9 as follows: "And the same (king of the north) shall come into the realm of the king of the south, but shall return into his own land." In fulfillment of this prophecy, Gaebelein comments, "In 240 B.C. Seleucus Callinicus the king of the north invaded Egypt. He had to return defeated. His fleet perished in a storm." [3] This was a further fulfillment of the prophecy in Daniel's vision.

> *But his sons shall be stirred up, and shall assemble a multitude of great forces: and one shall certainly come, and overflow, and pass through: then shall he return, and be stirred up, even to his fortress (11:10).*

The "sons" mentioned here are the sons of the Syrian king, Seleucus Callinicus: Seleucus III and Antiochus III.

---

[2] Leupold, *Daniel,* page 485.
[3] Arno C. Gaebelein, *Daniel,* pages 169-170.

The sons were stirred up because of their father's defeat and vowed to carry the fight to ultimate victory. One of the sons, Seleucus III, being a weak and undisciplined prince, came to an untimely end. His brother Antiochus III is the "one" in the text who should "certainly come, and overflow, and pass through." He assembled a large army, took full command, and marched through Palestine as far as Gaza, the Egyptian fortress. I take the words "pass through" to refer to passing through Palestine. After much killing and plundering, Antiochus returned northward to Syria, victorious as was prophesied.

Verses 11 and 12 record the next stage in this long series of wars, but now it is the king of the south who is the aggressor.

> *And the king of the south shall be moved with choler, and shall come forth and fight with him, even with the king of the north: and he shall set forth a great multitude; but the multitude shall be given into his hand. And when he hath taken away the multitude, his heart shall be lifted up; and he shall cast down many ten thousands: but he shall not be strengthened by it (11:11-12).*

The feelings of the Egyptian monarch are expressed by the words, "moved with choler," meaning he "became embittered." The people of Egypt rallied about their king to avenge themselves of Syria's attack, so that a great army stood ready to march northward toward Syria. The king of the north likewise had a great army to defend the attack; however, the southern army defeated him at Raphia, not far from the Gaza fortress. As a result of the southern victory, Ptolemy's heart was "lifted up" with pride. Even though he slew tens of thousands of the enemy, he did not remain strong, or, as was prophesied, "he shall not be strengthened by it" (11:12). He returned to celebrate his victory in a life of dissolution produced by sensual pleasures, therefore he did not prove himself strong.

For about thirteen years there were no open hostilities between the two warring kingdoms. In the meantime the king of the north, who had been chafing because of earlier defeat, was building a stronger army than any previous to that time. Let us look at the prophecy as given to Daniel more than three hundred years before its fulfillment.

> *For the king of the north shall return, and shall set forth a multitude greater than the former, and shall certainly come after the certain years with a great army and with much riches. And in those times there shall many stand up against the king of the south: also the robbers of thy people shall exalt themselves to establish the vision; but they shall fall. So the king of the north shall come, and cast up a mount, and take the most fenced cities: and the arms of the south shall not withstand, neither his chosen people, neither shall there be any strength to withstand. But he that cometh against him shall do according to his own will, and none shall stand before him: and he shall stand in the glorious land, which by his hand shall be consumed. He shall also set his face to enter with the strength of his whole kingdom, and upright ones with him; thus shall he do: and he shall give him the daughter of women, corrupting her: but she shall not stand on his side, neither be for him. After this shall he turn his face unto the isles, and shall take many: but a prince for his own behalf shall cause the reproach offered by him to cease; without his own reproach he shall cause it to turn upon him. Then he shall turn his face toward the fort of his own land: but he shall stumble and fall, and not be found. Then shall stand up in his estate a raiser of taxes in the glory of the kingdom: but within few days he shall be destroyed, neither in anger, nor in battle (11:13-20).*

Many details can be gleaned from historical records which would further reveal the accuracy of this amazing prophecy; however, we shall attempt to condense the highlights in as few words as possible.

This long series of wars between the Seleucidae, the rulers of Syria, and the Ptolemies, the rulers of Egypt, were fought over a period of approximately 130 years. While there were many kings who reigned and died during that time, the identity of those kings always remained the same, that is, "the king of the north" and "the king of the south." The records show a series of victories and defeats for both sides. The conflict now under consideration (11:13-20) took place during the reign of Antiochus III (the Great) of Syria, 224-187 B.C., and Ptolemy Philopator of Egypt, 225-205 B.C.

Having lost the previous battle, the king of the north was here the aggressor. He was well prepared for the battle (11:15). He marched southward through the "glorious land" (Palestine), taking possession as he went (11:16), and encountering practically no opposition. The last words in verse 16 mean that Palestine at that time was entirely in the hand of the king of the north. Already Daniel's people were feeling the pressure of that which would befall them, according to the angel's words to Daniel (10:14).

Verse 17 speaks of a fact that has since been verified by history. Antiochus was so intent upon victory that he proposed to Ptolemy Philopator that his young daughter Cleopatra be pledged in marriage to Philopator's infant son and heir to Egypt's throne. The ruling families agreed, and in the process of time the marriage was consummated. This seems to be the generally accepted meaning of the words, "and he [the king of the north] shall give him [the son of the king of the south] the daughter [in marriage]." Antiochus had schemed that his daughter would be faithful to her father, even after the marriage, thereby using her or "corrupting her" to gain an advantage over the king of Egypt. But the plot failed. Instead of remaining her father's ally and thus loyal to Syria, Cleopatra pledged her love and loyalty to her Egyptian husband. The girl felt it her solemn duty to be faithful to her husband, and so another phase of the prophecy in the vision was fulfilled, namely "she shall not stand on his side, neither be for him" (11:17).

When Antiochus' plot failed to control the young Egyptian king, he sought to gain control of the Mediterranean coastline of Asia Minor as well as the outlying islands. Such action aroused the ire of the Romans, who exercised a mandate over some of those islands. A Roman prince forced Antiochus to desist from his aggression, and so the Syrian king returned to his own country where he declined and was heard of no more. This explains in some measure the contents of verses 18 and 19. At this point in history we are introduced to the iron kingdom, that fourth kingdom of the dream image in Daniel 2.

> *Then shall stand up in his estate a raiser of taxes in the glory of the kingdom: but within few days he shall be destroyed, neither in anger, nor in battle (11:20).*

After the death of Antiochus, Seleucus Philopator his son attempted to rule Syria. His nation was so heavily indebted to the Romans, because of the poor condition in which his father had left the kingdom, the only way he knew to raise the enormous annual tribute was to levy heavy taxes. He is here called "a raiser [exactor] of taxes." After a short time he was broken (or overthrown). There was mystery attached to his demise, the Scripture merely stating that his death was "neither in anger, nor in battle."

When all of this was revealed to Daniel it was yet future, but now it has come to pass with remarkable accuracy.

FROM ANTIOCHUS TO THE ANTICIPATION OF ANTICHRIST (11:21-35)

And in his estate shall stand up a vile person, to whom they shall not give the honour of the kingdom: but he shall come in peaceably, and obtain the kingdom by flatteries. And with the arms of a flood shall they be overflown from before him, and shall be broken; yea, also the prince of the covenant. And after the league made with him he shall work deceitfully: for he shall come up, and shall become strong with a small people. He shall enter peaceably even upon the fattest places of the province; and he shall do that which his fathers have not done, nor his fathers' fathers; he shall scatter among them the prey, and spoil, and riches: yea, and he shall forecast his devices against the strong holds, even for a time. And he shall stir up his power and his courage against the king of the south with a great army; and the king of the south shall be stirred up to battle with a very great and mighty army; but he shall not stand: for they shall forecast devices against him. Yea, they that feed of the portion of his meat shall destroy him, and his army shall overflow: and many shall fall down slain. And both these kings' hearts shall be to do mischief, and they shall speak lies at one table; but it shall not prosper: for yet the end shall be at the time appointed. Then shall he return into his land with great riches; and his heart shall be against the holy covenant; and he shall do exploits, and return to his own land. At the time appointed he shall return, and come toward the south; but it shall not be as the former, or as the latter. For the ships of Chittim shall come against him: there-

*fore he shall be grieved, and return, and have indignation
against the holy covenant: so shall he do; he shall even
return, and have intelligence with them that forsake the
holy covenant. And arms shall stand on his part, and they
shall pollute the sanctuary of strength, and shall take
away the daily sacrifice, and they shall place the abomination that maketh desolate. And such as do wickedly
against the covenant shall be corrupt by flatteries: but
the people that do know their God shall be strong, and do
exploits. And they that understand among the people shall
instruct many: yet they shall fall by the sword, and by
flame, by captivity, and by spoil, many days. Now when
they shall fall, they shall be holpen with a little help: but
many shall cleave to them with flatteries. And some of
them of understanding shall fall, to try them, and to purge,
and to make them white, even to the time of the end: because it is yet for a time appointed (Daniel 11:21-35).*

These verses contain that part of the prophecy in Daniel's
vision which have to do with Antiochus Epiphanes, one of
the most infamous kings in history. His importance in history is suggested by the amount of space and detail given to
the description of his career. His reign extended over a period of approximately eleven years, 175-164 B.C. He is the
same person who was prophesied as the "little horn" in
Daniel 8:9-14. He was the younger son of Antiochus the
Great but without legal claim to the royal throne.

The prophecy described him as "a vile person, to whom
they shall not give the honour of the kingdom: but he shall
come in peaceably, and obtain the kingdom by flatteries"
(11:21). He distinguished himself among the people, who
knew him as a "vile" or contemptible person. He did not
become king by right or by popular demand but rather by
means of his own clever intrigues. He was a man of deceit

and reckless prodigality. He came to the throne with the promise of a program of peace, as will the Antichrist whom he foreshadows (cf., Revelation 6:2), but like the Antichrist will do, he showed himself to be a blasphemous madman with a hatred against Jehovah and the Jews. He has been called by many "the antichrist of the Old Testament."

Very early in his career Antiochus Epiphanes proved to be anything but a man of peace. The prophecy said, "And with the arms of a flood shall they be overflown from before him, and shall be broken; yea, also the prince of the covenant" (11:22). He swept all resistance before him, successfully defeating his enemies. It is not a simple matter to identify "the prince of the covenant," however several commentators link him with the Jewish high priest, Onias III. We do associate the "covenant" here with the holy covenant of God's people Israel (cf., verses 28, 30, 32). This king formed leagues with other nations, but being the cruel and crafty man that he was, his mode of operation was to practice deceit. The angel prophesied of him, "And after the league made with him he shall work deceitfully" (11:23).

By stealth he plundered the most fertile and productive spots in all the province and then under pretense of good will he distributed the spoils among the people (11:24). By making an exhibition of generosity he further deceived the people. His goal soon was to come out in the open when he used his power and courage in a military attack "against the king of the south" (11:25). He wanted control of Egypt and her wealth, and though many battles were fought and losses were heavy on both sides, Egypt could not stand against Antiochus. The end came as the prophecy said it would, "The king of the south shall be stirred up to battle with a very great and mighty army; but he shall not stand" (11:25). Notice once more that the victory of Antiochus was to be credited to "devices." Even those who worked closely with the king of the south, that is, men who ate at the king's table, turned against their ruler. We are not told how Antiochus successfuly operated his conspiracy within the top administration in the Egyptian government, but we do know his wicked plan worked, at least for awhile (11:26).

> *And both these kings' hearts shall be to do mischief, and they shall speak lies at one table; but it shall not prosper: for yet the end shall be at the time appointed. Then shall he return into his land with great riches; and his heart shall be against the holy covenant; and he shall do exploits, and return to his own land (11:27-28).*

The two kings are Antiochus and possibly Philometor, however we cannot be certain as to the occasion referred to in the text. We are told that when they sat down at the bargaining table neither had honorable motives nor employed honorable methods. They spoke lies to each other, and in the end neither prospered as the result of their treachery. Deceit and lying must ultimately fail because there is a "time appointed" when all that man builds up must face the final verdict of Almighty God. We have seen this principle at work in our own lifetime when the treaties of men who deceived and lied proved worthless and the men themselves toppled to the dust. Yes, such men appear to prosper for a season! Antiochus returned to Syria with many possessions which were the spoils of his military conquests. As he passed through Palestine to get to Syria he showed his hatred against the Temple of God and the holy covenant. But as the following verses show, his second campaign in Egypt was not successful.

> *At the time appointed he shall return, and come toward the south; but it shall not be as the former, or as the latter. For the ships of Chittim shall come against him: therefore*

*he shall be grieved, and return, and have indignation
against the holy covenant: so shall he do; he shall even
return, and have intelligence with them that forsake the
holy covenant (11:29-30).*

When Antiochus believed that he should begin another
campaign against Egypt, there were unseen forces at work
of which he knew nothing. Names and dates are not important here. What matters is that this campaign was "at the
time appointed," that is, at a time when divine providence
and power were at work. There are times when God sees to
it that the deeds of wicked men must contribute to the fulfillment of His purposes. The Psalmist wrote, "Surely the
wrath of man shall praise Thee: the remainder of wrath
shalt Thou restrain" (Psalm 76:10). History has borne this
out on not a few occasions. Our text in Daniel prophesied
that this later military campaign of Antiochus "shall not be
as the former." Although he arrived within a short distance
of the city of Alexandria, there he met disappointment when
a Roman leader confronted him with the demand that he
quit Egypt. At first Antiochus hesitated, actually stalling to
gain time, but the Roman staff demanded an immediate
decision. Antiochus knew well the strength of the Romans,
and so, though dissatisfied and disgruntled, he agreed to
withdraw from Egypt at once. All powers at that time had
to give way to the rise of the fourth empire, the Roman legs
of iron (2:33, 40). "The ships of Chittim" (11:30) are interpreted by most commentators to be the Roman fleet. They
are mentioned in the prophecy of Balaam (Numbers 24:24).
Chittim is the modern Cyprus.

"Therefore he shall be grieved, and return" (11:30). After
he was intimidated, Antiochus returned north. Embittered
by his humiliating treatment at the hands of the Romans,
he once more showed his hostility against the people of God.
Again he directed his hatred "against the holy covenant" as

on a previous occasion (11:28). However, this time there were apostate Jews who betrayed their own people and took sides with their enemy.

> *And arms shall stand on his part, and they shall pollute the sanctuary of strength, and shall take away the daily sacrifice, and they shall place the abomination that maketh desolate. And such as do wickedly against the covenant shall he corrupt by flatteries: but the people that do know their God shall be strong, and do exploits (11:31-32).*

The word "arms" here means "forces" or "armies." In 170 B.C. Antiochus came against Jerusalem, forebade the daily sacrifice in the Temple, and poured the blood and broth of a swine upon the altar. This, however, was not "the abomination of desolation" referred to by our Lord in Matthew 24:15 and Mark 13:14. The Lord Jesus spoke of that which was yet future in the coming days of the Antichrist. Antiochus not only took away the daily sacrifice, desecrated and profaned the sanctuary, but he also won over many Jews to his side by the use of smooth words. However, there was that class of Jews, "the people that do know their God," who remained faithful to Jehovah and the teachings of the prophets. Of these faithful ones the prophecy says they "shall be strong, and do exploits," that is, they shall ultimately achieve their purpose with a notable measure of success. But the final victory would not come until after there had come to the Jews much suffering, persecution, and death. Most of the prophecies in this vision up to this point were fulfilled during that period between the Testaments. Verses 33 and 34 assured Daniel that during those silent years God would have His faithful instructors among His people. No matter how bitter the persecution might become, there would always be that "little help" (11:34) until the great and final deliverance in "the time of the end."

FROM ANTICHRIST TO ARMAGEDDON
(11:36-45)

*And the king shall do according to his will; and he shall
exalt himself, and magnify himself above every god, and
shall speak marvellous things against the God of gods, and
shall prosper till the indignation be accomplished: for that
that is determined shall be done. Neither shall he regard
the God of his fathers, nor the desire of women, nor regard
any god: for he shall magnify himself above all. But in his
estate shall he honour the God of forces: and a god whom
his fathers knew not shall he honour with gold, and silver,
and with precious stones, and pleasant things. Thus shall
he do in the most strong holds with a strange god, whom
he shall acknowledge and increase with glory: and he
shall cause them to rule over many, and shall divide the
land for gain. And at the time of the end shall the king of
the south push at him: and the king of the north shall come
against him like a whirlwind, with chariots, and with horsemen, and with many ships; and he shall enter into the
countries, and shall overflow and pass over. He shall enter
also into the glorious land, and many countries shall be
overthrown: but these shall escape out of his hand, even
Edom, and Moab, and the chief of the children of Ammon.
He shall stretch forth his hand also upon the countries:
and the land of Egypt shall not escape. But he shall have
power over the treasures of gold and of silver, and over
all the precious things of Egypt: and the Libyans and the
Ethiopians shall be at his steps. But tidings out of the east
and out of the north shall trouble him: therefore he shall
go forth with great fury to destroy, and utterly to make*

away many. And he shall plant the tabernacles of his palace between the seas in the glorious holy mountain; yet he shall come to his end, and none shall help him (Daniel 11:36-45).

The prophecy here leaps forward from Antiochus to Antichrist. There is a time interval between verses 35 and 36. This part of the prophecy refers to the last great enemy of God and Israel at "the time of the end." A cursory reading would not detect a parenthesis beginning at verse 35; however, from the time of Jerome, 400 A.D., there has been a general unity of opinion that this part of chapter 11, commencing with verse 36, introduces the Antichrist. He is the "little horn" in 7:8, "the prince" in Daniel 9:26. For those of us who are presently studying the book of Daniel, at this point history ends and prophecy begins. It might help us to understand this a little more clearly if we keep in mind the stated fact in verse 35, namely the sifting and purifying of Israel through persecution is to continue till "the time of the end." That means that the trials of the Jewish people shall be the mark of all history from Daniel's day until the very end. The death of Antiochus was not to mark the end of Jewish persecution. There would arise another in "the time of the end," of whom Antiochus Epiphanes is a type. Between verse 35 and verse 36 over 2,000 years have passed, and there has been nothing in history which corresponds to verses 36-45. These closing verses in our chapter await a future fulfillment in the person of the Antichrist and his treatment of the Jews in the last days immediately preceding Messiah's return to the earth.

Observe the supremacy of the Antichrist (11:36-37). The first statement concerning this man is that "he shall do according to his will" (11:36). What is his will? It is to exalt himself and magnify himself above all other gods and to "speak marvellous [meaning *horrible*] things against the God of gods." Paul's description of this same person is quite similar: "Who opposeth and exalteth himself above all that is called God, or that is worshipped; so that he as God sitteth in the temple of God, shewing himself that he is God" (2 Thessalonians 2:4). He is the first beast in Revelation 13 who is worshiped by all who dwell upon the earth (Revelation 13:4, 8). From the beginning of his career Satan's chief aim has been to be worshiped as God (Isaiah 14:12-14). He pointed to the kingdoms of this world and said to our Lord, "All these things will I give Thee, if Thou wilt fall down and worship me" (Matthew 4:9). When at last he receives the worship of men, he will have reached the pinnacle of inflated pride (1 Timothy 3:6). The Apostle John wrote, "Ye have heard that antichrist shall come" (1 John 2:18).

"And shall prosper till the indignation be accomplished" (11:36). The supremacy of the Antichrist is for a limited time, "till. . . ." God has determined, or decreed exactly when this wicked one shall come to his end. He shall prosper only till the end of the great tribulation, the day of God's wrath, "the time of Jacob's trouble" (Jeremiah 30:7). The "indignation" in verse 36 is God's anger against the sins of His people Israel. He will use the Antichrist then, just as He used Antiochus Epiphanes to scourge Israel in past history. God had forewarned His people of this as far back as the time of Moses (Deuteronomy 4:30-31; 31:29). The supremacy of the Antichrist is a divinely-permitted one "till the indignation be accomplished." God sets the bounds of his supremacy. This willful king is but the instrument to fulfill the purpose of God. The indignation against Israel and the blasphemy against God is not to last long, only one week of seven years.

"Neither shall he regard the God of his fathers" (11:37). These words seem to indicate that the Antichrist will be an apostate Jew. It is not probable that one other than a Jew would present himself as being Israel's Messiah. If he were not a Jew he would be recognized at once as an impostor since the hope of Israel is to spring from within the nation.

A number of commentators have found it quite easy to argue against our interpretation, as stated above, on the ground that, in the expression, "the God of his fathers," the Hebrew word translated "God" is Elohim, which is a plural noun often translated "gods." Etymologically they are correct, but grammatically they are not necessarily correct. The same word is used in Genesis 1:1, and certainly they would not make that verse read, "In the beginning gods created the heaven and the earth." In both verses the translators have put the letter G in the upper case, referring of course to the one true God.[4]

"Nor the desire of women" (11:37). There is the strong possibility that this phrase refers to the desire of Hebrew women to be the mother of the Messiah, thus the word "desire" would refer to Messiah as in Haggai 2:7. The Antichrist is a hater of God and His Son the Lord Jesus Christ. "Who is a [the] liar but he that denieth that Jesus is the Christ? He is antichrist, that denieth the Father and the Son" (1 John 2:22). The Antichrist utterly denies Jesus Christ, pretending to be himself the promised Messiah, "for he shall magnify himself above all" (11:37).

"But in his estate [i.e., instead] shall he honour the God of forces" (11:38). "God of forces" should read "goddess of strongholds." Even though the Antichrist shall not have regard for any god at all, verses 38 and 39 seem to teach that he will create his own god, which is love of warfare and victory. With some people their god is sex, or money, or prestige, but with the Antichrist the pride of his heart will be to

---

[4] *Etymology* is that branch of philology treating the derivation of words. *Grammar* is the science that treats the correct use of words.

have men at his feet. If they will not yield to him willingly, then he will bring them there by force. Gold and silver and mere things hold no attraction for Satan. He is "the prince of this world" (John 12:31; 14:30; 16:11), and the whole world is his sphere of operation (1 John 5:19), but he must be the mighty master of men and angels. To bind the Antichrist to himself he will offer him particular honors and influence. The seventieth week will be Satan's greatest hour, and he will make the most of it. The Antichrist will be his willing tool, doing his bidding completely.

> *And a god whom his fathers knew not shall he honour with gold, and silver, and with precious stones, and pleasant things (11:38).*

It is possible that the god mentioned here is the image of Antichrist, the first beast in Revelation 13, whose design and construction were ordered by the second beast (Revelation 13:11-15). If we are correct in this, then that image will be made from gold, silver, and precious stones, as mentioned in Daniel 11:38. Satan knows that these things attract mankind, so he will use them to bring men to honor and worship him. With the aid of this "strange god" of his own creation, he will give to his worshipers honor and authority and land as their reward (11:39).

Note the suppression of the Antichrist. The closing portion of our chapter commences with the words, "And at the time of the end" (11:40). The time spoken of here is the end of the seventieth week which will be the "consummation of the age" in Matthew 24:3. It will mark the end of the career of Satan's man of sin.

Verse 40 speaks of a conflict in which the Antichrist becomes engaged.

> *And at the time of the end shall the king of the south push at him: and the king of the north shall come against*

him like a whirlwind, with chariots, and with horsemen, and with many ships; and he shall enter into the countries, and shall overflow and pass over (11:40).

The end of the seventieth week is likewise the end of this monstrous agent of Satan. The war mentioned here is the last conflict among men before the final conflict of Armageddon. The one precipitating influence is "the land" (11:39), "the glorious land" (11:41), which is of course Palestine. "The king of the south" (Egypt) and "the king of the north" (Russia) will combine in a simultaneous attack against him to wipe out the Jews and gain possession of Palestine. In Ezekiel 38 and 39 we are given a more complete identification of "the king of the north." When Russia comes down to join forces with Egypt against Israel, the final conflict of the ages will commence. The Lord Jesus Christ will not remain inactive when Satan begins his final push to annihilate the Jews and seize the land.

The land of Palestine was given by God to Abraham and to his natural seed for an everlasting possession (Genesis 12:1, 7; 13:15; 15:18; 17:8; 24:7; 26:2-3; 48:4). By creative right the land actually belongs to God (Psalm 24:1), therefore it is God who holds it in trust for the Jews (Leviticus 25:23). Now if any usurper assumes authority in that land, he should know that it must be for a short duration. The Antichrist will have success in his conflicts against Egypt (11:42) and Africa (11:43), but when in his madness he charges against Palestine, called here "the glorious land" (11:41), "he shall come to his end, and none shall help him" (11:45).

Verse 41 says the Antichrist will spare certain people. "These shall escape out of his hand, even Edom, and Moab, and the chief of the children of Ammon." Since these were the proverbial and perennial enemies of Israel, they stood for that for which Antichrist stands. But it seems as though God is preserving them for a special judgment because of their ill treatment of His ancient people. Isaiah and Ezekiel, writing of that day when Messiah comes to earth to rule in righteousness, includes Edom, Moab, and the children of Ammon with other nations for whom a special judgment has been reserved (Isaiah 11:11-14; Ezekiel 25:12-14). Obviously the Arab countries and Russia have turned a deaf ear to the warnings in the Word of God, therefore they must face their doom (Ezekiel 38:14-23).

The final push of the Antichrist and his hordes against Israel is described in verses 44 and 45. The words, "to destroy, and utterly to make away [or exterminate] many" (11:44), refer to Israel. This is strengthened by verse 45 which says he will set up his military headquarters in "the glorious holy mountain," which refers to the Holy Land. The exact spot where the Antichrist will gather his armies is designated by the Apostle John with geographical accurateness as " a place called in the Hebrew tongue Armageddon" (Revelation 16:16). The Hebrew word is Harmageddon from "Har" meaning mountain, and "Megiddo" meaning slaughter. This spot will one day be a literal mount of slaughter where the most awful conflict in human history will occur. It is at this spot that Antichrist will call the armies of the world together for the purpose of destroying Israel in her own land. The prophets saw many details of such a military gathering in the last days (Joel 3:1-2, 12-14; Zechariah 14:1-3).

But before the planned onslaught upon Israel can get under way, the Lord Jesus Christ will appear, and of the Antichrist our chapter concludes with the words, "none shall help him" (11:45). Just when it seems as if the Holy City must be destroyed by him against whom no nation could stand, he comes to his end by means of a single stroke of divine judgment at the appearing of Jesus Christ. The Antichrist, along with the false prophet, will be cast into the

lake of fire (Revelation 19:11-21). The Psalmist wrote prophetically of our Lord in that day, saying, "All nations compassed me about: but in the name of the LORD will I destroy
them. They compassed me about; yea, they compassed me
about: but in the name of the LORD I will destroy them.
They compassed me about like bees; they are quenched as
the fire of thorns: for in the name of the LORD I will destroy
them" (Psalm 118:10-12).

No man has been a match for the Antichrist, but the Lord
Himself will bring him to his end, "whom the Lord shall
consume with the spirit of His mouth, and shall destroy with
the brightness of His coming" (2 Thessalonians 2:8). "And
the LORD shall be king over all the earth: in that day shall
there be one LORD, and His name one" (Zechariah 14:9).

CHAPTER TWELVE

CHAPTER TWELVE

The opening words of this chapter, "And at that time," connect its contents with that which immediately precedes it. Chapter 12 is a part of one vision which began at chapter 10, not a new and separate vision. It is both the continuation and climax of one great disclosure which occupies the last three chapters of the book. All of these prophecies in this last great vision speak of Daniel's people (9:16, 19, 24; 10: 14; 12:1). The expression "thy people" has no reference to Gentiles nor to the Church.

The theme of the book of Daniel is the times of the Gentiles, portraying how and when Gentile dominion began and how and when it will end. Each vision in the book ends at this same point, namely the destruction of Gentile world power and the setting up of Christ's kingdom on the earth. G. H. Lang emphasizes this feature of the book in a way I had not seen heretofore.[1] He stresses a point I had completely overlooked, namely each vision in succession commences by turning back to some earlier point, covering part of the ground of the visions that precede it, introducing new features, and finally reaching the one goal. Thus:

(1) Chapter 2 commences with the beginning of Gentile

[1] Lang, *Daniel*, page 177.

world power (Babylon) and concludes with the stone (Christ) filling the whole earth (2:34, 44, 45).

(2) Chapter 7 begins part way through the image of chapter 2 and ends with the kingdom being given to Christ (7:13-14) and the saints (7:27).

(3) Chapter 8 shows the connection of the last emperor that will rule with the early Grecian Empire, and ends with his being broken by the Prince of princes.

(4) Chapter 9 opens with the decree to rebuild Jerusalem, continues with the prophecy of Christ's crucifixion (9:25-26), ending with the completion of the judgments upon both Antichrist and Israel, and the second coming of Christ.

(5) Chapter 11 starts again from the Persian and Grecian days, passes on to the rise of Antichrist, and carries the mind at verse 35 to the "appointed end" of the tribulation for Israel. It then turns back to some further details of the career of the persecutor, and at verse 45 reaches the same terminus, his end.

(6) Chapter 12 is the grand finale of all the preceding visions, and it brings us once again to the consummation of the times of the Gentiles. Only here we have some details of the end time which are not included in the visions that have gone before.

THE TRIBULATION (12:1)

And at that time shall Michael stand up, the great prince which standeth for the children of thy people: and there shall be a time of trouble, such as never was since there was a nation even to that same time: and at that time thy people shall be delivered, every one that shall be found written in the book (Daniel 12:1).

The expression, "at that time" seems to indicate the time of the end of the series of events recorded in the prophecies of Daniel, projecting the bounds of the prophecy to include the end of the seventieth week and the times of the Gentiles. It is used to equivocate the final fulfillment of all the prophecies in this book. It is mentioned three times here in verse 1 to assure Daniel that the point of time has not been shifted but remains the same as "the time of the end" in 11:40.

For the children of Daniel's people, "there shall be a time of trouble, such as never was since there was a nation even to that same time" (12:1). The prophecy is clear. The nation Israel can expect a time of unprecedented misery and woe before Messiah comes again. Our Lord described it as a time of "great tribulation, such as was not since the beginning of the world to this time . . . nor ever shall be" (Matthew 24:21). "For in those days shall be affliction, such as was not from the beginning of the creation which God created unto this time, neither shall be" (Mark 13:19). It is called the "great tribulation" (Revelation 7:14), "the abomination of desolation" (Matthew 24:15); the same abomination mentioned in Daniel 12:11. Our Lord and Daniel spoke of the same event and time. There are those who tell us that the great tribulation spoken of by our Lord was that time of suffering that came upon the Jewish people at the destruction of Jerusalem in 70 A.D. But both Daniel and John, and also the Lord Jesus, relate the great tribulation to a judgment that is to come upon the whole world immediately preceding the coming of the Son of Man to earth in power and great glory (Matthew 24:29). Our world has witnessed distress of serious magnitude, but the coming last distress will be unequalled. The world today gives little heed to this solemn prophecy, but the present indifference to it will in no wise lessen its fierceness when it comes.

The great tribulation is preceded by a conflict in the heavenly places. Michael, who was chosen by God for the defense of His people Israel (10:13, 21), will engage in combat against Satan and his angels. "And at that time shall Michael stand up, the great prince which standeth for the children" of Israel (12:1). John describes the conflict as follows: "And there was war in heaven: Michael and his angels fought against the dragon; and the dragon fought and his angels, And prevailed not; neither was their place found any more in heaven. And the great dragon was cast out, that old serpent, called the Devil, and Satan, which deceiveth the whole world: he was cast out into the earth, and his angels were cast out with him" (Revelation 12:7-9). Both Daniel and John have written about the same time and event in prophecy. The details of the warfare are set forth by John in Revelation, where we are told that, when the conflict is over, Satan will be completely overthrown and cast out of Heaven to the earth. This defeat will so enrage him as to precipitate his hellish designs against the Jews. It will be the prelude to the great tribulation when Israel shall "pass under the rod" (Ezekiel 20:34-38) and through the furnace of affliction (Ezekiel 22:18-22). The "woman" in Revelation 12:13, who is persecuted, I take to be the godly remnant in Israel who will be the main target of Satan's attack.

THE TRIUMPH (12:2)

And at that time thy people shall be delivered, every one that shall be found written in the book. And many of them that sleep in the dust of the earth shall awake, some to everlasting life, and some to shame and everlasting contempt (Daniel 12:1b, 2).

Following the victory of Michael over Satan in the heavenly places, there is a mighty triumph for Israel on earth. Their deliverance means a rescue from the awful conditions of the last three and one-half years of the great tribulation. At that time a remnant of Israel is preserved, the "elect" of whom our Lord spoke in Matthew 24:22, the 144,000 in Revelation 7:4, and the "saved" in Romans 11:26. There are two groups in Scripture called the *elect* of God. Israel, God's earthly people, He calls "Israel Mine elect" (Isaiah 45:4). But the New Testament saints, God's heavenly people, are also called God's elect (Romans 8:33; Colossians 3:12). Those to be delivered according to Daniel 12:1 are the elect of Israel. To read the Church into this passage is wrong. That there is a future salvation for the Jews is clear in such passages as Isaiah 11:11; 27:12-13; Jeremiah 30:7; Ezekiel 37:21-28; Hosea 3:4-5; Amos 9:11-15; to mention but a few.

But we must not fall into the evil that has ensnared those who teach that every Jew living on the earth at that time shall be saved. The prophecy in Daniel limits the deliverance to "every one that shall be found written in the book" (12:1). These are the godly Jews, the believing remnant on the earth at that time. Certainly the apostate Jews in that day are not included, but only the redeemed Israelites.

The "book" referred to could be the register of all who ever lived, giving the right to eternal life to those whose names had not been blotted out. This register of genealogy is possibly referred to by Moses when he prayed to Jehovah, "Oh, this people have sinned a great sin, and have made them gods of gold. Yet now, if Thou wilt forgive their sin—; and if not, blot me, I pray Thee, out of Thy book which Thou hast written" (Exodus 32:31-32). Now it seems that all Israelites were registered in the book, else how could some be blotted out, for God said to Moses, "Whosoever hath sinned against Me, him will I blot out of My book" (verse 33).

The Psalmist wrote, "Let them be blotted out of the book of the living, and not be written with the righteous" (Psalm 69:28). This verse seems to teach that the unrighteous had their names in the book and at a given time their names were erased so that only the names of the righteous remained. A word from Nehemiah seems to confirm this view: "And my God put into mine heart to gather together the nobles, and the rulers, and the people, that they might be reckoned by genealogy. And I found a register of the genealogy of them which came up at the first, and found written therein" (Nehemiah 7:5). Another significant verse which sheds light on this discussion comes to us toward the close of the Biblical record: "He that overcometh, the same shall be clothed in white raiment; and I will not blot out his name out of the book of life, but I will confess his name before My Father, and before His angels" (Revelation 3:5). Now since the overcomers are the believers (1 John 5:5), then it follows that they cannot be blotted out of the register. We conclude that it looks as though all names are there at some time, thereby giving all an opportunity to receive eternal life until the name is blotted out.

At which point is one's name blotted out? We cannot speak with dogmatic assurance about all of the details, but I would guess that the name of the unbeliever might remain until death, or the rapture of the Church, or the second coming of Christ to earth at the end of the seventieth week. Those in Daniel 12:1 who are delivered are the redeemed of the tribulation.

The triumph after the tribulation includes resurrection. "And many of them that sleep in the dust of the earth shall awake, some to everlasting life, and some to shame and everlasting contempt" (12:2). Interpreting this verse calls for prayerful and careful study, and most certainly the laying aside of harsh dogmatism. Whichever view one takes, there is a difficulty not easy to hurdle. What is this awakening from sleep, this rising from the dust of the earth? Let us examine our subject carefully and closely.

The Bible speaks of at least three kinds of resurrection:

First, there is a spiritual resurrection. This occurs every time a believing sinner becomes saved. The unsaved are described as "dead in trespasses and sins" (Ephesians 2:1) and as "being alienated [cut off] from the life of God" (Ephesians 4:18). When he is quickened by hearing the Word of God (Romans 10:17, cf., Hebrews 4:12), he "is passed from death unto life" (John 5:24), and thereafter his position is one of being "quickened . . . together with Christ . . . and . . . raised . . . up together . . . in Christ Jesus" (Ephesians 2:5-6). These passages are not referring to a literal death and resurrection of the body, but rather to the spiritual part of man.

Secondly, there is the physical resurrection of the body from death and the grave, as when our Lord raised up the widow's son (Luke 7:11-15), Jairus' daughter (Luke 8:49-56), Lazarus (John 11:43-44), or such as His own resurrection (Matthew 28:1-15; Mark 16:1-20; Luke 24:1-46; John 20:1-31; Acts 1:1-11), and the same kind of resurrection to which every believer in Christ looks forward (1 Corinthians 15:51-55; 1 Thessalonians 4:13-18).

Thirdly, there is a national resurrection for Israel, at which time all three kinds of resurrection will be experienced by Jews. Some living at that time will be spiritually reborn, others who have died will be raised from death and the grave, and there will be a national restoration to the land of Palestine when saved Jews from all twelve tribes will be reunited. For light on the national resurrection of Israel, the student should read Isaiah 26:12-19; Jeremiah 16:14-15; Ezekiel 20:33-44; 37:1-28.

Now which resurrection is meant in Daniel 12:2? It seems that all three might be included. Because they are "holy people" and are "written in the book," it follows that a spiritual resurrection would have had to occur at one time. Inasmuch as "holy ones" of past generations have died, and many more will die during the tribulation, it is reasonable to assume that a physical resurrection will be necessary. Finally, a national resurrection of Israel is necessary if she is to inherit the promises given to her as a nation by Jehovah.

But a bodily resurrection of individuals is most assuredly in view here as noted in the use of the words "many" and "some" and "dust of the earth." After our first parents had sinned, God said to them, "Dust thou art, and unto dust shalt thou return" (Genesis 3:19). Job said, "For now shall I sleep in the dust; and thou shalt seek me in the morning, but I shall not be" (Job 7:21). In both passages the death of the body is in view. These are human bodies of persons who had died, and there are definitely two classes here, the saved and the unsaved, those who are raised to everlasting life and those who are raised to everlasting shame and contempt. However both will not be raised at the same time. There will be a premillennial resurrection of the saved, who will live and reign with Christ a thousand years (Revelation 20:5); and after the millennium there will be another resurrection, of which it is stated explicitly, "the rest of the dead lived not again until the thousand years were finished" (Revelation 20:5).

It is true that Israel has been sleeping nationally in the dust of the earth, scattered among the Gentiles, and that a national restoration will take place as taught in the vision of dry bones in Ezekiel 37, but there will be also a physical resurrection of all dead Jews, the believers being raised to eternal life and the unbelievers for shame and eternal banishment from God. Our Lord said, "Marvel not at this: for the hour is coming, in which all that are in the graves shall hear His voice, And shall come forth; they that have done good, unto the resurrection of life; and they that have done evil, unto the resurrection of damnation" (John 5:28-29). The Old Testament saints will be raised at the end of the great tribulation but before the millennium; however, not with the New Testament saints who are raised and taken up to Heaven before the tribulation.

THE TEACHERS (12:3-4)

And they that be wise shall shine as the brightness of the firmament; and they that turn many to righteousness as the stars for ever and ever. But thou, O Daniel, shut up the words, and seal the book, even to the time of the end: many shall run to and fro, and knowledge shall be increased (Daniel 12:3-4).

The Revised Version describes those in verse 3 as "teachers" who instruct others in the way of righteousness. The tribulation will be one of the darkest periods in human history. However, during that time God will have his luminaries on the earth who, through their wise behavior and clear testimony, will teach others the way of righteousness. These are Jewish teachers whom God will raise up to be His ministers after the Church has been taken out from the earth. They are those referred to in Daniel 11:33-35; Revelation 7:4-8; 11:2-12; the remnant of the true Jehovah's witnesses who will point many to the coming Messiah. No matter how troublous the times have been, or will become, the darkest hours afford the largest opportunity for letting the gospel light shine. Daniel and John were speaking of those who will defy the decree of the Antichrist that all worship him, and courageously teach others the pure gospel of the kingdom (Matthew 24:14).

All true believers are exhorted to shine as lights in their own day. Our Lord said to His disciples, "Ye are the light of the world. . . . Let your light so shine before men, that they may see your good works, and glorify your Father which is in heaven" (Matthew 5:14, 16). He testified of John that "He was a burning and a shining light" (John 5:35). The Apostle Paul wrote to the saints at Ephesus, "For ye were sometimes darkness, but now are ye light in the Lord: walk as children of light" (Ephesians 5:8). This is wise counsel for all believers in the midst of troublesome times, and the wise among us will do well to heed it. "For God, who commanded the light to shine out of darkness, hath shined in our hearts, to give the light of the knowledge of the glory of God in the face of Jesus Christ" (2 Corinthians 4:6).

Daniel's vision, in its primary interpretation, had to do with Israel, and for those who witness faithfully during that midnight hour, they shall receive their reward. "They . . . shall shine as the brightness of the firmament . . . as the stars for ever and ever." Referring to the same people and time, our Lord said, "Then shall the righteous shine forth as the sun in the kingdom of their Father. Who hath ears to hear, let him hear" (Matthew 13:43). The world has its stars who appeal to the sensual in man and they receive their corruptible crowns (1 Corinthians 9:25), but God has His stars who appeal to the spiritual needs of men, and God's stars will receive their reward. The Apostle Paul wrote, "There is one glory of the sun, and another glory of the moon, and another glory of the stars: for one star differeth from another star in glory. So also is the resurrection of the dead" (1 Corinthians 15:41-42). Those faithful light-bearers will be assigned a position of authority and recognition commensurate with their devotion and diligence while they lived and labored on the earth (Luke 19:15-26).

> *But thou, O Daniel, shut up the words, and eat the book, even to the time of the end: many shall run to and fro, and knowledge shall be increased (12:4).*

There is a close relationship between verses 3 and 4 in their interpretation. Some ministers have taken the expression, "many shall run to and fro," to refer to much travel by means of high speed automobiles and jet aircraft, and the words, "knowledge shall be increased," to apply to the rapid program in scientific and technological research and development. If this is the correct interpretation of this passage, then there is abundant evidence of its accuracy and fulfillment.

I am inclined to agree with those teachers who link verses 3 and 4 together. In verse 3 Daniel was told that at that time teachers will arise who will turn many to righteousness. I take the "many" in verse 3 to be the same group as the "many" in verse 4.

Darby translates it, "Many shall diligently investigate, and knowledge shall increase."

Fausset says, "Many shall scrutinize it, running through every page."

Leupold writes, "Many shall diligently peruse it, and knowledge shall be increased."

Pember has it to mean, "Many shall search it through and through, and knowledge shall increase."

Pierson paraphrases it, "Many shall read and review the book, and knowledge shall increase."

Seiss says, "Many shall examine it."

Tregelles sees it, "Many shall scrutinize the book from end to end."

Daniel was instructed to "shut up the words, and seal the book, even to the time of the end," at which time, when the prophecy in the vision is fulfilled, many will examine those prophecies carefully and the knowledge of them will increase. The eyes of many will run to and fro across the pages eagerly. Israel is blind now so that she cannot see the great truths in this book, but the day is coming when many Jews will read and understand, even as our Lord predicted in Matthew 24:15. In view of the fact that we are in that time period immediately preceding the seventieth week, it would seem to indicate that this latter interpretation is the correct one. The Lord said to the Apostle John, "Seal not the sayings of the prophecy of this book: for the time is at hand" (Revelation 22:10). All that was sealed or shut up to Daniel and the Jews of that day is now unveiled to believers, so that with the book of the Revelation before us we may now understand the message in the book of Daniel. Knowledge of the book of Daniel is increasing and will continue to increase among the true believers in Christ, and this will be followed by the same increase of knowledge among Jewish believers in the tribulation.

The sealing of it by Daniel was for the purpose of preserving this inspired and informative document of divine revelation against any and all attempts to destroy its message or nullify its authority. And so the record has been guarded and protected in order that many will be able to examine its message. Satan would destroy every word of this book if he could, but God has protected it. In the light of the prophecies contained in it, Daniel might become one of the most widely read books in the last days preceding Christ's second coming to the earth.

THE TIME (12:5-7)

Then I Daniel looked, and, behold, there stood other two, the one on this side of the bank of the river, and the other on that side of the bank of the river. And one said to the man clothed in linen, which was upon the waters of the river, How long shall it be to the end of these wonders? And I heard the man clothed in linen, which was upon the waters of the river, when he held up his right hand and his left hand unto heaven, and sware by Him that liveth for ever that it shall be for a time, times, and an half; and when he shall have accomplished to scatter the power of the holy people, all these things shall be finished (Daniel 12:5-7).

We confess that there is difficulty in interpreting some of the features of the vision. The location of the vision is the River Hiddekel or Tigris, identified in 10:4. Keep in mind the fact that chapters 10 through 12 inclusive are one vision, therefore the "man clothed in linen" is the same here as in 10:5. In addition to the angel who had been explaining the vision, two other angels appeared in the vision, one on each side of the river, so that now there are three angels and Daniel in our study.

Why do two additional angels appear? The Scriptures tell us that at the mouth of two or three witnesses a matter will be established (Deuteronomy 19:15; 2 Corinthians 13: 1). Or, it is possible that they were present because these were the "things the angels desire to look into" (1 Peter 1:12). These are merely suggestions, for we do not profess to have an adequate answer as to why the two angels appeared.

The conversation in verses 6 and 7 is between the angels, Daniel being the silent observer and listener at this time. The one angel asked, "How long shall it be to the end of these wonders?" (12:6) The point of the question is, "How long will it take for the series of events foretold in the vision to be completed?" Then the angel clothed in linen lifted up both hands toward Heaven, as if to take an oath on the answer he was about to give. The raising of the hand was a gesture that accompanied the utterance of an oath (Genesis 14:22; Deuteronomy 32:40; Revelation 10:5-7). Usually one hand was raised for the giving of an oath. The solemnity of this oath is emphasized by the fact that both hands were raised. Whoever this angel is, described as "the man clothed in linen," he possessed information beyond that which other angels have. As was previously stated in our comments on chapter 10, there are those teachers who believe this angel to be our Lord Jesus Christ, who alone possesses full knowledge of things to come.

In response to the question, "How long shall it be to the end of these wonders?" the mighty angel answered, "For a time, times, and an half" (12:7). This expression is the same as "a time and times and the dividing of time" mentioned in 7:25, and is to be identified with "the midst of the week" in 9:27. This is the last half of the seventieth week, the duration of the great tribulation, when God through the Antichrist shall have accomplished His judgments upon Israel. It is that same period of time as the 1,260 days in Revelation 11:3 and the 42 months in Revelation 13:5. This time period, then, begins in the middle of the tribulation, with the setting up of the abomination of desolation to which our Lord referred in Matthew 24:15. The testimony of the two witnesses in Revelation 11:3 corresponds to this time. The duration of Israel's trouble is therefore announced once more. The prophecies in the vision will find their complete fulfillment when Israel's rebellion against God will have been finally broken. Israel's extremity will be God's opportunity, for then Messiah shall come and the nation will be led to acknowledge Him.

THE TERMINUS (12:8-13)

And I heard, but I understood not: then said I, O my Lord, what shall be the end of these things? And he said, Go thy way, Daniel: for the words are closed up and sealed till the time of the end. Many shall be purified, and made white, and tried; but the wicked shall do wickedly: and none of the wicked shall understand; but the wise shall understand. And from the time that the daily sacrifice shall be taken away, and the abomination that maketh desolate set up, there shall be a thousand two hundred and ninety days. Blessed is he that waiteth, and cometh to the thousand three hundred and five and thirty days. But go thou thy way till the end be: for thou shalt rest, and stand in thy lot at the end of the days (Daniel 12:8-13).

Daniel heard the conversation between the angels but without understanding. His finite mind could not comprehend the heavenly message, so he said, "O my Lord, what shall be the end of these things?" His question is actually an inquiry as to the final outcome, the terminus of all that the vision contained. It is not uncommon for a writing prophet not to understand all that he wrote. He knew the message was coming from God, but at times it came unaccompanied by explanation. Daniel was curious to know what the final end of this revelation would be and how the great struggle would end.

But it did not please God to tell all to His aged servant. He merely said, "Go thy way, Daniel: for the words are closed up and sealed till the time of the end" (12:9). It was not needful that Daniel have all the answers at that time. The vision would come to pass at God's appointed time, and that was all Daniel needed to know for the present. The Lord told Daniel that there was no further need to probe deeper into these matters. At the appointed time God will bring all to pass as revealed in the vision. Daniel was not to sit by idly and wait for the fulfillment of the prophecies, but he was told, "Go thy way, Daniel," that is, follow on in the way of obedient service as in the past.

Daniel had served God long and faithfully, and God had given to him all the knowledge He intended to impart at that time. If God chooses to conceal some of His future plans, He has a right to do so. The Bible is a thoroughly practical book revealing all we need to know, so we must rest content with what God has been pleased to tell us. Full knowledge will be revealed in God's time. Let us not waste time in speculating about the things God has not revealed in His Word, but let us occupy ourselves with those truths He has disclosed. We must be diligent in obeying what we know.

God did assure Daniel that at that time "Many shall be purified, and made white, and tried" (12:10). The reference is still to *the time of the end*, the terminus of the prophecies in the vision, the last three and a half years of the seventieth week. God's faithful remnant during the great tribulation will come through the purging purified and white. When God chastens His children in any dispensation the principle is always the same, "for our profit, that we might be partakers of His holiness" (Hebrews 12:10). In the tribulation many Jews will be saved. John heard the elders asking, "What are these which are arrayed in white robes? and whence came they? And I said unto him, Sir, thou knowest. And he said to me, These are they which came out of great tribulation, and have washed their robes, and made them white in the blood of the Lamb" (Revelation 7:13-14).

"But the wicked shall do wickedly: and none of the wicked shall understand" (12:10). Indeed this is a solemn note with reference to those who persist in willful unbelief. They have shut their eyes to the truth, therefore they shall not see the good when it is before them. "He that is unjust, let him be unjust still: and he which is filthy, let him be filthy still. . . . And, behold, I come quickly; and My reward is with Me, to give every man according as his work shall be" (Revelation 22:11, 12). The wicked do not understand now, nor will they in that day because "the natural man receiveth not the things of the Spirit of God: for they are foolishness unto him: neither can he know them, because they are spiritually discerned" (1 Corinthians 2:14). "And for this cause God shall send them strong delusion, that they should believe a [the] lie" (2 Thessalonians 2:11).

"But the wise shall understand" (12:10). Our Lord said, "Howbeit when He, the Spirit of truth, is come, He will guide you into all truth: for He shall not speak of Himself; but whatsoever He shall hear, that shall He speak: and He will shew you things to come" (John 16:13). The Apostle Paul added this word, "But as it is written, Eye hath not seen, nor ear heard, neither have entered into the heart of man, the things which God hath prepared for them that love Him. But God hath revealed them unto us by His Spirit: for the Spirit searcheth all things, yea, the deep things of God" (1 Corinthians 2:9-10). The Holy Spirit is the mighty Teacher of divine truth. The wise man is he who comes seeking that truth. "If any of you lack wisdom, let him ask of God, that giveth to all men liberally, and upbraideth not; and it shall be given him" (James 1:5). The wicked are those who willfully reject the truth, but the wise are those who seek to know it.

Verses 11 and 12 are difficult to interpret. We confess that at this writing we are in search of more truth. Why the difference in time between 1,290 days and 1,335 days, we are not told, nor have we found light upon these two time periods from other Scriptures.

DeHaan believes they are days of grace which the Lord will extend to the nations between the end of the tribulation and His personal appearing to judge the nations.

Ironside suggests that the extra days will be devoted to purging out from the kingdom all things that offend and are evil.

Talbot says it is the time when the sanctuary is cleansed and the earth purified.

Tregelles believes the extra time will be used to get all the Jews into the land.

Gaebelein wrote, "One might truly say, that the expositors whose commentaries are mostly used have only darkened this final word addressed to Daniel." Then he goes on to add, "But what is the meaning of these 1,290 and 1,335 days? Can there be anything plainer than the fact that these are literal days? . . . Now the great tribulation lasts for

1,260 days. But here we have 30 days or a whole month added. The Lord will be manifested at the close of the great tribulation of 1,260 days, three and a half years. Matthew 24:29-31 teaches us this. The extra month will in all probability be needed to make possible certain judgment events especially with the overthrow of the nations, which came against Jerusalem and the judgment of nations as given in Matthew 25:32. We cannot speak dogmatically on all this. But certain it is that 1,335 days after the antichristian abomination had been set up in Jerusalem, that is 75 days or two and a half months beyond the time of the great tribulation, the full blessing for Israel and the establishment of the glorious rule of Israel's King, the once rejected Lord Jesus Christ, will have come, for it is written, 'Blessed is he that waiteth, and cometh to the thousand three hundred and five and thirty days.' This is as far as any teacher can safely go and here we would rest." [2]

It was comfort enough for Daniel to hear the closing words of cheer addressed to his own heart, "But go thou thy way till the end be: for thou shalt rest, and stand in thy lot at the end of the days" (12:13). Here is a word of *rest* for the present and a word of *reassurance* for the future. God told Daniel that he would die, but He likewise gave to him the assurance that he would be raised from the dead to enter the millennium. "You are an old man, but keep on! Your strength is waning, but keep on! Persecution and tribulation will come, but keep on! And when life on earth is over, thou shalt rest. Then your day of resurrection and reigning will come."

Here is a challenge to us all: "Therefore, my beloved brethren, be ye stedfast, unmoveable, always abounding in the work of the Lord, forasmuch as ye know that your

[2] *Daniel*, pages 206-207.

labour is not in vain in the Lord" (1 Corinthians 15:58).
"Wherefore gird up the loins of your mind, be sober, and
hope to the end for the grace that is to be brought unto you
at the revelation of Jesus Christ" (1 Peter 1:13). "Be thou
faithful unto death, and I will give thee a crown of life"
(Revelation 2:10).

For Daniel and for all believers there is rest, resurrection,
and reward. God said to His servant, "For thou shalt . . .
stand in thy lot," which I understand to mean the reward he
earned in this life. It is written of the tribulation saints, "And
I heard a voice from heaven saying unto me, Write, Blessed
are the dead which die in the Lord from henceforth: Yea,
saith the Spirit, that they may rest from their labours; and
their works do follow them" (Revelation 14:13). The dead
who have died in the Lord are resting from their labors and
waiting for their lot which the Lord Himself will distribute
at His coming. Then shall every redeemed Jew occupy the
special place assigned him in the kingdom. "Many shall
come from the east and west, and shall sit down with Abraham, and Isaac, and Jacob, in the kingdom of heaven"
(Matthew 8:11).

Thus the book of Daniel comes to its terminus with a
ringing note of victory for the aged prophet of God. For
Daniel, and for all who trust in Daniel's God, the best is
yet to be. Daniel's God cannot be fully known apart from
Daniel's Messiah, our Lord and Saviour Jesus Christ.

If one reads these lines who has never received Jesus
Christ as Saviour and Lord, I urge upon you to accept Him
at once. "As many as received Him, to them gave He power
to become the sons of God, even to them that believe on
His name" (John 1:12).

BIBLIOGRAPHY

ARCHER, GLEASON. *Daniel.*

AUBERLEN, C.A. *The Prophecies of Daniel and the Revelation of St. John.*

AUCHINCLOSS, W.S. *The Only Key to Daniel's Prophecies.*

BEHRMANN, G. *The Book of Daniel.*

BOLL, R.H. *Lessons on Daniel.*

BOUTFLOWER, CHARLES. *In and Around the Book of Daniel.*

CALVIN, J. *The Book of the Prophet Daniel.*

COOPER, D.L. *The Seventy Weeks of Daniel.*

CULVER, ROBERT D. *Daniel and the Latter Days.*

DARBY, J.N. *Collected Writings, Prophetic,* Volume II.

DEHAAN, M.R. *Daniel the Prophet.*

DENNET, EDWARD. *Daniel the Prophet.*

DRIVER, S.R. *Daniel* (The Cambridge Bible).

EPP, THEODORE H. *Times of the Gentiles.*

FARRAR, F.W. *The Book of Daniel.*

GAEBELEIN, ARNO C. *Daniel.*

GOLLMICH, VICTOR G. *Daniel Sanely Explained.*

GREENE, OLIVER B. *Daniel—Verse by Verse.*

HENGSTENBERG, E.W. *The Genuineness of Daniel.*

HESLOP, W.G. *Diamonds from Daniel.*

IRONSIDE, H.A. *The Great Parenthesis.*

IRONSIDE, H.A. *Lectures on Daniel.*

JEROME'S *Commentary on Daniel.*

KEIL, C.F. *Biblical Commentary on the Book of Daniel.*

KELLY, WILLIAM. *Notes on Daniel.*

KELLY, WILLIAM. *Daniel's Seventy Weeks.*

KING, GEOFFREY R. *Daniel.*

LANG, G.H. *The Histories and Prophecies of Daniel.*

LARKIN, CLARENCE. *The Book of Daniel.*

LEUPOLD, H.C. *Exposition of Daniel.*

LUCK, G. COLEMAN. *Daniel.*

MAURO, PHILIP. *The Seventy Weeks and The Great Tribulation.*

MCGEE, J. VERNON. *Delving Through Daniel.*

NEWELL, PHILIP R. *Daniel—The Man Greatly Beloved and His Prophecies.*

PEMBER, G.H. *The Great Prophecies of the Centuries.*

PENTECOST, J. DWIGHT. *Prophecy for Today.*

PENTECOST, J. DWIGHT. *Things to Come.*

PETRIE, ARTHUR. *The Message of Daniel.*

PETTINGILL, WILLIAM L. *Simple Studies in Daniel.*

PHILLIPS, O.E. *When The Messiah Should Have Appeared.*

PUSEY, E.B. *Daniel the Prophet.*

SAMUEL AND DENMAN. *The Book of Daniel, Chapter Ten.*

SEISS, JOSEPH. *Miracles in Stone.*

SMITH, WILBUR M. *Egypt in Biblical Prophecy.*

STEVENS, W.C. *The Book of Daniel.*

TALBOT, LOUIS T. *The Great Prophecies of Daniel.*

TATFORD, FREDERICK A. *The Climax of the Ages.*

TATHAM, C.E. *Daniel Speaks Today.*

INDEX OF SCRIPTURE TEXTS